THE STORY OF EXETER SPEEDWAY

Volume 2

The Glory Years 1947–1953

Tony Lethbridge

Ali-Kat

ALI-KAT PUBLICATIONS
'Tresco'
6 Lower Kings Avenue
Exeter EX4 6JT
England

ISBN 0-9515149-2-X

Design and production by The Studio, 4A Brookside Units, Venny Bridge, Exeter EX4 8JN.

Contents

Ted Lethbridge
1916 – 1996

Acknowledgements

I cannot believe that it is more than twenty years since I began to write the history of Exeter Speedway. Naively I thought I could do the whole thing during the close season. Little did I realise just how much research and hard work would be required. The idea came about as the result of an exhibition I staged at St Thomas Library in the summer of 1979 to mark the fiftieth anniversary of speedway starting at the County Ground. Hearing of my interest Mr Sidney Salter generously gave me his pre-war scrapbook, which contained a wealth of information and set the ball rolling.

Volume 1 covering 1929 to 1945 was published in 1989 and I am delighted to say proved very successful. In fact it is still selling well. Since then we have constantly been asked 'when is the next book coming out?' No more excuses. Here it is.

A great many people have helped me achieve my goal and my sincere thanks go to them all. Fellow enthusiasts up and down the country have found lost scores, loaned programmes and supplied photographs, Mike Redfern even interrupted a holiday in Ireland to visit the National Library in Dublin and track down the scorers in the Shelbourne match. Goog Hoskin, Jack Geran and Neil Street have patiently answered all kinds of queries and provided countless anecdotes. In what other sport do your childhood heroes become your friends? Thanks also go to Francis Cann, Don Hardy, Wally Green, Herbie Plain, Alan Cowland, Cyril Lock and several riders who sadly are no longer with us, among them Bernard 'Broncho' Slade, Sid Hazzard, and Gordon Taylor; not forgetting long time supporters club secretary the late Mrs Winifred Kerr.

Special thanks go to my good friend Glynn Shailes as much for his encouragement and boundless enthusiasm for the project, as for his help in solving queries, and finding lost match reports which I would otherwise have missed. Thanks also to Gordon Gray, Reg Burrows, John Davey, Tony Ellis, Robert Doran, Don Miller, John Kitson, John Elmore, Ken Bessant and Mrs Edna Harris who have helped with photos and press cuttings. I must also mention Don Weekes' sister Edna who generously gave me her family's photo collection shortly before she died. I am also indebted to the late Ted Ottaway who bequeathed me two magnificent photo albums, the full contents of which will appear in a follow up volume.

Paul Eustace spent hours collating the match scorers from my collection of speedway magazines and John R. Smith put the original manuscript on computer disc, while Cyril J. Hart and Pat Gorman both generously volunteered their services as proof readers. I am indebted to both Peter Oakes and Colin Hill, who as promoters of Exeter Speedway, have given me their support as well as the opportunity to work within the sport we all love. Thanks too to my old pal Bob Radford for writing the foreword and not charging! I cannot close without mentioning a man I have yet to meet, John Dubarry, who now lives in Germany but used to follow the Falcons. He bought the first book ten years ago and regularly 'phones to ask where the next one is. Your wait is over John.

Last but by no means least my special thanks and love go to my wife Christine for her encouragement and constant help. Chris not only deciphered my handwriting so successfully that she was able to type the manuscript but also pointed out the bits that did not make any sense. She has done all the computer work, including the input of all statistics, and often came down in the middle of the night to save everything when I messed it all up on the PC.

Sadly the person I most wanted to read the finished work is no longer here, so it is with great affection that I dedicate the book to the memory of my Dad, Ted, who was there and saw it all right from the start.

Tony Lethbridge
March 2000

Foreword

After his first publication told of the earliest days of speedway in Exeter, Tony Lethbridge now brings us the historical details of the sport in the city from 1947 to 1953, and later this year 1954 to 1964. Tony originally intended these years to be covered in one book but discovered so much information that it has had to be split into two volumes.

This part of the story begins in post war Britain when Tony and I were born. The mass unemployment of the thirties was a thing of the past it was thought – until the 1980's at least. Television was in its infancy, the National Health Service was being introduced, along for the first time with free education.

With work for everyone most people had money in their pockets. Live sport boomed, not least this fast and exciting sport, which offered a form of escape from the austere post war rationing that did not end until the mid fifties.

By then speedway was on its knees and some of the attempts to run the speedway between the closure at the end of 1955 and the re-launch under Wally Mawdsley and Peter Lansdale in 1961 will be of great interest.

The Lethbridge family are synonymous with Exeter Speedway. Tony's late father Ted, a wonderful and kindly man, tended the track until almost eighty years of age. He remembered it all, and if there is a spirit world then he almost certainly resides at the County Ground on Monday nights during the summer.

Tony Lethbridge himself has been actively involved in Exeter Speedway for twenty years through the Peter Oakes and Colin Hill eras. He has the ability to look beyond the obvious, to paint the characters with the colour their talents deserved. He will always seek out the humour too.

Research and writing this book has taken Tony some time. I know his wife Christine has, as ever, supported him with practical help. It should be a darned good read and hopefully further volumes will follow in years to come.

Season 2000 will be Exeter Speedway's fortieth consecutive season, and that has been some achievement – a period of stability, whereas this volume contains what a hugely successful politician might refer to as 'Boom or bust.'

Writing a book like this will not make Tony Lethbridge rich. It might even cost him money. But as a librarian few know better than Tony how much pleasure the written record can be, and how useful it is for reference.

Enjoy the book. Well done, Tony, and I hope you will dedicate this one to the memory of your father Ted.

Bob Radford
Speedway Star Magazine

WARMING UP

The conclusion of the Second World War in May 1945 heralded the revival of speedway in Exeter. Leonard Glanfield introduced Speedway to the 'Ever Faithful' city, in March 1929. His flamboyant promoting style had at first attracted huge crowds, but he tried to do too much too quickly with the result that he was forced to close for financial reasons shortly before the end of the first season. The promotion was taken over by Freddie Mockford and Cecil Smith in 1930 but after initial success they, too, pulled out midway through 1931 to concentrate on their more profitable London tracks, Crystal Palace and later New Cross. A valiant attempt to stage amateur racing by the Exeter Motor Club in 1934 was also doomed to failure.

With the ending of the war two former Exeter riders, Frank 'Buster' Buckland and Bernard 'Broncho' Slade, felt the time was right to attempt another speedway revival. Their first effort, a VE Day grasstrack meeting in Exwick fields, proved a huge success despite an appallingly wet day. Thus encouraged, and with the help of local enthusiasts Bill Eastmond and Peter Jones, they set about building a track from scratch at Alphington as the traditional home of Exeter Speedway, the County Ground Stadium, was still in military hands.

Six highly successful meetings, involving the top stars of the day, were staged at the tiny 250 yard track before the Ministry of Agriculture stepped in and imposed a ploughing up order on the land.

This decision sadly ruined the promoters' hopes of introducing league racing at the new track in 1946, but the promoting consortium was determined to build on their early success and despite the loss of a complete season prepared to relaunch speedway back at the County Ground in 1947. Buildings of all kinds had stood on the track and against the grandstand, so concrete foundations had first to be removed. A new safety fence was required as the original wooden one was now in an advanced state of decay with 'just a few posts

The parade of riders at the VE Day meeting in Exwick Fields.

The star studded line-up for the ACU Southern Championship at Alphington. 16 August.
L → R Back: Jack Parker, Ron Clark, Oliver Hart, Mike Erskine, Fred Tuck. Front: Wally Lloyd, Ron Johnson, Colin Watson, Bill Kitchen, Eric Chitty.

and about six sound planks left'. The sight of it almost put Buckland off the idea all together, but Eastmond's enthusiasm for the task was undaunted and through one of the worst winters of the century, the track once again began to take shape.

Post-war austerity meant that building materials were in very short supply, and the biggest headache for Eastmond was finding a suitable safety fence. The answer came in the shape of the Morrison indoor air raid shelter. The Morrison shelter was a steel-topped table with mesh sides, which had saved many lives during the Blitz. Bill Eastmond acquired 242 of these now redundant 6' × 4' steel panels, which were set up around the track on posts obtained from air raid salvage dumps. At first there was uncertain opposition to the idea of a steel fence, not least from the Speedway Control Board. Eventually, the idea was approved and the fence is still in service today over 50 years later, although the original wooden posts were all replaced in the eighties; but there are still riders and some officials, who do not altogether approve of it.

While Bill Eastmond's resourcefulness and enthusiasm were channelled into rebuilding the track, Buckland was fully occupied finding a team. By the autumn of 1946 he had agreed terms with three un-named riders whom he described as among the 'finest in the game', and had also provisionally signed two Dutchmen and a Belgian.

Gordon Taylor practising prior to start of 1947 season.

1947

OFFICIAL PROGRAMME 6d.

EXETER SPEEDWAY

MOTOR SPORTS (EXETER) LTD.
COUNTY GROUND SPORTS STADIUM, ST. THOMAS, EXETER
Phone 5231

TUESDAY, 22nd APRIL, 1947 : : 7.30 p.m.

POSSIBLES v PROBABLES

Next Meeting: MONDAY, APRIL 28th, 7.30 p.m.

Grand Challenge Match

EXETER v EASTBOURNE

NO BETTING ALLOWED

W. V. COLE & SONS, EXETER

HEAT 1

Speedway's popularity had rocketed as the war-weary masses sought entertainment and excitement. The immediate post-war boom saw the National League reformed and in 1946 it once again boasted two divisions with six clubs operating in each, but such was the demand for speedway that a third division was planned for the following year using basically novice riders. This created problems for Buckland's previous plans as the Speedway Control Board decreed that first and second division riders could not compete on third division tracks, and third division was the only option for Exeter at that time. In speedway circles this was generally considered a non-starter as nobody believed that the public would turn out to watch inexperienced riders.

Another handicap to the newly formed teams was terrible winter weather, which had delayed the building work on their new tracks.

A further difficulty arose when the government threatened to place a ban on midweek sport. The financial after-effects of the war were still being felt throughout the country and the need to get Britain's industry back to full production was of vital importance. To this effect the government had imposed a new 2.00 pm – 10.00 pm industrial shift and the ban on mid week sport was a counter measure to possible absenteeism by the workers.

However, despite the difficulties the Third Division did get off the ground and all eight proposed clubs managed to open. Those eight clubs were Eastbourne – Eagles, Cradley Heath –

The 1947 Falcons – L → R Back: Tom Crutcher, Charley Hayden, Ted Moore, Ed Williams. Front: Allan Chambers, Les Trim, Broncho Slade, Don Hardy, Cyril Roger.

Heathens, Plymouth – Devils, Hanley (Stoke) – Potters, Southampton – Saints, Tamworth (Birmingham), and Wombwell (Barnsley) as well as Exeter.

The shortage of riders was eased by a training scheme run by former West Ham star Tiger Stevenson. The prospective Third Division clubs all contributed financially to the scheme, and over 1,500 applications were received from hopeful speedway stars. Stevenson whittled these down to 150 and the training schools were staged at Birmingham and Bristol, but to ensure a competitive team Buckland contacted his old boss Fred Mockford of New Cross and persuaded him to lend Exeter four juniors, Cyril Roger, Don Hardy, John Naylor and Bill Keen.

The Exeter team building continued with the arrival of Les Trim, who had ridden for Birmingham in 1938, then Crystal Palace and Rye House in 1939. Trim had recently bought the Redlands Filling Station on the Exmouth Road near Clyst St Mary and offered tuning facilities in his workshops.

The leading local riders were Broncho Slade, Reg Beer and Gordon Taylor, who had all ridden the County Ground in the '30s. While from along the south coast came a number of grass track riders and trainees from the Tiger Stevenson School, among them Tom Crutcher, Sid Hazzard, Allan Chambers and Dink Philpotts.

In fact 20 riders plus 4 reserves paraded for the Grand Opening Meeting, or, as it was subtitled, the Battle for Team Places, on Monday 14th April 1947. This was run to a rather odd formula but at the end of the 20 heats Charlie Hayden was the top scorer with 11 points from his 4 rides, having suffered his only defeat at the hands of Allan Chambers in heat 14. Chambers and Sid Hazzard tied for second on 10 each, while Slade and Londoner Ted Moore both notched 3 wins apiece. Broncho had also clocked the fastest time of the night, 84.4 seconds in the opening heat. The biggest disappointment was the form of Les Trim, who failed to score after breaking chains in his first 2 rides.

The four New Cross loanees were listed without their Christian names in the programme, although Keen never actually rode at the track. All races had to be started on the green light, as the new electric starting gate would not be delivered until the next day. The organisers were encouraged by the fact that 7,000 prospective fans turned up to witness the action. Many fans arrived long before the turnstiles opened and long queues formed along Church Road.

The second meeting took the form of a 'Possibles' and 'Probables' selection match but rather worryingly for the promoters this only attracted an attendance of 5,500. The match resulted in a win for the Possibles by 44–37. Their top scorer was Cyril Roger whose 12 point maximum was to be the first of many in Exeter's colours. Cyril had been an RAF dispatch rider during the war before applying to New Cross for trials. He had four outings at the Old Kent Road track in 1946 but fell each time.

At the end of the evening the team for the following week's challenge match against Eastbourne was announced: Broncho Slade/Les Trim, Cyril Roger/Allan Chambers, Ted Moore/Sid Hazzard with Don Hardy and Tom Crutcher as reserves. Trim was originally named as captain but he declined the honour, saying that it should instead go to Slade, as the local man. Broncho celebrated with an exclusion from his scratch race heat. After missing the start and charging past Philpotts and Moore he attempted to overtake Chambers. Unfortunately, their machines locked together and they crashed, luckily without injury, but Broncho was excluded for 'over enthusiasm'.

Exeter's first away match at Eastbourne set a trend, which continues to the present day. In Sussex the Exeter team finished on the wrong end of a 63–20 thrashing with Roger and Chambers top scoring with 4 points each! Buster Buckland commented that his team had already become so used to the big-banked County Ground track that they tried to go too fast around the tight Arlington bends.

Bernard 'Broncho' Slade.

Revenge came swiftly a couple of nights later when Exeter romped to victory over the Eagles by 52–32 back on home cinders. The 'Falcons' nickname would not be adopted until several weeks later, but their green and white race jackets were already a well recognizable symbol. Green and white had been chosen as these are the city's civic colours. At this time the Exeter team were occasionally referred to in the programme and the press as the 'Tigers' but this nickname obviously did not catch on.

Later that week, Exeter recorded their first away win in a challenge match at Plymouth and completed the double with a 47–36 home win over the Devils in front of nearly 9,000 spectators, their biggest crowd. Unfortunately, in this match, Exeter suffered their first casualty, Ted Moore breaking his kneecap when he clipped the fence whilst leading the third heat.

Exeter's first National League match took place at the County Ground on 12 May, when the Hanley Potters were the opposition. The match was raced in a steady downpour, but 6,000 spectators braved the elements to watch the homesters run up a succession of 5–1's and 4–2's to win by 62–20. The unfortunate Potters found the combination of the rain and the unique track too much to cope with.

This soon became the set pattern with the Falcons, as they officially became in June, winning convincingly at home, but invariably struggling to keep in touch away from the County Ground. The exception to this rule was at Plymouth where the Falcons enjoyed two victories that summer. The main problem was that the big 440 yard, steeply banked County Ground track was like no other. Visiting riders took time to adapt while the Exeter riders found the smaller, tighter flat tracks equally hard to adjust to.

The Falcons nickname came about as a result of an appeal by the newly formed Exeter Speedway Supporters Club, who invited the fans to send in suggestions for a nickname. Who actually suggested 'Falcons' is not recorded, but the nickname was first used against Cradley on 16 June. The previous week had seen the introduction of the well-known war cry:

1 – 3 – 5 – 7
Hear this roar from Glorious Devon
E – X – E – T – E – R   EXETER

This was attributed to Mr Hallett of St Thomas who was a member of the supporters club committee.

Due to a desperate shortage of soap, a further

Victory parade aboard the Peamore Jeep.

appeal by the supporters club ensured that the Falcons had an adequate supply to take into the showers with them!!

Meanwhile back on the track the Falcons, aided by their home track advantage, found themselves climbing the league and when they defeated Southampton at the County Ground on 23 June, they actually topped the Third Division for the first time. The clash with the Saints promised to be a real crunch match and the fans were not to be disappointed.

Exeter started well and were 10 points ahead after three heats, but the Saints quickly settled down and hit back over the next couple of races. With three races to go there were just 7 points separating the two sides. Roger and Hazzard gave Exeter a 4–2 in heat 12 but the Saints' Peter Robinson and Bert Croucher hit back with a vital 5–1, leaving Southampton needing another maximum heat win to force a draw. With 11,000 fans cheering him on, Don Hardy made a superb start to lead the final heat, but his partner Tom Crutcher crashed out on the first bend. Hardy's lead was short lived as Jimmy Squibb nipped past him, but Don had no trouble in holding off Pete Lansdale to give Exeter a narrow 43–41 victory and put the Falcons at the top of the league for the first time.

Exeter were to top the table for just 24 hours as the next evening at Banister Court the Saints won 47½ – 36½ . The match started well for Exeter with Hardy winning the opening heat and setting a new track record of 72.2, while Broncho dead-heated with Squibb for third place. Cyril Roger won heat 2, but a possible 4–2 was lost when Crutcher broke a countershaft while lying third. After a drawn third race the Falcons still led by one point, but from then on the Saints forged ahead. Exeter reduced the gap to just three points with a Roger/Hazzard 5–1 in heat 10, but thereafter victory slipped away.

The Falcons received vocal support not only from the travelling Exeter fans but also from a fifty strong Naval contingent of Devonian petty officers and ratings based at Portsmouth, who were led by a rather inexperienced bugler and a noisy drummer.

Southampton's reputation ensured that another huge crowd turned out when they returned to the County Ground for their second league match on 25 August. Over 11,000 fans flocked to see the Saints, but this time the Falcons won easily, and the main excitement occurred in heat 7 when Jimmy Squibb came from nowhere to pass first Sid Hazzard and then pip Stan Hodson on the line.

Hodson was making his debut for the Falcons, and was one of several popular riders who joined Exeter during the season. Nicknamed 'The Killer', Hodson had taken up speedway in 1945 after previously racing in the grass track meetings near his Nottinghamshire home. He had started as a novice at Belle Vue, Manchester, before joining Sheffield as a reserve and moving on to Wombwell. While with Wombwell, Stan was involved in an accident when his Buick car hit a telegraph pole as he was returning from a meeting at Plymouth. He was so shaken up by the incident that he decided to quit speedway and sell his bike, but after a few weeks Frank Buckland, the Exeter manager, contacted Hodson and persuaded him to make a comeback with the Falcons. Stan's trademark was a white pullover that he wore over his plain black leathers, and he soon became a big favourite with the fans.

Jack Parker, the British Match Race Champion was at the County ground at the end of June, but not to ride. Jack came along to present the prizes of cutlery and electric clocks to the winners of the Best Pairs Championship. This impressive meeting involved pairs from each league team and was won by the Southampton duo of Peter Robinson and George Bason from Ivan Kessell and Stan Lanfear of Plymouth. The Falcons representatives, Cyril Roger and Allan Chambers did not gate quickly enough and as the meeting was run in pouring rain found passing very difficult, though they managed fourth place.

Another new signing was John Myson, a grocer from Hoddesdon in Hertfordshire. Before the war he had worked at a hotel run by Australian speedway international Dicky Case. Case also ran the training school at the nearby Rye House track, and it was not long before Myson made it into the local team, which happened to be skippered by Les Trim. Earlier in 1947 Plymouth and Tamworth had shown an interest in signing him but a call to Trim's old mechanic, Stan Harris, resulted in a trial at the County Ground and the offer of a team place. Myson's first home appearance for the Falcons was against Plymouth on 7 July when he unfortunately sustained a fractured thumb.

Also in the wars that evening was Plymouth skipper Stan Lanfear who lost control while leading the first heat and hit the fence on the third bend. Lanfear bounced back into the path of Broncho Slade who rode over him before crashing

Johnny Myson.

Sid 'Hap' Hazzard.

himself. Lanfear was taken to hospital with fractured ribs but although Slade bravely continued his machine was so badly damaged that he was forced to ride the track spare. Sadly his efforts were to no avail as the spare had also been involved in a crash at Cradley the previous Saturday as a result of which the rear wheel was out of alignment. This caused the chain to fly off every time Broncho tried to broadside it and prevented him from scoring.

The following week Myson top scored with 10 points in the Falcons only away league victory of the season when they won 43–40 at Plymouth. Exeter started with a win thanks to a 4–2 from Don Hardy and Slade but the Devils quickly hit back and led until heat 7 when Myson and partner Tom Crutcher scored a 5–1 to put Exeter in the driving seat. With four races to go just three points separated the Devon rivals, but it was the Falcons who held on to win. Myson dropped his only points in the final heat when he finished third behind Ivan Kessell and Hardy. Cyril Roger crashed in his first race but won his remaining three. Charlie Challis was the Devils' top man backed by Kessell and Alex Gray.

The Falcons may have been running up regular cricket scores but the fans were still treated to some spectacular action from the home riders. While Cyril Roger's total County Ground supremacy ensured that he finished most of his races well in front, the likes of Broncho Slade provided plenty of thrills and of course spills. Sid Hazzard caused a sensation when he discovered that he could use the safety fence to drive around the outside of the bends. Buckland was so impressed that he offered 'Hap' Hazzard an extra fiver if he could get his back wheel up on the fence. Sid's reaction was to put both wheels up the fence and duly went home £10 better off.

With teams visiting each other twice in the league it is not surprising the second visits produced tighter scores. Wombwell were thrashed 50–31 on their first appearance but when they returned at the end of July the Colliers produced a real thriller before going down narrowly 43–41. Only Cyril Roger defeated their skipper, Harwood Pike. Ted Moore made his comeback for the Falcons, but fell in both of his races. In appreciation of the treatment Ted had received in the Royal Devon & Exeter Hospital, the Supporters Club held a collection to aid hospital funds.

Plymouth also pushed the Falcons to a last heat decider in the North v South Cup on August Bank Holiday in front of a huge 14,000 crowd. The Falcons had missed out by a single point at Pennycross a few days previously and were expected to walk this one, but it turned into a ding-dong affair with Plymouth needing a 5–1 in the final heat to draw. However, Roger and Myson saved the day with a timely 4–2, and Cyril completed a superb 15 point maximum before going on to clean up in the second half.

It was in the North v South cup that the Falcons were to suffer their first home defeat. This came at the hands of Eastbourne who won 45–51 at the County Ground on 18 August. Although the Eagles had obviously ridden well their chances had been enhanced by a run of machine problems for the Exeter boys, who ended the evening with just four fit bikes out of ten. Things started to go wrong for the Falcons when Chambers stopped when leading heat 4, while Hardy's bike was the

Cyril Roger in action.

next to go in the following race, and the Eagles found themselves in front 16–14. They still led 38–34 after 12 races but the Falcons appeared to be retaking control when Slade and Hazzard went ahead in heat 13, but when Broncho crashed on the first bend the heat was drawn.

Slade was involved in another desperate battle in heat 15. His partner Arthur Pilgrim's bike packed up as the tapes rose, and Broncho was left to fight it out every inch of the way with the Eagles reserves, Ron Clark and Bob Sivyer. At the flag it looked like a dead heat, but Clark got the decision and Eastbourne the match. Roger completed another 15 point maximum when he beat Wally Green and Jock Grierson in the nominated riders race but it was too late for the Falcons.

Arthur Pilgrim made his debut as Falcons reserve in this match following an impressive win in the junior scratch race the previous week. He too, had started on the grass tracks before riding speedway at Dagenham and Hall Green, Birmingham in 1938 without achieving too much success. After the war Arthur decided to have another go and started riding again early in 1947. Jim Edwards, the editor of Speedway World, noticed him and recommended him to Frank Buckland.

Pilgrim notched his first league win as Exeter beat Plymouth 53–30 on Monday 8 September. That night Stan Lanfear, having recovered from his earlier rib injuries, became the first visitor to score a 12 point maximum, while Sid Hazzard won his Christmas dinner! A group of supporters had offered to present a live goose, which they were feeding up for Christmas, to the most spectacular Falcons' rider of the match. Sid duly took the prize with another display of 'fence raising' form.

Buckland was by now looking to improve his side's away performances and had previously signed Cornish grasstrack champion Desmond Tamblyn who unfortunately failed to score in his only league appearance at Hanley.

On Monday 22 September Don Hardy suffered facial injuries, not on the track but in a train accident on the way to the meeting. Don was travelling down to Exeter from London on board the Southern Railways crack Atlantic Coast Express. Between Honiton and Sidmouth Junction the train was passed by another express, the London bound all-Pullman Devon Belle. Unfortunately the Devon Belle's three foot by two foot steel name plate became detached and swung into the path of the westbound Atlantic, tearing into the streamlined cowling of the locomotive and damaging the sides of the first seven coaches. Windows in the two leading coaches were smashed and Don was one of two passengers cut by flying glass. He received first aid from the kitchen car staff on the train before being taken by taxi from Exeter Central Station to the Royal Devon & Exeter Hospital for further treatment. The incident did not stop him, swathed in sticking plaster, from reaching the County Ground in time to score 8 points for the victorious Falcons who defeated the Rest 62–21.

The North v South competition, which perhaps should really have been known as the Midlands v South Cup, saw the Falcons grouped unsuccessfully with Eastbourne, Southampton and Plymouth. Having lost away at Plymouth and Southampton and at home to the Eagles, the Falcons did not progress to the final. The clash with the Saints again turned into a gala occasion for, not only did Exeter win convincingly, but the Royal Corps of Signals Olympic Team also treated the fans to a thrilling display. Among the riders taking part in the display was Vic Emms. After the meeting he had an impressive spin on Hardy's machine but unfortunately was unable to sign for the Falcons due to his military service. He was later to be a successful member of the Coventry Bees.

The 1947 season ended on an unusual note. Post war shortages were again creating real problems and petrol was in such short supply that it was decided that the away North v South cup match against Eastbourne should be staged at the County Ground as Arlington was considered to be so far out of the south coast resort that fans would not have the spare petrol to get there. The Falcons took full benefit of the situation to gain revenge for the previous slip up and won by 69–27. The evening ended with a spectacular firework display.

The Falcons had finished in fourth place in the league table and Cyril Roger was the Third Division Champion. Once again it had been proved that speedway could attract viable support in Exeter and even wet meetings, of which there had been several, had attracted crowds of 7–8,000. Since speedway had been re-launched more than 200,000 people from all parts of the Westcountry had passed through the County Ground turnstiles. The biggest disadvantage for the promoters was the newly imposed entertainment tax, which cost Exeter Speedway in excess of £10,000 that summer – a huge amount at the time. Unlike other sports such as football and cricket, speedway was not considered by the government to be a skilful sport and therefore was not exempt from tax.

Unfortunately, spectator facilities at the County Ground were not really adequate for the huge crowds of entertainment-hungry fans who flocked to the track every week. That first season it was not even possible to buy a cup of tea inside the ground. However, the Devon Athletic Company had drawn up elaborate plans to redevelop the ground. This futuristic design allowed space for crowds of up to 40,000 with underground car parking. Building costs in 1947 were an estimated £250,000 but sadly the project never got further than an architect's model.

Instead, the ever enthusiastic Bill Eastmond, the Falcons own Mr Fixit, together with a few helpers, spent the winter redeveloping the back straight terracing after hundreds of tons of rubble had been dumped there. The job was obviously done properly as the terracing is still in good repair today. Eastmond also carried out extensive work on the track, reducing the steepness of the banking and relaying the top surface with white sand and crushed granite.

Tom Crutcher in action.

1948

EXETER
SPEEDWAY
OFFICIAL PROGRAMME
PRICE SIXPENCE
Promoted by
MOTOR SPORTS (EXETER) Ltd.,
County Ground Sports Stadium, St. Thomas, Exeter Phone 5231
MONDAY, 12th JULY, 1948, at 7.30 p.m.
National League Match
EXETER v. SOUTHAMPTON
Sixteenth Meeting
NO BETTING ALLOWED
W. V. COLE & SONS, EXETER.

HEAT 2

Frank Buckland had spent the winter in Australia seeking out new talent. When he returned to a bleak and austere Britain in the spring of 1948 he brought with him three exciting Aussie prospects, Keith Gurtner, Hugh Geddes and Norman Clay.

Gurtner was the protégé of original Exeter track record holder Frank Arthur, and had learnt his trade at the Sydney Showground track, before moving on to Brisbane, where for two seasons he was reported to have been the top scorer. Gurtner had tentatively agreed to ride for Johnnie Hoskins at West Ham until Buckland persuaded him to sign for Exeter instead.

Geddes, too, had been trained by Arthur and speedway's first World Champion, Lionel van Praag at Sydney and Brisbane in 1946, before going to California where he regularly raced against the top American stars such as Wilbur Lamoreaux and 1937 World Champion Jack Milne.

Clay had inherited a bike from his brother Sid who had tragically drowned while on a fishing trip. After serving with the armoured division during the war Clay started racing again at Sydney and Newcastle but was involved in a serious crash in which he suffered a fractured skull and other injuries. Remarkably, he was back on the track within six months, where Buckland spotted him and quickly offered him an Exeter contract. His wife Muriel accompanied Clay to England.

Several familiar faces would be missing from the new look Exeter team. Tragedy had struck the Falcons during winter when Tom Crutcher had been killed in a car crash. Meanwhile veteran Les Trim had decided to call it a day at 43 years of age. This decision followed a serious leg injury, which

The 1948 Falcons L→R back: Norman Clay, Bert Sibley, Frank Buckland, Hugh Geddes, Arthur Pilgrim, Gordon Taylor. Front: Stan Hodson, Cyril Roger, Bert Roger, Don Hardy.

had spoilt his 1947 season with Exeter. Several of the Hampshire-based riders had been lured away by the opening of a new speedway track at Poole, among them Allan Chambers, Sid Hazzard and Charlie Hayden. Hayden was destined to ride for the Pirates in the ill-fated opening race at Wimborne Road during which Yarmouth's Reg Craven suffered fatal injuries in a first bend crash. Hazzard rode as reserve in the rerun.

The Third Division now boasted twelve teams. Apart from Poole new tracks had opened at Coventry, Hull and Yarmouth while Eastbourne, the 1947 champions, moved along the coast and become Hastings.

A late edition to the Exeter line-up was Cyril Roger's younger brother Bert. Bert, an accomplished all-round motorcyclist, had only taken up speedway the previous summer after starting his racing career on the grass tracks. He had achieved a high degree of success road racing and finished eleventh in the Junior TT on the Isle of Man as well as doing extremely well at Scarborough. New Cross quickly spotted his potential and signed him up before loaning him out to the Falcons.

The Exeter season opened at the County Ground on Easter Monday morning with an individual event, the Tom Crutcher Memorial Trophy. Bert made an immediate impact scoring 12 points. The meeting was seen as a team trial and the majority of riders taking part were Exeter assets, the only exceptions being the Plymouth duo of Billy Newell and Pete Lansdale.

Heavy drizzle had soaked the track overnight and the rain steadily increased during the morning, but fortunately stopped in time to allow racing to go ahead. Cyril Roger maintained his '47 form by winning the meeting with a 15 point maximum, but it was Johnny Myson who stole the glory. Myson had ridden at Plymouth on Good Friday in a big individual meeting and finished second in front of a 20,000 strong crowd which included Clay and Geddes, both of whom had paid to get in after the pits gatekeeper refused to believe that they were new Exeter riders.

Back at the County Ground Myson was unbeatable in his first four races and the meeting reached a magnificent climax in heat 20, when he lined up at the tapes with Cyril Roger. Myson made the start, but Roger overtook him on the first bend. For two laps Myson trailed his skipper, then made his move going down the back straight. Having closed right up on Roger, Myson attempted to overtake but only succeeded in clipping his opponent's back wheel on the third bend. Myson was instantly hurled head over heels along the track, but happily, after prompt attention from the first aiders he was able to walk back to the pits. Bert Roger made an immediate impact at his new club, finishing joint second with Myson overall on 12 points.

The three new Australians all got their first experience of the Exeter track under racing conditions. Geddes, although the lowest scorer of the trio, appeared to be the most accomplished rider, despite injuring his leg in an early heat. Clay notched 9 points in smooth fashion, but although Gurtner struggled in his early races he came good towards the end. It is interesting to note that his rear wheel was fitted with an old motorcar tyre!

Broncho Slade returned to form with some lively racing but a number of broken chains, each time while leading, kept him out of contention. Arthur Pilgrim showed a marked improvement on the previous season, but Stan Hodson was forced to miss the opening action following a crash during an earlier practice session which left him with an injured hand.

During the interval Frank Buckland announced the Falcons' line-up for their first match against Plymouth the following week. Cyril and Bert Roger were paired together at one and two, with Myson and Geddes, Slade and Gurtner forming the other two pairings. Pilgrim and Clay were named as reserves. Up until that point Don Hardy had not enjoyed a good meeting but the Londoner was so incensed at being left out of the team that he immediately came out and scored a convincing win in his next race.

Not only did Exeter have more than enough riders to fill the team places but the club also sported an impressive list of up and coming juniors eager to make it into the line-up. Two new faces that appeared at the County Ground that spring were Bill Elliott and Art Hood, both newcomers via the 'Speedway World' training schools, and they joined local second halfers Reg Robins, Herbie Plain, Gordon Taylor, 'Dingo' Davey and John Hancox.

The strength of the new line-up was evident when the Falcons thrashed Plymouth 68–28 a week later in the first round of the four-leg Devon Derby competition. 11,000 fans watched Exeter, now sporting a smart new Falcon emblem on their race jackets, dominate the Devils in what was generally a processional match. The main excitement came in heat 7 when, after missing the start,

Frank Buckland & Bill Eastmond welcome Keith Gurtner, Hugh Geddes & Norman Clay to the County Ground.

Cyril Roger was forced to carve his way through from the back eventually snatching victory from Pete Lansdale on the final corner.

Despite the impressive victory Hardy was quickly recalled and replaced Gurtner as reserve for the first league match away at Southampton the following evening. It was not an auspicious start as the Falcons were hammered 57–27. Worse was to follow at Tamworth the next evening where, in the first leg of the Daily Mail National Trophy, the Falcons were annihilated 82–26 over 18 heats.

Back in Exeter the awful news was broken to stunned fans at a Supporters Club Dance, where a highly optimistic M.C. cheered them with the fact that the Falcons "would only need to score 5–1's in every heat in the home meeting, to go through to the next round".

His optimistic prediction was almost fulfilled at the County Ground on Monday 12 April when the Falcons won the return leg 81–27, and only engine failures for Bert Roger and John Myson, in heats 3 and 7, prevented Exeter from pulling off the comeback of the century. Exeter were in fact 50 points ahead after 16 heats and just needed maximums from the last two heats to win on aggregate. Unfortunately disaster struck in the penultimate race when Hardy punctured a tyre, this allowed Steve Langton and Basil Harris to go in front, but only until Slade burst around the fence in a shower of sparks to take the lead. Although the Roger brothers duly took a 5–1 in the final race Exeter's chance of progress was gone. Myson had bravely ridden with stitches in his jaw following a crash in the first leg at the Fazely Stadium.

The Falcons achieved their first away victory of the season at Plymouth three days later when they won the second leg of the Devon Derby 52–44. This was followed by two good home league wins over newcomers Hastings 'Saxons' and Hull 'Angels' at the County Ground.

Prior to the Hull match Cyril Roger beat Southampton's Bob Oakley 2–0 in the Third Division match race championship. In winning the first race Cyril also set a new track record of 78.4 seconds.

Exeter's first league double was achieved at Hastings' newly constructed Pilot Field track on Wednesday 28 April. This proved to be a real

Tapes go up at the County Ground.

nailbiter, which ended with a last heat decider. Exeter opened with a 5–1 courtesy of Cyril Roger and Broncho Slade, but the Saxons quickly retook the lead and forged ahead. Undaunted, the Falcons fought back and another 5–1 in heat 10, this time thanks to Bert Roger and Arthur Pilgrim, put them back in front. Hastings drew level twice more and with one race to go the score was 39–39, but Slade and Hugh Geddes clinched victory for the Falcons with a last gasp 5–1.

A qualifying round of the Sunday Dispatch Speedway Riders Championship was the next event at the County Ground. The World Championship would not be revived until the following year so this competition was seen as the alternative.

The Exeter round produced several upsets as well as one legendary race. Cyril Roger naturally started as favourite, but his challenge suffered a setback in his second outing. For once Cyril was a little slow out of the start, which allowed Ken Tidbury of Hastings and Tamworth's Steve Langton to get ahead of him. He quickly made up the lost ground and swept into the lead only to crash on the fourth bend. Although Cyril won his next two heats he was content to finish behind brother Bert in heat 17. This allowed Bert to finish with 13 points, a total which could only be beaten by Hastings' Wally Green, who after four rides had scored 11. Green seemed certain to win the final heat and take the winner's cheque, but everyone had reckoned without Broncho Slade.

When the tapes were released Broncho made a terrific start and headed Green into the first bend. From then on the Kennford leg-trailer rode the race of his life successfully blocking every move that Green made to overtake him. This tremendous duel lasted for the whole four laps and although Green made a superhuman effort to pass on the run in to the flag, Slade managed to maintain his slender lead, to the huge delight of the crowd.

Former track manager, Ted Lethbridge, recalled that this race produced probably the noisiest crowd reaction he ever heard at the County Ground. This view is borne out by the following week's programme in which Frank Buckland described the race as:

> "82.2 seconds of continuous cheering, the like of which has never been heard before in Exeter".

Wally Green's own recollections of the race appeared in the Express & Echo's Pure Nostalgia column during November 1996 and put a slightly different slant on the incident.

> "My race against Broncho should have been a formality once I had gained the lead, but to my astonishment, although I was only a yard or so

away from the white line, Broncho, a leg trailer who always rode round the fence, came inside, and as he passed he winked at me with his right eye. That completely distracted me and try as I might I couldn't catch him."

Green's defeat meant that he tied with Bert Roger for first place and so the two riders shared the £25 first prize, which was presented by the Sunday Dispatch sports editor Pat Reekie.

Bert Roger's other two qualifying rounds were at Hanley and Wombwell where he scored 10 and 14 points respectively. This gave him a total of 37 which was equalled by Wally Green and Hanley's Dave Anderson and it was decided that the three should take part in a run-off at Cradley for the third qualifying slot in the second division rounds with Jock Grierson and Alf Bottoms who had scored 40 points each. Anderson pulled out due to a hand injury but Bert in his first appearance at Dudley Wood beat Green and went through. This was no mean achievement for a first year rookie. The Division Two rounds saw Bert score 9 at Middlesbrough, 8 at Birmingham and 3 at Norwich but his total of 20 points was only good enough for 26th place. The championship final was staged at Wembley in September and won by Harringay Racers' Vic Duggan who received the trophy from the Duke of Edinburgh.

Around this time the Exeter track came in for some criticism from visiting riders. Ken Tidbury of Hastings complained that the concrete starting gate was like a 'sheet of ice' and gave little grip.

Bert Roger takes mascot Gordon Gray on parade.

Other riders were unhappy with the fine white sand, which was used as top dressing, claiming that it cut the skin and was bad for the eyes. Wally Green was able to substantiate this, as grains of the sand thrown up by the back wheels of other riders had infiltrated under his goggles and into his eyes. Later while driving to London Wally was reported to have suffered from temporary loss of vision and was forced to pull off the road. Fortunately Arthur Pilgrim saw him, stopped and rendered first aid to both of his eyes, which had become badly swollen. Arthur then drove Wally's car for him, while Mrs Pilgrim took over the wheel of their transport.

Cradley Heath was the next team to visit the County Ground, being decisively dispatched 65–18. Cyril Roger claimed a full maximum, despite having injured his leg at Plymouth riding for a 'West Select' side against second division Birmingham the previous week, while brother Bert scored 10 paid 12.

Exeter's 51–33 victory over the Norwich Stars in a challenge match on Whit Monday afternoon, 17 May, was particularly significant as it was the first appearance by a second division side at the County Ground. The Falcons also made history by becoming the first junior side to beat a team from a higher division. This was achieved in front of a crowd of 11,000. Cyril Roger got Exeter off to the best possible start by beating Stars' skipper Paddy Mills. In doing so Cyril broke his own track record by 1.4 seconds, setting a new record time of 77.0 seconds.

The Stars line-up that season included pre-war Exeter favourites Bert Spencer and Ted Bravery. Bravery proved that he had not forgotten the way around and recorded three wins for a total of 9 points, but sadly Spencer was unable to ride due to injury. With George Harper also on the injured list Norwich had booked West Ham's Howdy Byford as a guest. Byford's scoring was restricted thanks to a couple of spills and a controversial clash with Clay. Howdy also had something of a reputation as crooner and happily was still in good voice later on at a dance organised by the Supporters Club at the nearby Buller Hall in Cowick Street. During the evening he entertained the fans, if not the still irate Clay, with three songs.

The following Monday the Plymouth Devils made their third appearance of the season at Exeter, this time in the North v South Cup. This match would make the headlines in the Daily Mirror, sadly not for the quality of the racing but for a pre-match incident in which two of the Devils' machines were apparently sabotaged.

When Plymouth's Pete Lansdale went to warm up his bike prior to the match he found that the filler cap of his fuel tank was loose and crusted with sugar. His team mates' machines were immediately checked and skipper Peter Robinson's bike was also found to have been 'nobbled'. Approximately two ounces of sugar, sufficient to choke the carburettor, was found in each tank. Frank Buckland immediately condemned the incident as a 'filthy trick' but pointed out that the sabotage had not necessarily taken place in the Exeter pits as both machines had been sent, unescorted, by rail from London. Nevertheless pits security at the County Ground was to be tightened up.

The match itself resulted in another comprehensive victory, this time 65–31, for the Falcons. Although the Devils only managed to win one heat, they showed considerable improvement on their previous visits. This, it was suggested, was due to the influence of Wembley's Bill Kitchen, who was currently sidelined with a broken arm, and had been engaged as an honorary team coach.

Peter Lansdale's performance was obviously effected by the sugar incident, as he managed to score only a single point, and it was left to Plymouth reserve Vic Gent to top score with 7 points. During the previous winter there had been much speculation that Gent was on the Falcons' 'wanted' list although Buckland denied the rumours. After the match Kitchen was besieged by young autograph hunters, but still managed to give an interview to the 'Falcon Fanfare', the local speedway paper. In this interview the idea of a pre-match parade was suggested as a way of giving the visiting riders the opportunity to ride the track before racing commenced.

Whilst big wins were good for the Falcons' league position, the management were now looking for ways of reducing the home advantage and improving the racing. Bill Eastmond had managed to obtain a tractor complete with hydraulic grader to replace the Peamore Garage jeep that had previously dragged a grader around when required. As the tractor was much easier to get on and off the track grading could now take place between each race.

Exeter were now well into an unbeaten run which by mid June would be extended to a record 15 consecutive wins, and as a result put the Falcons at the top of the table. Meanwhile changes were also being made on the team front. With nine riders vying for eight team places it was decided that Johnny Myson, who had suffered a niggling series of minor injuries, should be allowed to go on loan to Bristol. Keith Gurtner, who had never settled at the County Ground, went to Newcastle in exchange for Bonny Waddell, who with no immediate prospect of a team place agreed to go on loan to Plymouth.

May ended with a 65–19 home victory over Poole and a week later Hanley were dismissed 66–18. That evening, 7 June, also saw Cyril Roger maintain his hold on the match race championship. Prior to the Falcons match against the Potters he beat Southampton's Alf Bottoms 2–0. 10,000 fans had turned out to watch and they were not disappointed as Roger won the first heat in a new record time of 76.2 seconds. In the second race Bottoms unfortunately seized his engine and Cyril toured the last two laps unopposed to finish in 80.4.

The following Monday the public obviously felt that the newly formed Coventry Bees, made up mainly of Belle Vue juniors, would not offer much of an attraction as only 4,000 fans turned up to watch. As so often happens on these occasions, the 'stay aways' missed the most exciting match of the season to date. The Falcons won easily 57–27 even though Cyril Roger had a rare off night and only scored 5 points. For the Bees Vic Emms, previously seen at Exeter in 1947 as a member of the Royal Corps of Signals White Helmets Display team, scored ten points, the highest so far by a visiting rider, and his clash with Slade in heat 3 was the highlight of a meeting packed with thrills and spills. Later in the dressing room Emms told George Selley, the Falcons' veteran trainer and masseur, that for several years he had suffered with a dislodged cartilage in his left knee. Within half a minute George had obligingly put it back in place.

The second half proved just as exciting. A junior match between Exeter and Poole resulted in 13–10 victory for the Falcons' reserves. Exeter's Johnny Hancox was given a particularly warm welcome having been married earlier that afternoon. Johnny had apparently enjoyed himself a little too much at the reception and as a consequence found avoiding the safety fence rather tricky, but still managed to win both his races.

As soon as the meeting was over the Falcons set out on the long journey to Yarmouth where they were due to race the following evening. The riders and officials travelled by train, arriving at Paddington station in London at 7.30am. Here the bikes were loaded on to a lorry provided by

British Railways that was to take them and the team across London to Liverpool Street station. However the driver had to stand guard over the equipment while everyone went off for 'a wash and brush up and breakfast'. Once at Liverpool Street they transferred to more comfortable reserved accommodation on the train, which took them the rest of the way to Yarmouth where they arrived at 4.30pm

The track at Caister Road had acute bends with a surface layer of four inch deep cinders and it appeared at one stage as if Exeter's winning streak had run out. The biggest crowd Yarmouth had seen so far saw Exeter trail for most of the match before finishing strongly to win 45–35. Cyril Roger notched yet another maximum, while Bert dropped his only point to 18 year old Billy Bales in his first race. This was no disgrace as in beating Bert the Bloaters' teenage sensation broke the track record.

Cyril's continued success was beginning to bring its own problems. He was by now riding regularly for parent club New Cross in the First Division, and it looked increasingly likely that the Rangers would recall him permanently, although it was hoped that he would be allowed to stay until the end of the season.

Post-war shortages still prevailed as borne out by one irate lady who complained in the weekly 'Falcon Fanfare' that although she had paid for her supporter's club badge the previous season, it had still not been received. The ESSC secretary explained that not enough badges had been delivered to meet the demand due to a limited supply of materials.

The Falcons' away success continued with a 56–26 away victory at Coventry. The scoreline was particularly notable in that it was the highest ever away win by a team in any of the three divisions since the war. The Exeter score was boosted by two 5–0s, the second of which was caused by a collision between the two Bees riders, George Smith and Fred Yates. Sixty-two Exeter fans travelled to Brandon by coach at a cost of £1.7s.0d (£1.35p) each. The evening proved slightly more expensive for Cyril Roger who, following a heated dispute with a Coventry rider in the pits, was fined £10.

Back at the County Ground the Falcons scored another massive win over Wombwell, who were decisively dismissed 69–15. Harwood Pike was the only rider to split the Falcons, coming second behind Cyril Roger and ahead of Hugh Geddes, in the opening race after which he failed to score another point. This race apart it was very definitely one-way traffic, with Broncho Slade producing the ride of the night, in heat 9, when he came through from last to first.

Off track, Norman Clay and his wife, Muriel, were reported to be seeking a suitable beach where they could go surfing. An appeal in the programme resulted in several suggestions, but their final destination is uncertain.

The Falcons' impressive on track success was unfortunately not being reflected at the turnstiles. Before the match against Cradley on June 28, the fans were stunned to hear Buckland announce over the tannoy that he was prepared to close Exeter and move the riders to another venue near London if attendance did not improve. In a hard-hitting programme editorial Buckland followed up by explaining that a regular attendance of 8,000 was required, whereas the crowds had only been averaging around 6,500. The cost of staging a meeting in 1948 was £450. Prize money needed to be at least £208; riders' expenses, including travelling expenses averaged out at £5 a head totalling £40 and the annual rental of the stadium

Stan Hodson is pushed off watched by a huge first bend crowd.

was £500. Exeter also employed 60 track officials and 5 permanent office staff. The Speedway Control Board took 2½% of the takings, while £450 in every £1,000 taken at the turnstiles went to the government in entertainment tax. The riders pay scale in the third division at this time was the equivalent of 75p a start and £1 a point.

6,800 paid to watch Exeter beat Cradley 67–16 that evening but the meeting was marred by a horrific sixth heat crash. Heathens' Jimmy Wright was first out of the gate and well out in front when his engine cut out coming off the second bend. Arthur Pilgrim passed him, followed by the other Cradley rider, Phil Malpass. Unfortunately for Wright he forgot about third place man Slade and instead of pulling onto the grass, turned right across the track towards the pit gate. This proved to be an almost fatal error as Broncho, head down, flat out, left leg trailing, came blasting around the boards in a desperate bid to make up lost ground. At full bore he hit Wright amidships and the impact sent both men and machines somersaulting down the straight.

Slade was bleeding so profusely that a blanket covered his face as he was carried to the first aid room, in an attempt not to alarm his mother, who was watching from the grandstand. It had the reverse effect and the rumour rapidly spread that Broncho had been killed. Happily he 'only' suffered concussion, shock and facial cuts and was not detained in hospital. Wright was not so lucky having suffered serious fractures to his right arm, leg and pelvis, and underwent surgery at the Royal Devon & Exeter Hospital later that evening.

While Wright was in the operating theatre the Falcons, with John Hancox a last minute addition to the party in place of Slade, were once again travelling through the night to Yarmouth, where this time they lost by a single point. After a good start Exeter let slip a 9 point lead and went into the final heat just one point in front. Billy Bales won the race for the Bloaters, but on the last bend Cyril Roger crashed into Reg Morgan while battling for second place. As a result Roger was disqualified, Hugh Geddes finished second and Morgan, who had been stretchered off, was awarded third place. Thus Yarmouth won 42–41.

Gordon Taylor came into the Exeter team to replace Slade at Plymouth a couple of days later for a thriller of a league match. The lead yo-yoed from Exeter to Plymouth and back again until heat 8 after which the Falcons forged ahead, helped by a heat 13 5–0 in which both Plymouth riders fell. The Roger brothers top scored once again with Bert producing a superb ride in heat 6 during which he battled his way past Lansdale and Newell to win.

Quite clearly the fans had not forgotten the nobbling incident at the County Ground a month earlier, as the Devils' supporters has dreamt up a new warcry ending:

> 'S-U-G-A-R SUGAR'.

Exeter responded with:

> '5 10 15 20
> Sugar's scarce, but we've got plenty'

One lad in green and white was even seen waving a Tate & Lyle box on a pole. Despite the war having been over for three years sugar remained in short supply and was in fact still rationed.

Exeter suffered a further defeat at Coventry on Saturday 10 July, where they were beaten 47–35. The Falcons were without Bert Roger, who was riding in the Riders Championship at Norwich, and Broncho Slade who was injured. They also suffered a spate of engine problems, and twice suffered the ignominy of seeing both riders fail to finish. In heat 3 Stan Hodson and Norman Clay both fell and in heat 9 Hugh Geddes and Cyril Roger went out with engine trouble. Geddes' machine had earlier let him down while leading heat 5.

The Coventry fans were reported to be more 'spirited' in their reactions to the racing and were armed with bigger and noisier rattles, an innovation that was becoming increasingly unpopular. Many fans had acquired the big wooden devices previously used by ARP wardens during the war, and their use had already been banned at New Cross, partly due to complaints from the neighbours and because indiscriminate use on tightly packed terraces had injured some spectators. A survey showed that over two thousand rattles had been in weekly use at the Old Kent Road track that season but had now been replaced by bells, whistles and bugles.

The visit of championship rivals Southampton Saints to the County Ground on Monday 12 July was a gala occasion. The evening opened with the first leg of the match race championship in which Cyril Roger defeated Hastings' Jock Grierson 2–1. Although Cyril fell in the opening run he came back to win the other two races.

In the vital league match that followed, the Falcons faced their toughest opponents so far. The Saints refused to allow Exeter to build up much of a lead. Thanks to wins by Southampton's Alf Bottoms and Jimmy Squibb, the first two heats were drawn. Don Hardy was Exeter's first winner of the evening in heat 3 and although the Saints never managed to get ahead, there was never more than six points in it until the last three races when Exeter finally broke away to win 48–36. A 5–1 by Hardy and Pilgrim in the last race rounded things off neatly for the Falcons.

Again the Roger brothers headed the Exeter score chart while Clay also showed impressive form and included two wins over Bob Oakley in his 8 point tally.

A new look programme cover was used for this meeting with an up to date action photo of Cyril Roger replacing the pre-war picture of Tiger Stevenson. The programme was not the only thing to be revamped as at 6.30am the next day work began on major alterations to the track. The work was supervised by track manager Bill Eastmond, and involved laying 40 tonnes of red ash from Stoke on the fourth bend just for starters. If the experiment proved successful a further 100 tonnes of ash would replace the unpopular silver sand.

Major Fearnley of the Speedway Control Board had been at the County Ground to watch the Southampton match and stayed over to see the track work. He later carried out a track inspection, paying particular attention to the concrete starting grid, before expressing his general satisfaction.

That evening Cyril Roger was in action at Hastings where he again defeated Jock Grierson to retain his match race title. Grierson looked set to force a decider on a neutral track as he led the final race, but on the last turn Roger found some extra speed and burst through to win by a bike's length. All three races were run within the existing track record and Cyril had the satisfaction of establishing a new record time of 71.8 seconds for the 388 yard circuit.

Later that week the Falcons suffered defeats at Cradley and Hull. On the way up to Dudley Wood from Chelmsford Don Hardy and Arthur Pilgrim, who were travelling together, broke down and arrived at the stadium so late that the reserves had to take their places in three races. When Pilgrim eventually got out on to the track in heat 11 there were further problems. The referee excluded Heathens' Phil Malpass for crossing the inside white line, but the cover of the **blue** exclusion light was broken and Pilgrim seeing a **white** light, together with the start marshal displaying the black flag, thought it was meant for him and promptly stopped. Uproar ensued with the 15,000 strong crowd loudly voicing their opinions. The result was declared as a 3–2 in Cradley's favour.

Exeter's first visit to Hull the following night was a total disaster for the league leaders as they were mauled 63–21. The D shaped Hedon track, laid out on the edge of a disused airfield, saw the Falcons heaviest defeat not only of this season, but also since joining the league the previous summer. The track effectively had five corners, thanks to a substantial bulge in the back straight, which the Exeter riders failed to master. These two away defeats allowed Cradley to become joint top of the table with Exeter on 29 points each.

Back at the County Ground the Falcons found the new ash surface very much to their liking and used it to great effect by beating Plymouth 58–25 in their next home league match on Monday 19 July. Unfortunately the ash had to be riddled for clinker before it could be used, which limited the amount laid to 40 tonnes per week.

The victory over Plymouth was the Falcons' sixth consecutive success against the Devils. Bill Kitchen was still acting as Plymouth's team trainer, but his skills were to no avail when Peter Robinson lost a chain and Vic Gent lost control gifting Exeter a 5–0 in the opening race. Later in the match Ivan Kessell took a spectacular tumble while racing neck and neck with Slade. After hitting a bump at the end of the back straight he hurled into the safety fence, but although badly shaken, was fortunately able to walk back to the pits.

Another busy week on the road saw the Falcons suffer defeats at Tamworth (46–38) and Hanley (51–33), but they redeemed themselves by beating the Colliers at Wombwell, 47–37.

The adventures encountered by the Falcons on this trip highlight the difficulties of travel in those austere post war years. With no team coach available the riders and officials set off for Tamworth on Tuesday morning in two taxis with the bikes following behind in a lorry. The day started badly as the party was two hours late leaving Exeter. Just before they reached Bristol one of the taxis, containing Frank Buckland, Broncho Slade, Hugh Geddes and mechanic Bert Sibley, seized it's engine. The two riders were put in the other cab and sent on their way but valuable time was lost while the motor was allowed to cool. Buckland and Sibley eventually fixed the engine and continued towards the Midlands, but once through Bristol, it broke down again. Undaunted they made their way to a railway station and caught a train to Birmingham, from where they took yet another taxi to Tamworth, eventually arriving at the track in time for the second heat! All the delays, however, meant that the team had only reached the track with half an hour to spare. Although the start was delayed to enable them to get ready, the last minute machine checks were rushed and they suffered several engine problems.

By the end of the week everyone was glad to be going home. Buckland, Geddes and Roger forsook the delights of travel by taxi and decided to return to Exeter by train. Having changed trains at Bristol, they sat back for the last leg of their stressful jaunt. But to their horror the train steamed straight through both Exeter St Davids and St Thomas stations and looked set to carry the three weary travellers a further forty miles to Plymouth. Fortunately the signals were against them on the approach to Dawlish Warren and the train slowed almost to walking pace. The Falcons trio did not hesitate. They leapt out of their carriage, walked along the line to the seaside station and three minutes later gratefully caught a local train back home to Exeter.

By now visiting teams were beginning to get to grips with the peculiarities of the County Ground and the home match with Hanley produced a good meeting. The rapidly improving Norman Clay had a particularly successful night scoring 10 as the Falcons won 53–30.

The following weekend was August Bank Holiday when not one but two home meetings were scheduled, an inter league challenge against the Bristol Bulldogs was arranged for Saturday afternoon and an individual event, the Froud Trophy, on Bank holiday Monday afternoon.

The Falcons beat the second division Bulldogs 57–27 thus maintaining their impressive form against teams from a higher league. Don Hardy and Arthur Pilgrim were Exeter's top scorers with 11 apiece, while Cyril Roger suffered a couple of breakdowns. Johnny Myson made an unsuccessful return to his old track, scoring but a single point for Bristol. Broncho Slade was missing again having broken his pelvis in a midweek grass track meeting at Middlemoor. Ironically he now found himself in the next bed to the unfortunate Jimmy Wright at the Royal Devon & Exeter Hospital.

Bank Holiday was wet and the County Ground track extremely heavy after 12 hours of continuous rain. It was common knowledge that Cyril Roger was facing an imminent recall to New Cross as a replacement for George Newton who was suffering from a mysterious illness.

Understandably Cyril wanted to leave Exeter in a blaze of glory. He started well winning his first three races, but Norman Clay was going equally well and both were unbeaten when they met in heat 14. Despite the continuing rain, the pair battled neck and neck for two laps before Cyril attempted a big sweep round the outside but overslid leaving the way open for his opponent. Clay still had to race Bert Roger in the final heat. Bert had recorded three wins and a second so needed a win to force a run off. Clay made the start, and although Bert tried to come back under him the move failed and he fell, leaving Clay's way clear to win the meeting. The Roger brothers finished joint second.

Fortunately for the Falcons only seven fixtures were scheduled for August allowing breathing space to rearrange the line up. Bert Roger inherited the captaincy from his brother, and three weeks later his photograph replaced Cyril's on the cover of the programme. Cyril's move to the first division also forced him to relinquish the match race championship. Bert was nominated to race against Wally Green from Hastings for the vacant title. At the same time Gordon Taylor retired from speedway to concentrate on running his family paint business.

On Monday 9 August Exeter's new look line-up defeated Wombwell 61–23. The re-arranged pairings were Hodson/Hardy, Roger/Geddes, Clay/Pilgrim with Herbie Plain and Mike Wood, a novice from the Rye House training school, as reserves. Clay was again in unbeatable form and recorded his first league maximum.

The Falcons maintained their drive for the championship with another away win at Hastings two days later. Later in the week Exeter also rode a challenge match at Rayleigh, a new venue in Essex. As a one off Arthur Pilgrim, who lived in Chelmsford, was allowed to guest for the Rockets but the Exeter management made it clear that there was no question of a transfer. The freshly laid Rayleigh track also gave cause for concern and drew complaints about the number of bumps and holes. With Exeter's league prospects very much in mind Frank Buckland told his riders not to take any unnecessary chances and as a result the Rockets won narrowly by 41–40.

The team's journey home was equally bumpy as their coach suffered several punctures in various out of the way places en route.

A 53–30 home success over Poole saw Clay score his third successive County Ground maximum in as many weeks. The followed evening, Tuesday 17 August, saw the Falcons travel to Southampton for what promised to be the most important match of the season.

Exeter had again edged clear at the top of the league with 37 points from 25 matches, ahead of Hastings (32 from 27) and Cradley (31 from 24) but it was the Saints (30 points) who now posed the major threat as they had five matches in hand and were unbeaten on their own track. Victory at Southampton would be a major boost for the Falcons at this vital stage of the season, but without Cyril Roger and Broncho Slade even the most optimistic Exeter fan could not be sure of the outcome.

Nevertheless, plenty of fans made the journey in coaches, cars and on motorcycles to support the Falcons at Banister Court where they boosted the crowd to over the 17,000 mark. Exeter supporters who stayed at home were able to hear a 15 minute commentary by Frank Buckland broadcast on 'BBC West of England Wavelength Service'.

With so many matches in hand Southampton naturally fancied their chances of overtaking Exeter in the race for the championship. The Saints also had team problems as both Bob Oakley and Bert Croucher were injured. Exeter had meanwhile recalled Bonnie Waddell from Plymouth, a move that brought strong objections from Southampton promoter Jimmy Baxter, who was also in charge at Pennycross. Waddell had accepted the recall and scored just one point against Poole the previous night. He arrived at Southampton, unloaded his machine and wheeled it into the Falcons section of the pits. But after a discussion with Baxter, he was seen to load his bike back into his car after which he took no part in the meeting. Frank Buckland immediately announced that Waddell was banned from the team saying, 'I would rather pay him £3.00 a week to stay away', and planned to take the matter up with the Speedway Control Board.

The match itself was equally exciting. Southampton's Alf Bottom won the opening race from Don Hardy and Stan Hodson. When Norman Clay failed to get the better of Jimmy Squibb in heat 2 and Arthur Pilgrim dropped back with engine trouble the Saints, as expected, moved into the lead. Southampton's advantage was extended to four points in the following race when Hugh Geddes, already riding with an injured foot, crashed while in front and Bert Roger was unable to snatch the lead from George Bason.

Chaos reigned in heat 4. Saints' Bill Griffiths crashed and brought down Exeter's last minute reserve Doug Smith. Simultaneously Pilgrim, now mounted on the track spare, stopped when the throttle twist grip came off in his hand. The race was halted and Griffiths excluded. Smith failed to start in the rerun leaving just Pilgrim, back on his own machine, and Bottoms to battle it out. Bottoms went ahead at the first corner but on the second lap his bike failed which left Pilgrim to amble around on his own.

The Falcons looked set to take a 5–1 from heat 5 until Squibb powered past both Hodson and Hardy. The next race was also drawn with Cecil Bailey just managing to hold off Clay and Pilgrim. Southampton led 17–16 but to the huge delight of their followers Exeter went ahead when Roger beat Kaines and Geddes finished third in heat 7. The Falcons now held a single point advantage 20–19.

Clay won the eighth heat from Squibb and Ernie Rawlins before Exeter edged further ahead thanks to a Hardy/Hodson 4–2 over Bailey in the next race. The next four heats were all drawn which only added to the increasing tension. With just heat 14 to go the Falcons held a three point lead, 39–36, so nothing less than a 5–1 could save the match for Southampton. With 17,000 fans cheering themselves hoarse Kaines and Bailey came to the tapes alongside Hodson and Geddes. The Saints pairing made the perfect start and led around the first bend but second time around everything changed as Bailey's machine suddenly ground to a halt and Geddes overtook Kaines for first place.

Exeter had achieved a memorable 43–38 victory, ended Southampton's unbeaten home run and considerably strengthened their own chances of winning the championship.

Those with a superstitious leaning put Exeter's splendid victory down to Arthur Pilgrim, who on the way to the track had stopped to pick sprigs of lucky heather that he attached to the handlebars of the Falcons' machines.

Exeter's successful week continued with another win at Wombwell, this time by 43–41. Mike Wood and Herbie Plain filled the reserve berths but failed to score.

The Falcons were next in action at Poole on Monday 23 August, where they lost 46–38. With the team away in Dorset a Best Pairs competition was staged at the County Ground, involving riders from other tracks. The line-up included riders from Bristol, Hastings, Hanley, Tamworth, Plymouth and Coventry, but victory went to pre-war Exeter regular Ted Bravery and his partner Paddy Mills from Norwich. Heat 17 was to prove unlucky for Wally Green who crashed breaking his right collarbone, just a month after recovering from a fracture of his left one.

The Falcons had now won ten away matches and topped the third division table with 45 points, well clear of Southampton, Hastings and Cradley, all of who were on 32. The Exeter fans were confident that the Falcons would collect two more league points when Plymouth returned to the County Ground on 30 August, but this time is was the Devils who would produce a shock result.

Things began to go wrong for Exeter well before 7.30 pm when the car in which Arthur Pilgrim and Don Hardy were travelling from Chelmsford was delayed by three burst tyres and engine trouble at Salisbury. Subsequently they did not arrive at the track until an hour after the start of the meeting so did not ride. John Hancox and Lew Coffin were drafted in to replace them, and Exeter were forced to rely on Hodson, Clay and Roger, who scored 9 points each. Geddes only managed one win, as he was hampered by a knee injury while Stan Lanfear, who had joined the Falcons from Plymouth scored 4, which was a reasonable start as he had missed most of the season thanks to a broken ankle.

The Falcons opened with a 4–2, but Plymouth took a 5–1 in heat 2 and after five races led 16–14. Further misfortune hit Exeter in heat 6 when Roger suffered engine failure after overtaking Len Read for the lead. This left Geddes to chase the diminutive Read, but after a couple of spirited attempts his bike too began to misfire and within yards of the finish Gibson nipped through to grab the Devils' second 5–1.

A tangle at the start of heat 7 resulted in Hodson losing his footrest after a collision with Waddell, who was back with Plymouth after the Southampton debacle. Hodson ended up on the grass and was forced to ride the track spare in the rerun, which was drawn. Clay won heat 8, while Coffin earned a huge cheer when he held off Bill Sobey all the way to the finish giving Exeter a much needed 5–1.

Exeter now trailed by just two points and the deficit was maintained until heat 13, when Waddell and Sobey extended the Devils lead with a vital 4–2. In a dramatic finale Geddes tore past Lansdale, who had made the start, while Lanfear, after taking Vic Gent, made a desperate last bend attempt to go around the outside of Lansdale. Sadly, Stan did not quite make it and so Plymouth gained a totally unexpected 43–31 victory, in what had been the most thrilling match seen at Exeter that year.

It was later reported that as a result of the breakdown en route to the County Ground, Don Hardy was actively seeking a flat in Exeter, which would enable him to cut down on travel. The end of August also saw Johnny Myson asking for a return to the County Ground as he had been given few rides at Bristol and was forced to live on his weekly £3 machine maintenance money.

The Falcons hoped to gain rapid revenge over their Devon rivals when they visited Pennycross later that week. The Supporters Club had booked no less than nine official coaches while a number of private buses were also expected to make the trip west. Even British Railways had laid on a speedway special excursion train at a cost of 5/6d (27½ p). Sadly all these plans were to no avail as the meeting was rained off. The supporter's coaches actually set off but were stopped at Chudleigh by a local fan following an urgent phone call from the speedway office at the County Ground.

The beginning of September brought news of a major change to the Falcons' management team. Frank 'Buster' Buckland had decided to emigrate to Australia and his position as clerk of the course and general manager was to be taken over by Bill Eastmond. Former rider Les Trim had also decided to quit as team mechanic due to the demands of his garage business.

The rider crisis had by now been overcome and it was confirmed that Stan Lanfear had signed on a permanent basis after Exeter had paid a £100 transfer fee. Lanfear had been signed from his parent club, Wembley, and although he never rode regularly for the Lions, Stan had gained plenty of experience on loan with Sheffield and Plymouth.

The Falcons' first match in September was at Tamworth, and again it was not a successful trip. Due to the revival of greyhound racing at the Fazeley Stadium the match had been brought forward by 24 hours from Wednesday to Tuesday. Unfortunately the Exeter management had overlooked this and they had to hurriedly call the team together and pack them off to the Midlands at extremely short notice. Trips to Tamworth seemed to have been fated and this one was no exception. The lorry carrying the bikes broke down and only arrived at the track with five minutes to spare. Although the start was delayed for 10 minutes it was not surprising that the Exeter team's preparation was not up to their usual standard and consequently the Falcons lost 50–33.

Exeter gained ample revenge the following week by winning 65–19 when the Hounds visited the County Ground. Don Hardy scored his first full maximum of the season while Clay also rode unbeaten. During the evening Exeter registered their 1000th match point.

Two more valuable league points were gained at Hanley where, without Stan Hodson, who was nursing a leg injury, the Falcons produced a magnificent performance to win 45–39. Stan Lanfear moved up into the team to replace Hodson and Lew Coffin was given another chance at reserve. Hodson's absence was not so easily covered at Cradley the next evening where the Falcons had to wait until heat 7 before recording their first race win. The Heathens won comfortably by 55–29.

The season was now reaching its climax. Exeter remained 6 points clear at the top of the table, but

Don Hardy.

second place Southampton still had six matches in hand, although five of these were away.

A 10,000 crowd saw the Falcons beat the Coventry Bees 48–36 in a thriller at the County Ground on 20 September. During the evening the Royal Corps of Signal motorcycle team gave a display on the centre green. The previous season, Coventry's Vic Emms had been a member of the 'White Helmets'. This time around he was the Bees joint top scorer. Both he and Lionel Levy scored 11 points in the league match and lost out only to Bert Roger who duly collected another 12 point maximum.

The most poignant part of that evening was Frank Buckland's farewell to the County Ground before leaving for Australia. Frank had decided to emigrate for health reasons and planned to start a sheep farm near Melbourne where he intended to look up his old friend 'Wizard' Frank Arthur.

Buckland had been involved in speedway at Exeter since its launch early in 1929. He had been responsible for installing the original floodlighting but quickly made his name as a rider. A farewell luncheon was held in honour and his last official duty was as BBC radio commentator at a match between Poole and Plymouth. Frank Buckland was to return to his native city just once, in the mid-sixties. During his short visit he attended a Rotary Club lunch where among the guests was the late USA team manager John Scott, who at that time was manager of the AA office in Exeter. 'Buster' died in Australia in 1973 after a lengthy illness.

The Falcons went back to Poole on Monday 27 September, and this time, under newly installed floodlights, won 52–31 to take another step nearer the championship.

As had become usual when the Falcons visited Dorset an open meeting was staged at the County Ground. This time it was Cornishman Bruce Semmens, then a big star with Sheffield in the second division and Britain's top ice racer, who created the thrills and won the pairs event. Semmens, whose son Mike was to ride for the Falcons in the 80's, swept to a 15 point maximum. His partner should have been Jack Bibby, but he was unavailable so John Hancox stood in and contributed 3 points. Semmens was untouchable even though the rain, which fell continuously all evening, had thoroughly soaked the track. Earlier in the day Bruce had arrived in his smart Allard sports car and after taking his first look around the County Ground declared that this was the kind of track about which he had dreamed.

The rearranged trip to Plymouth took place the following night. The needle between the two sides had increased even more since the Devils had won at the County Ground. This time around the Falcons stormed to victory by 46–38. After two drawn heats the Falcons went ahead and although the Devils managed a 5–1 in heat 6 Exeter were never seriously troubled. Stan Hodson rounded off a fine evening's work by winning the Derby Scratch race final from Hardy and Pilgrim.

Two more big home wins over Yarmouth and Tamworth further reinforced the Falcons position at the top of the table as the season entered its final month. Four Falcons – Clay, Pilgrim, Hodson and Geddes – went to Bristol and won a five heat challenge match 17–13, much to the surprise of the Bulldogs' fans.

The Falcons travelled away for the last time that year on Saturday 16 October when they paid their second visit to Hull. Eager to put their previous defeat behind them Exeter started confidently. The lead changed hands several times and after seven races the scores were level at 21–21. At that point Don Hardy crashed heavily and broke his collarbone. The scores remained level for a couple more races after which the Angels gradually pulled away to win comfortably 50–34. It was a disappointing result, not only for the team, but also for the coach load of fans who had set out from Exeter at midnight on Friday to make the long journey to Hedon.

There was far worse news for the members of the Supporters Club the following week when it was discovered that their treasurer had absconded to London with the club's funds of over £400. He later gave himself up to the police and served a term of imprisonment following an appearance at the Exeter Assizes.

At that time the Supporter's Club also boasted an expert forger in 20 year old Tony Hallett but his activities were perfectly legal. Still a regular follower of the Falcons today Tony carefully copied the riders' autographs on to ladies' silk scarves, which were sold at the track shop.

Just two home matches now stood between the Falcons and the championship. The last major hurdle was overcome when they defeated their nearest challengers Southampton 46–38 in front of a 12,000 crowd on a pouring wet night at the County Ground on Monday 18 October. By the

The victorious Falcons receive 'The People' Trophy after winning the National League Division III championship.

fourth heat Exeter led by 4 points but the Saints were level by the halfway stage. Once again the Falcons edged ahead thanks to a magnificent ride by Stan Hodson, but Alf Bottoms retaliated with a victory over Bert Roger next time out and again the Saints were level. Pilgrim and Clay scored the only 5–1 of the match in heat 10 after which Exeter gradually pulled away to win by eight points.

The Falcons clinched their first league title seven days later when amid great rejoicing, they easily swept aside the challenge of the Hull Angels to win the last match 62–22. Already without Dick Shepherd and skipper Mick Mitchell, who had been injured together in a previous crash, the Angels had no answer to Exeter's all round superiority.

Hugh Geddes finished on a high note with his first maximum and Bert Roger was also unbeaten in his four races. Both Clay and Myson notched paid maximums while Bert Roger scored 12. It was a well deserved reward for the Falcons who had been supreme at the County Ground all season.

Alderman F P Cottey, who had been one of the original directors back in 1929, presented the 'People' Division Three trophy. All the Falcons riders received league winners' medals, as did the team mascot Gordon Gray. Amid the celebrations reserve Herbie Plain was presented with the Peamore Trophy in recognition of his second half successes.

A spectacular firework display rounded off the proceedings, and everyone went home happily anticipating promotion to the second division in 1949.

1949

EXETER
SPEEDWAY
OFFICIAL PROGRAMME
PRICE SIXPENCE
Promoted by
MOTOR SPORTS (EXETER) Ltd.,
County Ground Sports Stadium, St. Thomas, Exeter Phone 5231
MONDAY, 4th APRIL, 1949, at 7.30 p.m.
Daily Mail National Trophy
EXETER v PLYMOUTH
Second Meeting
BETTING STRICTLY PROHIBITED
W. V. COLE & SONS, EXETER.

HEAT 3

No sooner had the excitement of the Falcons' League Championship victory settled down than the Exeter management set about applying for promotion to the Second Division. But to the dismay of both the promoters and the fans alike the Speedway Control Board turned the application down.

The Falcons' promoters dispatched a strong protest but this too was refused. Directors F. P. Harding and R. M. Howell of Motor Sports (Exeter) Ltd along with Mr H. H. Bryant, the secretary of the Supporters Club, were invited to London for a hearing and explanation of the Board's decision. The meeting was chaired by Lt Col. R. C. V. Brook who explained that attendances at the County Ground in 1948 were not sufficient to warrant promotion and he pointed to the infamous programme article by Frank Buckland which threatened to move the whole set up to a better supported area. This, Col Brook claimed, implied that Exeter would not be able to meet the higher financial cost of Division Two racing. The Falcons had attracted an average crowd of 7,400, whereas the Board felt that Second Division tracks required gates of between 10,000 and 12,000.

It was also felt that the County Ground lacked the kind of spectator facilities such as bars, a restaurant, terracing and covered spectator stands, demanded by the higher status. Another point of concern to the Board was the Exeter track itself, particularly the very steep banking, which tended to put many visiting riders off. Mr Harding tried to point out that the stadium capacity was 18,000 but the Board would not reconsider and so Exeter faced another year of Third Division racing. Meanwhile Cradley, Southampton and Coventry, who had finished second, third and eighth were all allowed to move up.

The Third Division now consisted of Exeter, Hull, Hanley, Hastings, Poole, Yarmouth, Tamworth and Plymouth along with new tracks at Oxford, Liverpool, Rayleigh, Leicester and Halifax.

A second blow to the Falcons' hopes came with

The 1949 Falcons L → R Back: Bill Dutton, Major W. Fearnley (SCB), Johnny Myson, Norman Clay, Broncho Slade. Front: Vic Gent, Don Hardy, Arthur Pilgrim, Gordon Gray (mascot), Hugh Geddes, Stan Hodson.

the news that New Cross had recalled Bert Roger. The move back to the Old Kent Road came as no real surprise as Bert had scored a record 419 points from 43 matches producing an 9.74 average during 1948 which, it must be remembered, was his first full season of speedway. Bert's tally would remain the Exeter Club record until 1955.

The Rangers' management dropped a further bombshell when they also let it be known that Don Hardy would also be required to return to the London track as their No 9. Exeter promptly offered to buy the rider outright, but this was refused. Although Hardy was in the pits at the County Ground on the opening night in company with the Roger brothers, he had to content himself with the role of spectator and did not ride.

A great deal of work had been done to the track during the winter, 250 tonnes of brick rubble from local bomb sites had been used to raise the level of the third bend over a distance of 120 yards. The whole track had been resurfaced with 70 year old decomposed red ash slag from a coalmine. The controversial starting grid had temporarily been resurfaced with embedded granite chippings as previously visiting riders had claimed that it was too slippery.

Following the departure of Bert Roger, Arthur Pilgrim had been appointed skipper. Vic Gent had finally joined the Falcons from Plymouth and was programmed as first reserve along with John Hancox. The opening line up was announced as Pilgrim/Hodson; Myson/Geddes; Clay/Slade.

In the opening meeting the Falcons successfully defeated Poole Pirates 54–30 in a National League match at the County Ground. Norman Clay was in fine form. Slade, defying rumours that he would never ride again following his broken pelvis, made a good return scoring 8, as did new signing Gent. Myson was the most outstanding rider of the night, and appeared to have thrown off the ill luck that had dogged him the previous year. Nevertheless in the second half he still managed to hit the fence spectacularly, but escaped without injury.

Arthur Pilgrim.

The second half also saw the debut of a local youngster, 'Goog' Hoskin, who, having just been demobbed from the RAF, was keen to make his mark in speedway after practising at Alphington. He made a good start by winning one of his races. Another new face among the Exeter juniors was Cornishman Bill Rundle.

The traditional rivalry between Exeter and Plymouth got off to an early start when the two sides met in the Daily Mail National Trophy. Exeter won the first leg convincingly by 62–45. Clay looked like going through the card but missed out to Lansdale in heat 13 and then had to be content with third behind Lansdale and Pilgrim in the final heat.

A fleet of coaches made the trip down to Pennycross the following Thursday and a special railway excursion was also laid on. The fans were not disappointed as the action proved to be the most spectacular seen at Plymouth since racing was revived in 1947, which made up for the bitterly cold wind that swept across the stadium. Exeter took an early lead but Plymouth fought back to earn a well-deserved draw. Fortunately it was enough to put the Falcons through to the next round. Norman Clay was again in grand form, equalling the track record and scoring 16 points. In the last race of the match he and Pete Lansdale were involved in a superb tussle, which ended with the Exeter man snatching victory by half a yard.

As well as supporting their team the fans were also turning out on Sunday mornings to carry out further improvements to the stadium. Workshops were now under construction in the pits where two old railway coaches supplied by Bill Eastmond had also been put to good use.

The Falcons' hopes of retaining their third division championship suffered an early set back when they lost the services of Norman Clay in their home league match against the Yarmouth Bloaters. This match also saw Stan Lanfear brought back in to replace Hancox at reserve.

Exeter started well, but disaster struck in heat 3 when Clay's frame snapped coming out of the start, causing the bike to rear and throwing the unfortunate rider under the machine. Meanwhile in a totally separate incident the Bloaters pairing of Bill Carruthers and Billy Bales fell on the first bend. The race was stopped and Clay assisted from the track having broken two bones in his foot. The rerun took place without Clay but Bales whose fall had caused the pile-up, was allowed to restart. The Yarmouth pair duly took a 5–1 over Slade.

Bert Rawlinson won Heat 4 to reduce Exeter's lead to just one point. Myson's chain then broke in Heat 5 with the Falcons on a possible maximum, while Gent split Rawlinson and Hipperson to prevent another Yarmouth 5–1 in heat 6. Pilgrim fell on the first bend of heat 7 but Stan Hodson led for almost the whole 4 laps only to let Carruthers and Bales nip through and win thanks to some clever track craft. Myson failed to leave the start line in Heat 8. Rodwell fell and in doing so forced Lanfear over the white line. Stan managed to stay on but finished second with a puncture. Yarmouth were now 6 points in front. Slade lost first place to Morgan for a shared 9th Heat. Heat 10 was also shared, but Yarmouth went further ahead thanks to a Bales and Carruthers 4–2 over Geddes. With a scoreline at 28–36 Exeter started to pull back thanks to a 5–1 by Gent and Lanfear. A 4–2 reduced the deficit to just 2 points leaving Exeter needing a 5–1 to win but despite an all out attempt Hodson and Slade could not catch Billy Bales whose victory gave Yarmouth the match 42–40.

It was strongly suggested that the Exeter management should protest over Bales, the cause of the stoppage, being allowed to take part in the rerun of the third heat as the steward's decision had cost the Falcons two vital league points. However the Falcons quickly made up for their loss by winning their first ever match at Halifax.

The steeply banked Shay track was fairly similar to the County Ground and so suited most of the Exeter riders, but the meeting was not without problems. The top dressing was between 9 and 12 inches deep and very rough in places. The track in fact was so deep that the sumps of the machines were actually running through the cinders. Afterwards Myson had to replace his motor because the sump was badly damaged owing to the depth of the cinders. Even so Geddes, Slade, Pilgrim, Hancox and Lanfear all won races. The meeting took place on April 13 and the highlight for Exeter was Heat 13, which resulted in a 5–1 for Hancox and Gent.

Things did not go so well two nights later at another new track, Liverpool. The track at Stanley Street had teething problems and Falcons Manager Bert Sibley had to protest at the exclusion of Hugh Geddes in Heat 2 for tape breaking after the starting gate did not release properly on his side. Geddes was duly reinstated but then the gate failed completely and all races had to be started on the green light. Later another Falcon was excluded under two minutes but this went unnoticed in the pits because the klaxon was not working.

The Falcons were also handicapped by the non-arrival of Arthur Pilgrim, who had been stuck in Hanley when the ignition on his car caught fire. Arthur had tried in vain to contact the speedway office at the Liverpool track, but eventually got through to a greyhound racing official. By the time his message reached Sibley it was far too late to send transport to collect the stranded skipper. Not surprisingly Liverpool won 55–29. The track record, which had been held by Bill Kitchen since 1937, was broken by 3 seconds in Heat 2, by ex-Plymouth rider Alex Gray who set a new time of 80.00. His teammate Chads skipper Harry Welch went even quicker in Heat 5, lowering the record to 77.5. By comparison Geddes was Exeter's quickest rider with 84.8.

Goog Hoskin travelled with the Falcons on this trip to gain experience and was given rides at both Halifax and Liverpool.

Back at the County Ground on Easter Monday the Falcons satisfied a big crowd by beating another new team, Oxford, 60–24. This was the first occasion Oxford rode as the Cheetahs and although the result was never in doubt Broncho Slade gave the fans their money's worth. Many had thought that his broken pelvis, suffered in a grass track crash the previous summer, would end his career, but Broncho had other ideas. He won all his four races against Oxford in thrilling style and also clocked the fastest time 80.2.

It proved 6th time lucky for the Plymouth Devils when Exeter travelled to Pennycross for a league match later that week. The Falcons had won all 5 of their matches there since the start of 1948, but this time the Devils took their revenge on the depleted Falcons, who suffered a number of accidents. With Clay already sidelined for several weeks, the Falcons were further weakened by the loss of Lanfear with an ankle injury, which he sustained during the Oxford match. Then at the last minute it was realised that Geddes had not arrived having broken down en route. But the busloads of Exeter fans that had made the trip over Dartmoor were delighted to discover that Don Hardy was a surprise addition to the Falcons line-up. The injury crisis had forced the Exeter management to approach New Cross again. The Rangers' promoter, Fred Mockford, had previously priced Hardy at £500, which apparently had been beyond Exeter's budget. However Mr Harding, the Falcons' general manager, had persisted and eventually a deal was struck for an undisclosed fee late on the Wednesday night which allowed Hardy to make the dash West to Pennycross, where he received a great welcome from the Falcons' supporters and duly responded by top scoring.

The crowd that night was unusually small by Plymouth standards for a local derby, the Devils having been beaten by Poole the previous week. Plymouth were without Peter Robinson due to a bout of 'flu and also novice Alan Smith, while Bonnie Waddell was riding with strapped up ribs.

As usual there was no lack of thrills. Pete Lansdale broke the track record in the opening heat, and his new time of 76.8 was exactly one second inside Clay's previous time. The track rode particularly fast that night, Hardy later equalled, then went under the old record, while Lansdale again came close when he clocked 77.2 in Heat 10.

The Devils took the lead from the start and although the Falcons were never far behind, Plymouth stayed in front to win 44–40. Len Read scored a fine 12 point maximum for the Devils.

Hanley were Exeter's opponents in the next round of the National Trophy. A new concrete starting grid had been laid at the County Ground over the weekend, and while this suited the Potters it took the Falcons a while to settle. As a consequence plenty of extra time was spent on starting practice at the regular Tuesday morning practice sessions. Despite these difficulties Exeter still managed to run out winners by 57–51 after 18 heats and thus became the first team to beat Hanley in 9 matches.

Don Hardy received a great welcome from the home fans when he came to the tapes for his first race, but it was to prove a disappointing start. Don lost his chain almost as soon as he came out of the gate.

This was to be Exeter's last win for several

Stan Hodson and Arthur Pilgrim in action at Rayleigh. 18 April.

meetings. Defeats followed at Rayleigh, home and away against Leicester and then at Hanley in the second leg of the National Trophy where a 75–33 scoreline put Exeter out of the competition.

Although the Falcons were successful against Rayleigh at home, they also went down at Tamworth and Oxford where Ernie Noakes made his debut alongside Goog Hoskin at reserve but failed to score.

No Exeter riders were scheduled to take part in the newly revived Sunday Dispatch World's Speedway Championship, the first qualifying round of which took place at the County Ground on the 16th May, but Vic Gent came in at the last minute to replace Hull's Norman Johnson. It proved to be a dull meeting and was won by Bristol's Jack Mountford with a 15 point maximum, while Len Read of Plymouth finished second with 13. Sweden's Bertil Carlsson came over especially for this meeting and scored 7 points. He was accompanied by Mr C. G. Ringblom, a senior Swedish speedway official and a young rider by the name of Olle Nygren, who in the afternoon prior to the match had a practice spin around the County Ground track, his first ever ride on a British circuit.

A week later the Falcons returned to form with a 61–23 home victory over Hastings. Norman Clay returned to the saddle and was joint top scorer with Vic Gent. Unfortunately the Australian failed to score at Hanley at the end of that week, when he picked up another injury in a crash with the Potters' Lindsay Mitchell. As a result Clay did not ride in the home challenge against the Norwich Stars 48 hours later. His place in the line-up was taken by Hugh Geddes, who in turn was replaced at reserve by George Nicholls.

Australian reserve Bob Leverenz became the first visitor to score a maximum at the County Ground that summer, but his efforts did not stop Exeter from beating the Second Division Stars Select for the second year running. Pilgrim also scored 12 points, but it was not a good night for Norwich's original Exeter pioneer Bert Spencer who found points hard to come by. The veteran Aussie, known as the 'Baby Cyclone' in pre-war days, injured his ankle in his first race and it was later announced that it would be his last appearance.

That week the Exeter directors announced that Bill Dutton would be taking over as team manager from Bert Sibley, who had found the role tough going.

Whit Monday saw the Falcons beat Hanley fairly comfortably by 48–36. Although at the time nobody realised it the home clash with the Potters would be Stan Hodson's last County Ground appearance.

Hugh Geddes, Gordon Gray & Stan Hodson on their way to the pits prior to the Falcons' Whit Monday match with Hanley. This was the last picture taken of Stan before his untimely death a few days later.

This match was filmed by local cine enthusiast George Parsons and was later shown at the Supporters Club AGM. Fortunately a copy of this short but splendid film still exists, vividly bringing back to life the atmosphere of the post war speedway boom and is featured as the climax to 'ReRun Videos' 1994 production. 'The Western Wonders – Part I: The 40's & 50's'

That week the Falcons returned to Liverpool and Halifax where they were beaten by identical scores 49–35. Hodson was Exeter's top scorer in both these matches. Sadly, however, Stan had been ill all year with TB, but few realised just how serious his condition had become. On his return from the Northern tour he collapsed and 'Killer' was immediately admitted to a Paignton nursing home, where he died shortly afterwards.

Popular legend has it that Stan, who was 27

years old, was buried in the famous white jersey that he always wore over his racing leathers. Prior to the funeral his mother was taken to the County Ground where she filled a small bag with shale from the track, which was also placed in the coffin.

Obviously the death of such a popular team-mate deeply affected the other riders, but they still managed to defeat Hull by 48–36 in the next match at the County Ground in what was described as the 'quietest meeting ever at Exeter'. Before the first race both teams, the officials and track staff lined up on the centre green, where they observed a minute's silence after which an army bugler from Topsham Barracks sounded the last post.

Three days later, the Falcons were beaten for the second time at Plymouth. Home wins over Tamworth and Poole followed, interspersed with an away defeat at Yarmouth. Another home defeat followed this time at the hands of Halifax, for whom the up and coming 17 year old Arthur Forrest topped the Dukes score with 10. A big crowd had been drawn by Forrest's appearance. The fans were not disappointed and by the end of the evening Arthur had established himself as a firm favourite with the locals.

Victories followed against Liverpool at home and Leicester and Hull away. The Hull win showed that the Falcons had finally got to grips with the difficult Hedon track.

The August Bank Holiday weekend was a busy one for the Falcons. They started by beating Plymouth 54–29 in the Devon Derby at the County Ground on the Saturday afternoon and followed up with a convincing 53–31 home victory over league leaders Yarmouth on the Monday afternoon.

Exeter at this time were seventh in the League Table, while local rivals Plymouth were third. Devil's Pete Lansdale was the only opponent to inflict a defeat on Norman Clay over the weekend. Billy Bales came very close to breaking the 76.2 track record, when he managed to clock a time of 76.6, but was twice beaten by the Exeter star. Clay also made an attempt on the track record but the best time he could achieve was 77.0.

Exeter followed this with a 52–31 home win over Hastings, but then went down away at both Tamworth and Rayleigh.

Thanks to a spell of extremely dry weather Tuesday morning practice sessions at the Alphington training track had to be suspended, due to the lack of watering facilities. The trainees, who included locals, Bob Turner, Tom Dell, Dennis Baker and Rusty Russell had attempted to keep the dust down with buckets of water and a stirrup pump, but as this proved totally ineffective practice sessions were relocated to the County Ground until the fine weather broke.

Plymouth were beaten again in the Devon Derby at the County Ground on 15 August. Broncho Slade broke his collarbone in a second bend fall in heat 2 after clipping Alan Smith's wheel, while Goog Hoskin, making his Falcons' debut at reserve, had a couple of pointless rides before coming out to replace Stan Lanfear in Heat 12. In that race Geddes made the start and quickly pulled away from Robinson. Hoskin had also started well and reached the first bend in third place ahead of Johnny Bradford. Gradually he made ground on Robinson and, much to the delight of the home fans and the surprise of Plymouth skipper, passed him in splendid style to take a vital second place. Goog later won his scratch race heat and qualified for the final.

The Falcons picked up another away win at Oxford, this time by the narrowest of margins. 42–41. Exeter's hero at Sandy Lane was Don Hardy, who was involved in a tangle with both Cheetahs' riders in his first race and took a nasty bump on the head as well as cuts to his face. Against the track doctor's advice Don insisted on riding in the rerun, but twice had to lay down his machine in later races to avoid fallen riders. His efforts were greatly appreciated by the home fans. Clay meanwhile scored a superb maximum despite suffering from 'flu.

The Falcons were also victors back at the County Ground where they easily disposed of the Leicester Hunters, who provided very poor opposition. Such was Exeter's supremacy that Clay, Hardy and Geddes all scored 12 point maximums. Pilgrim gave another great captain's performance, finishing second to his partner in each outing. Harwood Pike was the Hunters only race winner.

The second half was equally disappointing as four visiting Swedish riders who had been booked to appear failed to do so. Apparently their ship from Sweden was due to dock at Tilbury at 6.00 am but remained anchored off Southend Pier for several hours due to fog. As a result Olle Nygren, Eskil Carlsson, Einar Lingqvist and Lennart Carlstrom were unable to reach Exeter in time. Bill Dutton hastily looked for alternative riders and discovered that two Bristol Bulldogs, Eric

Salmon, and Jack Mountford, were due through Exeter at any moment on their way to Cornwall for an open meeting at St Austell the next day. John Hancox and mechanic Don Weekes were dispatched to hijack them. The police and AA were also asked to keep a look out for a car and trailer, registration number LAE 100, while John and Don duly stationed themselves out on the A38 in a bid to wave the Bristol lads down. At 6.25 Salmon phoned the stadium and Dutton breathed a sigh of relief.

Rayleigh were no match for the Falcons at the County Ground on Monday 29th August. Exeter were just too good for the Rockets and cruised to a 60–24 victory. Pat Clarke however kept them on their toes by scoring 10 points. Another Rayleigh youngster Wally Mawdsley, later to become the Falcons' promoter, was making his first visit to Exeter but failed to score. Prior to the league match Don Hardy beat Billy Bales in the first round of a special match race. Bales levelled the score at the interval but Hardy won the decider.

Away defeats at Hastings and Hanley marked the end of August and the beginning of September. The County Ground visitors on Monday 5 September were the Oxford Cheetahs who now included Jimmy Wright, who after many months in Royal Devon and Exeter Hospital following his 1948 smash had made a return to the saddle. Unfortunately another injury prevented Jimmy from actually riding at this meeting, but he still travelled down with the Cheetahs to meet up with all the people who had visited him during those long months in hospital. Also missing from their line-up was Dennis Gray, who had not been allowed leave for the match from the RAF, with whom he was still serving. The Cheetahs were beaten 52–30.

Halifax's Arthur Forrest made a guest appearance in the second half, beating Norman Clay 2–0 in a match race series.

The Falcons were in action at Poole the following Monday evening, so a Best Pairs Competition was arranged at the County Ground. While Exeter was losing 45–39 at Wimborne Road, the Fleetwood Pair of Wilf Plant and George Newton were taking the honours back in Devon. Arthur Forrest and Vic Emms also rode in this meeting, and before moving on to St Austell the next day they asked Don Weekes, the Exeter team mechanic, to accompany them. Don already intended to go to the Cornish track with a team of Exeter juniors, but it was a tribute to his mechanical skills that the Halifax duo should also seek his assistance.

Forrest and Emms were back at the County Ground a week later with the Dukes on league business. Halifax dominated the early heats and were 18–12 up after five races, but then Emms crashed and was excluded. In the rerun Bill Crosland was hampered by engine trouble and the Falcons gratefully grabbed a 5–0, which brought them right back into the match. Exeter squeezed ahead thanks to a 5–1 by Geddes and Pilgrim in Heat 10, but Halifax immediately struck back with 4–2 by Al Allison and Dick Sears over Norman Clay, which reduced the Falcons' lead to a single point, 33–32. As the next three heats were all drawn Exeter hung on to win by the narrowest of margins, 42–41.

Disaster had befallen the Hull Angels who had been forced to close down in August. The Angels' track at Hedon airfield was located too far out of the town to attract big enough crowds despite the fact that a railway halt ajoined the stadium. The Angels' place in the third division was offered to the newly hatched Swindon Robins who took over the remaining fixtures.

The Robins made their first appearance at the County Ground on Monday 26 September. That evening also saw Rusty Russell make his debut for the Falcons at reserve in place of Lanfear. The fledgling Robins relied heavily on George Craig and Bob Jones, and the Falcons cruised to an easy 58–26 victory with Russell contributing two points.

That proved to be the Falcons' last win for a while as they lost 53–51 at Yarmouth the next evening and suffered another defeat, 53–52, at the hands of champions elect Hanley back at the County Ground a week later.

Monday 10 October saw Exeter make another trip to Poole resulting in yet another defeat – this time by 46–38. Norman Clay scored 11 points but blew his engine in his last race.

A welcome victory came 24 hours later back at the County Ground where the Falcons achieved a 57–27 win over the Liverpool Chads in the final home league match of the season. Clay, riding a borrowed machine, recorded an immaculate 12 point maximum and also clocked the fastest time of 78.6 seconds, in what, tragically, was to be his last County Ground appearance. His teammate Don Hardy was also unbeaten by a Liverpool rider.

As Clay was due to return to Australia at the

weekend, he did not take part in the last two away matches at Plymouth on Thursday, and at Swindon two days later. Both matches resulted in defeats for the Falcons. Clay was present to see his Falcons' team-mates go down 56–28 in their first league appearance at Swindon's Blunsdon Abbey Stadium, before journeying through the night to Tilbury where he would board ship for Australia. Exeter had previously raced at Swindon in a challenge match, where, also without Clay, they had been defeated narrowly 42–41.

The season ended at the County Ground on Monday 17 October when Tamworth's Harry Saunders won the Froud Trophy with a 15 point maximum. Exeter skipper Arthur Pilgrim finished second with 14, and Lindsay Mitchell of Hanley was third with 12 points. The evening was marred by a serious accident. Saunders and Pilgrim both went into heat 18 unbeaten and while they were battling for the lead and the win that would decide the night's victory, Hasting's Ken Middleditch fell behind them. Middleditch's rider-less bike continued along the track and struck Rusty Russell. Both machines careered into the fence just before the pits gate and were catapulted high into the air taking Russell with them. The unfortunate rider then fell back across the safety fence with such force that he fractured his spine and broke his pelvis in two places. Total silence fell on the crowd as he was carried from the track with his head covered.

Rusty was 23 at the time and had just completed his first season at Exeter, having decided to become a speedway rider rather than go to university and study architecture. Incredibly he would recover in time to race again in 1950.

Thus 1949 ended on a sad note, and tragically worse was to follow. Hanley won the Third Division title on race points-difference only from Yarmouth after both teams finished on 71 points each. Exeter finished in seventh place, one slot below arch rivals Plymouth. Despite the disappointment of the Falcons not retaining the championship, racing had generally been much closer and more exciting at the County Ground.

Norman Clay had become a star in his own right and not surprisingly had aspirations of moving up to the First Division in 1950. It was strongly rumoured that a probable transfer to either New Cross or Bristol was very much on the cards. Alas Norman was never to get his wish. On 20 January 1950 he was killed in a track crash at the Sydney Showground, which also claimed the life of Harringay's Ray Duggan.

1950

EXETER
SPEEDWAY
OFFICIAL PROGRAMME
6D.
Promoted by
MOTOR SPORTS (EXETER) Ltd.,
County Ground Sports Stadium, St. Thomas, Exeter Phone 5231
FRIDAY, 21st JULY, 1950, at 7.30 p.m.
National League Match
EXETER v. ALDERSHOT
NINETEENTH MEETING
BETTING STRICTLY PROHIBITED
W. V. COLE & SONS, PRINTERS & STATIONERS, EXETER

HEAT 4

1950 was not an auspicious season for the Exeter Falcons or for that matter speedway in general. It was a wet summer and declining attendances indicated that the immediate post war speedway boom was over. Alternative attractions were becoming more readily available thanks to the ending of petrol rationing.

Halifax, Hanley, Yarmouth and Plymouth had all been promoted to the Second Division. Promotion for the Devils sadly ended those emotionally charged and economically attractive Devon Derbies and as a result both tracks suffered. Aldershot and St Austell joined the Third Division and although the Gulls down at the Cornish Stadium provided the next best thing to a local derby the atmosphere was never the same as at those notorious clashes with Plymouth.

Several changes had been made to the Falcons line-up. Even before his tragic accident Norman Clay was expected to move to a team in a higher division, while veterans Broncho Slade and Stan Lanfear had retired, although in Broncho's case the decision would be short lived. Two new Australians, Ken Walsh and Jack Bedkober, had been signed, and Ted Moore, who rode briefly for the Falcons early in 1947 before suffering a serious leg injury, made a welcome return. Rusty Russell had also successfully recovered from his injuries of the previous autumn, and was eager to return to the saddle. However the main talking point that summer as far as the Exeter fans were concerned was the decision by the Falcons' management to switch the regular race night from Monday to Friday.

The announcement of the decision caused a flurry of letters to the Editor of the Express and

1950 Falcons L → R Back: Vic Gent, Jack Bedkober, Don Weekes, Ken Walsh, Hugh Geddes. Front: Ted Moore, Don Hardy, Bill Dutton, Arthur Pilgrim, Johnny Myson, Gordon Gray (mascot).

Echo. One correspondent, 'LGG of Heavitree', pointed out that local farmers would already have returned home earlier in the day from the weekly cattle market so were unlikely to come back again for the speedway; working men now had Saturday as their half day, so often worked late on Friday, while many other fans would be unable to attend as Friday was also choir practice night. Many other letters were published in similar vein, and all eventually proved correct. It was subsequently announced that no meeting would take place on Good Friday as the management wished to avoid offending churchgoers.

Practice sessions started at the County Ground in March and were held three times a week prior to the start of the season.

The first major speedway event in the city that year was the wedding of former Falcon Bert Roger to Miss Jose Huxtable at St Thomas church close by the County Ground on Saturday 18 March. A huge crowd turned up to see the happy couple leave the church, including a party of 40 New Cross supporters who had travelled down overnight from London dressed in the Rangers' orange and black colours.

Cyril Roger was responsible for persuading new signing Ken Walsh to join the Falcons. Cyril, who had toured Australia with the England team, saw Walsh in action as reserve at Melbourne in the sixth test and suggested that as he planned to come to England he should join Exeter. Walsh, a 22 year old motor engineer and a protégé of Jack Biggs, had received three other offers from British clubs, but had not rushed to make a decision. In fact he was at sea for two weeks before he finally made up his mind which team to join. By coincidence one of his best friends in Melbourne was a midget car driver called Bill Dutton. On discovering that this was also the name of the Exeter manager, Walsh decided that this was as good a reason as any for joining the Falcons.

The Falcons' other new Aussie, Jack Bedkober, came on the recommendation of Birmingham star, Graham Warren, but at first it looked as though he would not arrive until half way through the season. The earliest ship on which Bedkober was able to book a passage was not due to reach England until the end of July. In an attempt to speed things up Bill Dutton contacted the P & O Steamship Company, who readily agreed to give the new Falcon the first available cancellation. P & O were as good as their word although Bedkober had to fly from Sydney to Adelaide to board a liner on which a last minute vacancy had occurred.

Exeter's Australian trio – Ken Walsh, Hugh Geddes & Jack Bedkober.

Bedkober lived at Bondi Junction, Sydney and had been a near neighbour of Norman Clay. Shortly before leaving for England he finished third, with 12 points in the New South Wales junior championship.

The Falcons' season got underway with a challenge match at St Austell on Tuesday 28 March. The Gulls, with Broncho Slade a last minute signing at reserve, won narrowly 43–41. Exeter skipper Arthur Pilgrim made a good start scoring 11 points mounted on his brand new Martin–JAP machine. Walsh, who had only arrived the previous Saturday, did not ride as the management decided to allow him time to settle in.

The purpose built St Austell track had first operated the previous summer regularly attracting crowds of 10,000 plus to watch the sports top stars competing in open licence meetings. Unfortunately the Gulls promoter, 'Chirpy' Richards, found it a much harder job to put together a competitive third division team and the Cornish outfit subsequently suffered defeat in their first 15 league matches.

The Gulls did not do too well in challenge matches either and the Falcons comfortably won the return 53–30. The St Austell mainstay was Norman Street who was beaten only by Don Hardy. A most encouraging sign for the Falcons was Ted Moore's reserve maximum. Team manager Dutton again decided against introducing newcomer Ken Walsh into the side, so the Australian spent the evening as an interested spectator.

Amazingly Rusty Russell had recovered sufficiently from his 1949 injuries to ride in the second half. A freshly laid top dressing of copper sand coupled with a newly introduced narrower type of tyre gave the riders a few problems. There were several spills and over-slides culminating in Goog Hoskin falling three times in one race. Dutton however pointed out that this was due to over enthusiasm on Goog's part rather than any fault with the track.

As part of a promotion for the Australian film 'The Rugged Riordans', featured at the Gaumont in North Street that week, a special trophy was donated by the cinema management for the top scoring rider – Don Hardy. Several of the riders had gone along to see the film, and a few days later when the star, Australian actress, Wendy Gibb visited the city to promote the picture, the Falcons' two Aussie riders Hugh Geddes and Ken Walsh were at Central Station to greet her.

The Falcons rode their first league match of the new campaign away at Poole on Monday 3 April. Exeter started well, but after leading throughout the match, missed out in a last heat decider, and lost narrowly 43–41.

In deference to churchgoers the management decided against staging a home meeting on Good Friday. Instead the Falcons rode away at Leicester where they were beaten decisively 66–42 in the National Trophy. Walsh finally made his team debut at Blackbird Road but failed to score. It would take the Australian a little while to adjust to English tracks with their unfamiliar concrete starting grids.

Walsh 'enjoyed' another pointless evening at Oxford on Easter Saturday where the Falcons suffered their third defeat of the week. A twenty point deficit in the challenge match at Cowley only served to increase the management's concern over the team's poor start to the season.

Easter Monday morning saw the Leicester Hunters at the County Ground for the second leg of the Daily Mail National Trophy, which to the surprise and delight of the management and fans alike the Falcons won 65–41, therefore forcing a 107–107 draw on aggregate. Don Hardy was in fabulous form scoring a full 18 point maximum.

Jack Bedkober reached England on Easter Saturday and made his debut for the Falcons in their 46–35 National League victory over Swindon the following Friday. The next evening in the return at Blunsdon the Robins gained prompt revenge by winning 54–30.

Bedkober's inclusion in the Falcons' line-up at Swindon was obviously unexpected, as his name did not appear in the Blunsdon programme. When the teams were announced Exeter's reserve was incorrectly named as 'J. Cooper'. Down in the crowd a 14 year old schoolboy loudly disputed this information telling the fans around him,

> "It's Exeter's new Australian, Jack Bedkober. Look, I've just got his autograph and you can read it quite clearly."

Unfortunately this gem of information did not reach the steward and so 'Cooper' was duly written into the official programme. As a result of this oversight the single point scored by 'Cooper' was actually listed among the Exeter scorers in the 1951 edition of the famous Stenner's Speedway Annual.

That schoolboy was Glynn Shailes who has since become one of Britain leading speedway historians and Press Officer at both Swindon and Oxford. He later acquired that official programme, and generously passed it on to me during the preparation of this book. Obviously the speedway reporter of the Swindon Advertiser heard Glynn's protests as Bedkober's name was spelt correctly in his match report.

A new innovation that summer was the Division Three Riders Championship. Qualifying rounds were held in the second halves of all league matches in which the four top scorers from both teams took part in four individual races. The points from all these races were totalled up and the top 16 scorers would qualify for an end of the season championship final to be staged at neutral Walthamstow.

The Speedway Control Board announced that the rerun of the drawn National Trophy tie with Leicester would be staged on Monday 17 April. The Falcons won 62–45, and then for good measure went to Leicester's Blackbird Road the following Friday and beat the Hunters 55–33. Exeter's 117–93 aggregate victory earned them a place in the divisional semi final in which the Falcons were drawn against Oxford.

While Exeter were at Leicester an individual meeting, the Falcon Trophy, was being staged at the County Ground. Swindon's George Craig flew off with the trophy, with Norman Street of St Austell second, leaving Bill Downton, Ken Middleditch and Mick Mitchell all to tie for the third spot.

Exeter returned to St Austell for their second

Leicester v Exeter L → R: Johnnie Carpenter, Johnnie Myson, Jock Grierson, Ted Moore.

challenge match of the season at Cornish Stadium on Tuesday 25 April, but torrential rain and a soaked track made good speedway impossible. After 10 heats of very slow racing the match was abandoned with Exeter leading 31–29. Several spills occurred in the first few races as the conditions steadily worsened.

Two days later Exeter went to Oxford for the first leg of the National Trophy match. The meeting was a disaster for the Falcons who were humiliated 83–24. The Cheetahs stormed to 5–1 maximums in 14 of the 18 heats.

The surprise of the night as far as Exeter were concerned was the performance of Goog Hoskin who top scored with five points. Team manager Bill Dutton was quick to explain that the cause of the Falcons' downfall was twofold, gearing and gating. For their previous visit to Cowley when the track had been wet, the Exeter riders had used an 868 gear ratio. They decided to stick with this even though this time around track conditions were dry and it was noted that the Cheetahs were pulling 895. The exception was Hoskin who preferred to use as low a gearing as possible, on this occasion 910. Nearly 50 years on Goog looks back on Dutton's explanation with a certain amount of cynical amusement.

Twenty four hours later Oxford inflicted a further defeat on the Falcons at the County Ground. This surprisingly was not the second leg of the National Trophy but a National League match. Nevertheless the Cheetahs started just as they had finished the previous evening – with a 5–1. On a wet night Oxford opted to take gates two and four thus taking full advantage of the shelter provided by the roof of the grandstand. However after two races Dutton stepped in and watered the grid nearest the safety fence with the hosepipe thus ensuring fair conditions for all. After six heats the Falcons had managed to level the scores, but the Cheetahs' superior gating again put them ahead and a trio of 5–1s from the last three heats ensured another Oxford victory. The only bright spot for Exeter was a 12 point maximum for Don Hardy.

Naturally the situation did not go down well with the local fans and the tension increased when two of the Oxford riders, Pat Clarke and Bill Kemp, were excluded for dangerous riding after bringing down Hardy and Vic Gent in separate incidents. Gent was particularly incensed by his rough treatment, which left him on the wrong side of the safety fence and his machine extensively damaged.

A week later Oxford were back at the County Ground again, this time contesting the National Trophy tie. The Cheetahs held a 59 point lead from the first leg so on recent form there was only going to be one outcome. The match proved a much closer affair than many expected with the Falcons clinching victory by a single point 54–53. Hardy was in brilliant form, breaking Cyril Roger's two year old track record in the opening race before scoring 15 points from six rides. Don missed out only in heat 8 when he finished last behind Ernie Rawlins, Bob MacFarlane and team mate Hugh Geddes. His new record time was 76.0 seconds.

Arthur Pilgrim produced a workmanlike 13 points, while Ken Walsh chipped in with a useful nine, but an indication of Oxford's all round strength was illustrated by the fact that of their top three scorers two were the reserves, Rawlins (15 from 6) and Jimmy Wright (10). The Cheetahs went on to defeat Tamworth in the Third Division Final before suffering a narrow 111–105 aggregate defeat at the hands of the Halifax Dukes in the first of the Second Division rounds.

The Falcons' next league match was at newly opened Aldershot with its unusual pear shaped track on which they were beaten 55–29. From the start Exeter never looked like winning and the best they could muster was five drawn heats. Vic Gent's 10 point tally included two victories, while Hardy was the Falcons' only other race winner.

Another splendid Don Hardy maximum saved the Falcons from a second humiliation at Oxford the next evening, and although it was something of a one man effort the rest of the team did enough to keep the Cheetahs on their toes and the scoreline to 49–35.

The Falcons' black week ended back at the County Ground with their third successive defeat in as many days, where in a challenge match against second division Southampton, the visiting Saints romped home to a 50–33 scoreline. Veteran Steve Langton, who had never had a great liking for the Exeter track, was complimentary about the improved surface and demonstrated his approval by notching 10 points. The Falcons were without Pilgrim and Bedkober, who had both picked up minor injuries. In their absence Herbie Plain and Bill Grimes rode at reserve.

Exeter's disastrous run of results continued with another narrow home defeat by Leicester, who won a closely fought encounter by a single point even though Pilgrim and Bedkober were back in action for the Falcons.

After such a dismal run Exeter were glad to secure a comfortable 58–25 home victory over the Liverpool Chads on 26 May. Hardy scored a maximum, while Pilgrim and Walsh backed him up with 10 points each.

An additional attraction at this meeting was a match race between the 'White Ghost' Ken Le Breton, from Glasgow Ashfield, and Hardy. Don won the first leg, but the white leathered Aussie clinched the rubber 2–1.

Whit Monday afternoon saw another challenge match at the County Ground, this time the opposition was Plymouth who won 43–41. The Devils had not won at the Exeter track since 1948 but their visit attracted the largest and most enthusiastic crowd of the season. A close match ended with a last heat decider, but both Ted Moore and Vic Gent were forced to come out on borrowed machinery, a situation that the Plymouth pairing of Cecil Bailey and Alan Smith exploited to the full. Gent's motor had earlier blow itself apart to such an extent that the remains were placed on display in the window of Ernie Pile's cycle-shop at the corner of Wardrew Road and Cowick Street.

Behind the scenes concern was growing at the County Ground. Crowd figures had plummeted alarmingly in the light of the Falcons' disastrous form, and it was announced that admission prices would rise by 3d on the 2/- (10p) and 3/- (15p) tickets. The cost of running a third division meeting at Exeter in 1950 was £500 and with 45% of the gate money going in entertainment tax, there was not a great deal left from a gate of 7,000 to 8,000. Due to their lack of on track success the Falcons were now only attracting around 6,000 on a regular basis, and up to June only two meetings had shown a profit making closure a very real possibility unless crowd figures improved. The increase of 3d did not effect entertainment tax as this was charged at varying fixed levels.

The Falcons put their financial problems out of mind and concentrated instead on a tough schedule of matches that weekend. The home meeting on Friday 2 June saw Exeter beat St. Austell 60–24 with Don Hardy notching no less than eight race wins, a 12 point maximum against the Gulls and four further wins in the second half.

Don Hardy leads Ken Le Breton.

Early next morning the team set off in their coach transporter on a three match tour with the first stop in Dublin and a challenge match against the Shelbourne Tigers. This was to be the Falcons only appearance in Ireland to date.

After a very long tiring day on the road the Exeter party arrived at Holyhead ten minutes before midnight and spent two hours getting their machines and equipment through customs and on to the ferry. The boat sailed at 3.40am and arrived at Dublin at 8.am, where it took a further hour to disembark and clear the Irish customs. After a hastily snatched breakfast a lorry arrived to take the riders and their equipment to the track four miles away where they prepared for the afternoon meeting.

Speedway had been introduced at Shelbourne Park the previous month by Wimbledon promoter Ronnie Greene and was attracting average crowds of 18,000. Not surprisingly the 385 yard track resembled Plough Lane but instead of shale was surfaced with brick dust, which for this meeting was bone dry. Sadly the Falcons maintained their English form and were beaten 59–49 over 18 heats by a Tigers' side, which included several Wimbledon riders.

The legendary double world champion, Ronnie Moore, then just 17 years old and in his first British season, partnered his father Les in the opening race. Although Ronnie was unable to make up lost ground after a bad gate, Les Moore won the heat and broke the track record. Ronnie, however, went on to win his other four races including a last gasp victory over Hugh Geddes after chasing him for three laps. The future champion's efforts obviously impressed Bill Dutton who prophetically commented in a later programme column, 'Keep an eye on this New Zealander, as I believe he will become one of the outstanding stars in speedway.' Hardy won two races and Myson and Moore one each, but Walsh suffered an early set back when he discovered that he had left his leathers in Exeter.

Immediately after the meeting the Exeter riders and officials made a return dash to the docks and by 8.30pm were aboard the ferry and sailing back to Holyhead. They remained in their cabins overnight catching up on some sleep before spending another hour and half getting the bikes through customs. Then it was back on to the team coach and another long drive to Liverpool where they were due in action that evening against the Chads in a league match. The Falcons were beaten 47–35 but the match was not without incident. In one heat Liverpool's Reg Duval attempted to go around the outside of Don Hardy, but their

Ken Walsh.

handlebars tangled making it impossible for Hardy to knock off the throttle. The Exeter rider managed to wrench his bike away, but in doing to sent Duval into the fence. Hardy was able to continue and won, but a protest from the Liverpool manager resulted in his exclusion even though Duval sportingly admitted that he was at fault.

After a rest day spent in Southport the team were back on the road on Wednesday morning heading south to Tamworth and another defeat. The 51–32 score line again endorsed the urgent need to strengthen the team, plans for which were already underway. The American rider Bud Reda had visited the County Ground for a trial after the St. Austell match, accompanied by the great Australian Ron Johnson, who had ridden in Exeter's opening meeting in 1929. Reda was given a three week temporary contract, but did not return. The Ministry of Labour had written to the Exeter management informing them that the signing of an American rider would not be approved. The Speedway Control Board was also unlikely to allow a third division side to track a foreign rider even if government approval was forthcoming. Meanwhile it was announced that Bill Downton had been purchased from Swindon for £190.

The Falcons' hectic week finally came to a successful end when they beat Tamworth 55–29 in the return match at the County Ground on Friday 9 June. Up and coming youngster Eric Boothroyd, later to become Chairman of the BSPA, topped the Tammies score chart with 8 points, but Hardy led the Falcons to victory with another fine maximum.

Oxford's Bob MacFarlane won the Exeter World Championship round a week later, with Tommy Miller from Glasgow White City second. Macfarlane's Cheetahs team mate Pat Clarke finished third. International interest in the meeting was created by the appearance of Eskil Carlsson from Sweden. Carlsson was the younger brother of Bertil, who had ridden at the County Ground the previous season. Another new name also appeared in the programme that evening; Johnny Sargeant was listed as stand by reserve along with Goog Hoskins. But Sargeant, who made his County Ground debut in the previous week's second half, failed to score in both of his outings.

New signing Bill Downton wore the reserves race jacket for the Falcons' home match against Poole on Friday 23 June but only scored a single point. The Pirates' No 1 Ken Middleditch inflicted Don Hardy's only defeat in a thrilling opening heat, and went on to record a paid maximum after following his partner Charlie Hayden home in heat 7. The Dorset outfit looked to have the match under control, but the Falcons came good in the second half of the match and gained a morale boosting victory. After eight heats Poole held a six point lead, but 5–1s for Geddes/Gent and Hardy/Moore in Heats 11 and 12 put Exeter in the driving seat, and Geddes and Downton clinched it for Exeter with a 4–2 in the penultimate race. The arrival of Downton marked the end of Johnny Myson's near four year spell with Exeter, his name being circulated as available on a free transfer.

The rivalry between Hardy and Middleditch continued in the second half when they met in the Division Three Riders Championship qualifier. Middleditch won the first heat, but in a classic final Hardy was the victor, after a race in which the two principal contenders passed and re-passed in exciting fashion. Afterwards an excited Dutton commented that this race 'would still be talked about in 1980'

The following night the Falcons lost 50–34 at Rayleigh, but a week later, Friday 30 June, they came close to snatching their first away league win when they travelled to Leicester's Blackbird Road. The Hunters were only two points in front at the halfway stage and it looked as though the Falcons could spring a surprise, but again success eluded them and they lost 48–35.

That same evening back at the County Ground an experimental three team tournament, the first to be staged at a third division track, proved to be a dull and uninteresting affair. The quartet from top of the league Oxford won easily with 40 points from Aldershot 29, and Swindon 25.

There was however some welcome success for the Supporters Club at the Annual Speedway Sports Day held at Dawlish Warren that weekend. The Exeter fans were the overall winners with 32½ from Plymouth 31½, and Bristol on 19. The Falcons' junior fans made a good start by winning both the sack and wheelbarrow races, while two Exeter ladies beat all-comers, even Johnny Sargeant, in the 'Bun and Treacle' race!

Better track action was in store at the County Ground in the first meeting of July. The Falcons, aided by the 'Black Prince' from Halifax, Arthur Forrest, took on and beat a Ken Le Breton select side. This fixture attracted a much bigger crowd and the match got off to a shattering start with Le Breton carving a whole second off Hardy's track record reducing it to 75.0. The White Ghost lowered it further with a time of 74.6 in heat 4, which he equalled three heats later. Swedish rider Sune Karlsson was on maximum form, partly due to Walsh suffering an untimely puncture, which allowed the Swede to pass him. A puncture in his last ride also robbed Le Breton of a maximum.

That same evening Hugh Geddes rode in a world championship round at second division Halifax, where he scored 11 points. Hardy had also fared well against first and second division opposition scoring 10 points at Norwich. Both riders went through to the third round.

The Falcons were still lurking very near the bottom of the table, with only Rayleigh and St Austell below them. Even the struggling Gulls beat Exeter at the Cornish stadium on Tuesday 11 July. The Falcons however managed to win at home against Leicester later that week even without Hardy who had damaged ligaments in his leg in a crash at St. Austell. But victory over the Hunters

Riders night out at the Savoy cinema. Don Weekes receives a marrow from Vic Gent, watched by Johnny Sargeant, Ken Walsh, Ted Moore, Rusty Russell and Goog Hoskin.

did not come without cost. Bill Downton suffered serious head injuries when he crashed in Heat 8 while trying to avoid Johnny Carpenter. Downton careered onto the centre green and hit the steel railings of the dog track. X-rays taken the following Sunday revealed a fracture at the base of his skull.

During July the Falcons failed to top the 30 points mark at Poole, Aldershot and Oxford, but towards the end of the month managed to achieve an away win at newly opened Long Eaton, and a home victory over Aldershot.

Unfortunately the numbers attending matches had reached crisis proportions and the fans were stunned to learn that Hugh Geddes had been transferred to Swindon for £550 in a bid to keep Exeter alive. The news broke at a Press Conference given by Bill Dutton who said:

> 'Geddes had scored a 12 point maximum in his last match against Aldershot. This unfortunately had to be done to enable us to carry on speedway in Exeter. We have very many commitments to meet and we have used most of the capital put up by directors at the beginning of the season. It was the only way to meet our liabilities and carry on'

Dutton pointed out that it was all down to finance and if speedway had the same rate of Entertainment Tax as football – 15%, then meetings could be run even with the attendances of 4,400, which was currently the average Exeter gate. The recent matches against Leicester and Aldershot had lost the management £100.

With Geddes gone to Swindon, Bob Wigg was signed and made his debut against Oxford at the County Ground on Friday 28 July. Wigg made a successful start by winning Heat 2, but next time out Cheetah's Frank Boyle over slid on the second bend taking both Wigg and his partner Johnny Sargeant into the fence. Sargeant crawled uninjured from the tangled mass of men and machines but Boyle, who had been excluded, and Wigg were both taken to hospital. The new Falcons signing was reported to be 'seriously ill' with fractured ribs while Boyle had a bad foot injury. Despite this setback the Falcons still managed a notable success by defeating the high flying Cheetahs 48–36 with Ken Walsh collecting a hard earned maximum.

Another sad occurrence at the end of July was the demise of the excellent Falcon Fanfare newspaper, which, since the end of 1947, had provided comprehensive details of local speedway matters. The falling attendances had effected weekly sales so badly that the publishers could not afford to carry on.

August began with another away defeat at bottom of the table St Austell, and then Exeter just managed a draw at home to Poole. To add insult to injury Geddes was in the Swindon team, which beat the Falcons home and away over the August Bank Holiday weekend, the scorelines being 53–30 at Blunsdon and 36–48 at the County Ground on the Monday afternoon. Hughie marked his re-appearance at Exeter with a 12 point maximum. The Bank Holiday programme also contained a questionnaire to discover whether the fans would prefer a switch back to the traditional Monday race night.

The injury problems continued into August. Both Wigg and Downton were now expected to miss the remainder of the season. Jack Bedkober was ruled out of the home match with Swindon, with his place being taken by Sargeant, while Rusty Russell made it back as reserve alongside another new signing Larry Young.

Veteran racer Fred Tuck started coaching the team at the weekly Tuesday morning practice, and the Falcons duly won their next two home fixtures against St Austell and Rayleigh. Even Broncho Slade made a comeback, first in the second half and then in the team. Don Hardy, returning from

The Falcons return to the pits on the Jeep.

injury, rode as reserve in the St Austell match and won both his races. Don moved back in the team proper against the Rockets and scored a convincing 10 points.

Australian international Les Hewitt was the second half attraction for the St Austell meeting at the County Ground, taking part in a match race series against Ken Walsh. Walsh won 2–1 and also claimed a new track record – 74.2 seconds. Hewitt was hampered by engine problems and asked for a return later in the season. Walsh's success was not confined to the track. He was also the winner of a competition to guess the number of Smarties in a 2lb jar at a supporters' dance at the Buller Hall. Ken's guess was exact – 360.

The Supporter's Club, whose accounts had now fully recovered from the disaster of two years previous, had made some generous donations to the riders. Johnny Myson had received £5 in appreciation of his efforts in the past; Don Hardy also received £5 whilst injured, whereas Hugh Geddes received an electric clock as a farewell present. A cheque for £325 had been sent to the unfortunate Bill Downton, who had a wife and five children to support, while a collection had been made for Bob Wigg.

Towards the end of August the Falcons' luck began to improve. A trip to Plymouth for the first leg of the Devon Derby saw Exeter lose by just four points to the second division Devils – 44–40. Although Exeter again lost heavily, 59–25, the following evening at Leicester they rounded off the week with a 43–41 victory away at Rayleigh.

September got underway with two big home wins – 66–18 over Liverpool, and 65–19 against Tamworth. It was to be the Tammies final appearance at the County Ground as the Staffordshire track closed, never to reopen, at the end of the season. Lack of support was again the cause but fortunately the Fazeley stadium closure did not take place until after the Falcons succeeded in winning 46–38 there on Wednesday 13 September.

Another boost came with the news that the Control Board had given permission for Exeter to revert to the more popular Monday race night and the last Friday meeting on 15 September resulted in another big win for the Falcons, this time a 61–23 victory over Aldershot.

Exeter's fortunes improved still further on Monday 18 September when the Falcons beat their old rivals Plymouth Devils 54–30 to win the Devon Derby on aggregate in front of a bumper 7,000 crowd. Two new novices rode in the second half of this meeting: Bob Roger, the youngest member of the famous Roger family, and Rex Hardy, younger brother of Don. Bob won his first race in the reasonable time of 79.6.

Rain forced the final league match against Rayleigh to be abandoned after Heat 7 with Falcons leading 27–14. What should have been the final meeting at the County Ground saw the revitalised Falcons defeat newly crowned league champions Oxford 48–36, but a week later the curtain thankfully fell on the traumatic 1950 season when the restaged league match against Rayleigh saw Exeter round off with a 55–29 victory.

The final programme included a letter written by Lt Col R. Vernon C. Brook, Chairman of the Speedway Control Board, which highlighted the discriminating way in which entertainment tax had virtually crippled British speedway that summer. Col. Brook pointed to the World Final at Wembley where of £22,500 taken in gate receipts £10,200 had to be paid in tax. Had this been football, rugby or ice hockey the tax bill would only have been £3,070.

The last event to involve Exeter riders was the Third Division Riders Championship at Walthamstow, where 23,000 fans watched Oxford's Pat Clarke win the title with a 15 point maximum. Trevor Redmond was second and Ken Middleditch third. The Falcons representative, Don Hardy, only managed to score 3 points, while Arthur Pilgrim, riding as reserve notched a single point.

Veteran Alf Kaines splashes his way around the County Ground.

1951

EXETER
SPEEDWAY
OFFICIAL
PROGRAMME
9D.
Promoted by
MOTOR SPORTS (EXETER) Ltd.
County Ground Sports Stadium, St. Thomas, Exeter
Phone 5231
MONDAY, 15th OCTOBER, 1951, at 7.30 p.m.
Challenge Match
EXETER v. WEMBLEY
TWENTY-NINTH MEETING
BETTING STRICTLY PROHIBITED
W. V. COLE & SONS, LTD., PRINTERS & STATIONERS, EXETER

HEAT 5

Having survived the traumas of 1950 Exeter were determined to enjoy a better season. Three new tracks, Cardiff, Long Eaton, and Wolverhampton had joined the Third Division but the best news as far as the Falcons were concerned was the return of their archrivals, the Plymouth Devils. The Devils had, rather unjustly, been demoted from the Second Division on purely geographical grounds. Leicester, Liverpool and Oxford were all promoted but sadly Tamworth had closed.

Another boost for Exeter was the news that the ban on first division riders appearing at third division tracks had been lifted. The County Ground had also been named as a venue for a test match against the Swedish national side.

Pre-season practice day at the County Ground was very wet, (not an unusual occurrence at Exeter), but the day was brightened by the news that the youngest member of the Roger clan, Bob, had been signed on loan from New Cross despite considerable competition for his signature from other clubs. Bob practised at the track along with Cyril and Bert, and agreed to join the Falcons on the recommendation of his brothers, having completed his National Service as a paratrooper.

During the winter the Falcons' skipper Arthur Pilgrim had decided to retire from speedway and planned instead to concentrate on 500cc Formula III car racing. However, he was eventually persuaded to make a comeback shortly afterwards with the newly formed Cardiff Dragons. Vic Gent was named as the Falcons' captain in his place. The opening line-up was announced as Gent/Sargeant, Hardy/Hoskin, Walsh/Moore, with

The 1951 Falcons L → R. Back: Bob Roger, Goog Hoskin, Don Weekes, Don Hardy, Bill Williams. Front: Jack Bedkober, Johnny Sargeant, Bill Dutton, Vic Gent, Ted Moore.

Bedkober and Roger as reserve. Bedkober unfortunately missed pre-season practice, as his wife had been ill.

The Falcons' aspirations suffered an early set back when Ken Walsh was injured at Plymouth on Good Friday where the Australian was riding for a Devon select side in a challenge match against an all-star line-up. Heavy rain had turned the Pennycross track into a quagmire and kept the crowd for the opening meeting down to under 4,000. In his second race Walsh made a bad start and tried desperately to make up the lost ground. But on the last lap he slowed up having somehow torn the sole from his right boot, broken a toe and badly bruised his leg. Walsh was taken to hospital where it was announced later that he would be sidelined for three weeks. The upshot was that Bob Roger was given an early opportunity to move up into the team proper, while another new face, Bristol based Paul Best, took over the No 8 race jacket.

Walsh was not the only rider in trouble. Second halfers, Tom Dell and Bob Emery, had been injured while riding at the newly opened practice track, which had been constructed behind the Peamore Garage on the main Plymouth road just outside Exeter. Dell had unfortunately fractured a thigh, while Emery had torn muscles in his left leg.

Mr Spurway, who built the new track, was the proprietor of the garage, and the president of the Exeter Speedway Supporters Club. The track, sporting a corrugated iron safety fence, was intended to replace the original Alphington practice circuit, which dated back to 1945. Sadly Peamore's future would be short term thanks to the efforts of local residents.

The Falcons' season opened on Easter Monday morning with a 42–37 victory over Swindon in a challenge match at the County Ground. The wet weather had left the track so slippery that Vic Gent was the only rider to finish the first heat. Both Hugh Geddes and Johnny Sargeant fell, the latter crashing into the fence on the second bend after being blinded by flying mud, while Buster Brown suffered an engine failure. Gent went on to top score for Exeter with 10 points while Roger made a quiet debut scoring just three points.

The relaxing of the ban on first division riders

Easter Monday. Exeter v Swindon. Pre-match parade of riders. Vic Gent stays on the jeep along with Don Weekes.

was quickly exploited with Wembley stars Bill Kitchen and Eric Williams appearing in a match-race series before taking on Gent and Geddes in an all-star final. Gent beat Williams in a qualifying heat but narrowly lost out in the final after leading all the way.

The Express & Echo encouragingly reported that the meeting had attracted the second largest crowd since the war, with an official attendance of 9,800, a figure bettered only by the 11,000 who had watched the Falcons race Southampton back in 1947.

Good crowds would be essential, as later in the month speedway would suffer a major financial blow when the Chancellor of the Exchequer announced in the budget that he intended to raise the level of entertainment tax. Manager Bill Dutton writing in the Exeter programme urged the supporters to lobby their M.P. and get speedway reclassified. He also pointed out that as a direct result of the Chancellor's action Sheffield had been forced to close less than a month into the season. A supporter from Chulmleigh made the suggestion that "trade union members should get a resolution passed at their local branch, deploring the high rate of this taxation, and that its termination through any circumstances would deprive the workers of one of his most valued forms of recreation."

The first month of the season saw the Falcons competing in two major competitions: the long established Daily Mail National Trophy and the newly introduced Festival of Britain Trophy. The Festival of Britain itself was devised to boost the country's morale after several years of drab post war austerity and also mark the centenary of the Great Exhibition of 1851. The Festival was centred on London's South Bank exhibition site but cultural events took place all over the country and speedway certainly took the opportunity to get involved.

The competition was run as a number of regional mini leagues with the Falcons grouped with Poole, Plymouth and Aldershot. Matches were run over twenty heats using ten man teams, six in the team plus four reserves who effectively rode their own match within a match. Riders for the twentieth heat were nominated. Exeter's reserve squad at the time included, Ivan Sparkes, Bob Legge, Maurice Hard and Bert Fryer as well as Paul Best and Rusty Russell.

It did not start well for Exeter who were thrashed 89–30 at Aldershot on Saturday 7 April, but bounced back to beat the Shots 71–47 back at the County Ground two days later. Paul Best made a good impression for the Falcons, with a fine 11 point score, before crashing in a later heat and breaking his nose.

Exeter's second Festival match was at Poole on Tuesday 24 April where they lost 70–50. The return was also staged on a Tuesday, 1 May, when although the Falcons won 67–53 they again lost on aggregate. Another big disappointment that evening was the non-appearance of the Pirates' 16 year old sensation, Brian Crutcher who had scored nine points in the first leg. Brian was the son of Tom Crutcher who had ridden for Exeter in 1947.

The Falcons wound up the Festival rounds with an aggregate win over Plymouth, when after losing 69–51 at Pennycross on 3 May Exeter demolished the Devils 81–39 at the County Ground. Plymouth's Alan Smith spoilt Don Hardy's hopes of a maximum in heat 11 while Bob Roger continued a string of double figure scores with 11 points.

Bob Roger – Top Falcon of 1951.

The highlight of the night however was the appearance in the second half of First Division riders Dick Bradley of Bristol, and Harringay Racers' colourful star Split Waterman. Bradley beat Waterman in the first of their match races but suffered a puncture second time out. Hardy then gave Waterman a terrific race in the top scorers' final. At the first attempt Bob Roger hit the fence and fell, but in the rerun although Hardy shadowed Waterman all the way he was unable to find a way past his opponent. It was reported that Split's front wheel hardly touched the ground the entire race.

The Daily Mail National Trophy proved to be a much more successful competition for the Falcons. They began with a 77–30 win over Plymouth at the County Ground on Monday 2 April. Bob Roger made a terrific impact by top scoring with 16, but Exeter's injured list grew when Devils' Dennis Hales crashed on the main straight directly in front of Goog Hoskin. Goog, unable to avoid the fallen rider's machine, was thrown into the air hitting the ground just short of the concrete starting area, while his bike broke in two on impact with the track. Although Hales escaped unhurt, Goog suffered a fractured collarbone, one of the few injuries of his career.

With both Hoskin and Walsh missing Exeter did well to force a 54–54 draw in the second leg at Pennycross three days later which was enough to give the Falcons aggregate victory by 131–84 and a place in the Third Division semi final

The semi final saw Exeter gain an aggregate win over the Rayleigh Rockets. The Falcons went down narrowly 56–52 at the Weir on Saturday 14 April, but two days later demolished the Rockets 73–35 back at the County Ground.

The first leg of the Division Three final took place later that week when the Falcons notched their first away win of the season, a crushing 61–47 victory over Swindon at Blunsdon. Bob Roger top scored with 13. Exeter then duly clinched their first piece of silverware since 1948 by winning the second leg 63–45 at the County Ground on Monday 23 April.

The next stage of the competition was against second division opposition in the form of recently promoted Oxford Cheetahs, Exeter's bogey team from 1950. The first leg at Cowley not surprisingly saw the Cheetahs win 80–28. Although Hardy won the opening heat it was to be Exeter's sole victory. The return took place at the County Ground on Whit Monday and although Exeter did well to win 60–47, Oxford went through on aggregate. Naturally the meeting was not without an element of controversy as Cheetahs' Pat Clarke broke his leg in a collision with Roger's machine after the Exeter rider had fallen in front of him.

Bob Roger leads Vic Gent & Harry Saunders – Exeter v Oxford, National Trophy, Whit Monday.

With their National Trophy dreams at an end the Falcons could now concentrate on the league championship. The campaign began with an away win at St. Austell. Exeter led 9–3 after just two heats, and although Allan Quinn and Bill Rundle raised Cornish hopes with a 4–2 in the fourth heat the Falcons were quickly back in the driving seat. Exeter provided the winner in all but one of the fourteen heats although eight races were drawn. The match was also notable as it saw Goog Hoskin score his first maximum.

Ex Falcon Arthur Pilgrim made a welcome return to the County Ground with the new Cardiff team on Monday 21 May. Pilgrim was skipper of Dragons but his 9 point tally could not save the Welsh outfit from a twenty point defeat. However New Zealander Mick Holland prevented Don Hardy from notching a maximum with a win in heat 5. After the match the Supporters Club presented Pilgrim with a clock in appreciation of his past efforts for the Falcons.

Exeter were by now displaying a considerable strength in depth and this was evident at Long Eaton that week where they sported a ten point lead with fives races to go. Despite their riders being involved in a number of pile-ups in the remaining races the Falcons held on for their second away win.

Further success followed at Wolverhampton the next night. Their first ever visit to Monmore Green saw the Falcons record their biggest ever away victory, 62–22, with every rider except Hoskin claiming at least one race win. Vic Gent scored a full maximum while Hardy was unbeaten by an opponent. Such was Exeter's superiority over the new Wasps, as they were then known, that one Midlands reporter described the evening's action as "the worst massacre he had ever witnessed".

Long Eaton Archers paid their first visit to the County Ground on Monday 28 May and were promptly swept aside 65–18. The main interest of the evening however surrounded the revived Division Three Match Race Championship in which Don Hardy unsuccessfully challenged Aldershot's Trevor Redmond. Redmond had previously ridden against Ken Middleditch for the vacant title, but the Poole Pirate had been forced to withdraw having broken a collarbone when the series was drawn at 1–1. Exeter's hopes were dashed when Hardy fell in the first race and was beaten in the second.

There was plenty of entertainment on the programme that night and the fans were also treated to a first division match race between World Champion Freddie Williams from Wembley and West Ham's Australian international Aub Lawson, which Williams won 2–0. Bob Roger later challenged Williams but team-mate Ken Walsh beat fellow countryman Lawson in a thrilling finale.

Twenty-four hours later Redmond retained his match race title by winning the second leg 2–0 at Aldershot. Hardy led the first race for nearly a lap but overslid allowing his opponent through. Redmond made the start in the second race and won easily as Don again had problems with the tricky fourth bend. The big problem with the Aldershot track as far as Exeter riders were concerned was the unusual 'pear' shape. The first bend being wide and sweeping proved no problem, but at the other end of the circuit the track tightened up very sharply forcing the riders to slow considerably.

Winning away from the County Ground was suddenly becoming a habit for the Falcons. On Thursday 24 May they beat the 'old enemy' Plymouth by the narrowest of margins, 42–41, at Pennycross. The Devils took an early lead but Exeter levelled the scores at 18–18 thanks to a Walsh/Roger 5–1 in heat 5. Alan Smith and George Wall, who both scored maximums, led the efforts to put Plymouth back in front, which they were until the final heat. Exeter trailed 40–37 going into that race but thanks to a 5–1 by Johnny Sargeant and Walsh the Falcons snatched victory.

May came to an end with yet another away win on a new track. Exeter went to Ipswich's Foxhall Heath stadium where they won 45–39 in a challenge match.

Monday 4 June saw a qualifying round of the world championship staged at the County Ground. The line-up included two American riders, Don Hawley and Nick Nicholaides, members of the United States touring team who were based at Dublin's Shelbourne Park that summer. Also competing were Harold Fairhurst and Eddie Lack from second division Edinburgh Monarchs. Lack would return to Exeter in 1979 to spend a couple of seasons as track curator.

Hawley won the opening race, but Exeter riders won all the next ten heats. Fairhurst offered the main threat to a home victory. The Monarchs' rider was involved in a terrific duel with Bob Roger in heat 11. Roger made the start and led almost the whole way but unfortunately overslid twenty yards before the finish allowing Fairhurst to nip through for his first win. He followed this up with a win over Sargeant and Walsh in his next race, which left him needing a win in heat 17 to clinch the round. In that heat he faced Poole's Charlie Hayden, Nicholaides, and reserve Ted Moore who was replacing Ernie Rawlins. Hayden took the lead but when Fairhurst attempted to go around him on the fourth bend the bikes locked together and they crashed heavily. Hayden's leathers were badly torn and Fairhurst severely shaken but both came out for the rerun only to be beaten by Moore.

Sargeant and Hardy both finished the meeting on 13 points. In the run-off for first place Hardy made the start and led Sargeant by several lengths. However after a couple of laps Sargeant caught and passed his team mate and although Hardy raced neck and neck with him to the finish Johnny hung on to claim the winner's £20 cheque provided by the Sunday Dispatch newspaper. Vic Gent overcame a first race crash to finish joint third with Fairhurst.

Goog Hoskin, Bill Dutton and Don Weekes all missed the meeting as they were in Sweden with the England 'C' team for a three match test series. That evening the England team was staying at Sodertalje, near Stockholm and discussing who would win at Exeter. Also enjoying the party was the local newspaper proprietor who offered to find out the result. By 10am the next day he was able to give the Exeter contingent not only the news of Sargeant's victory but the full details of the meeting, all as Dutton put it "thanks to the marvels of the modern age."

Goog Hoskin.

A week later Exeter beat Swindon 45–38 in a vital but wet league encounter. The Falcons now topped the table with 12 points ahead of the Robins who were on eight.

Swindon hit problems even before the start when Danny Malone failed to arrive at the stadium. Then further difficulties arose in the first heat. Hugh Geddes took the lead until his engine blew up causing him to crash and unable to take any further part in the meeting. This left Bedkober and Hardy to take a 5–1.

Swindon riders – Ray Ellis, Buster Brown and Bob Jones, won the next three heats but another Bedkober/Hardy maximum extended the Falcons lead. Had the Robins been at full strength Exeter could well have been hard pushed to win, but Swindon were only able to track a single rider in three of the closing heats.

Man of the match was undoubtedly Robins' Buster Brown who scored a superb maximum despite the track being extremely wet and difficult. Brown's 'full house' was the first by a visitor that season.

RKO Gaumont sponsored the second half and Brown continued his successful evening by winning both his heat and the final. The sponsorship was tied in with the film 'Circle of Danger', starring Ray Milland and Patricia Roc, which was then showing at the Gaumont in North Street, Exeter. A special prize presentation was arranged to take place at the cinema later in the week. Unfortunately Brown had racing commitments with the Robins and was not able to attend, so Vic Gent accompanied by the management and riders received a cigarette lighter on his behalf.

The difficult Aldershot track ended Exeter's unbeaten league run on 16 June. The Falcons problems started when Roger got lost en-route forcing Exeter to go into action one man short. Ken Walsh was injured in his third ride when he tried to avoid Bert Edwards who had crashed in front of him. Altogether it was not a happy night for the Falcons who found themselves on the wrong end of seven 5–1s before finally going down 59–23.

The Falcons expected an equally tough encounter when Aldershot visited the County Ground two days later, but in reality it proved to be a relatively easy 56–28 victory for Exeter. Trevor Redmond again kept the home side on their toes by winning his first three outings but missed out to Bob Roger in his last race. In the second half Aub Lawson and Split Waterman made welcome re-appearances. Ken Walsh again defeated Lawson in a revenge challenge match, while Sargeant came out on top in his race with Waterman.

During this time the Supporters Club was working hard to raise funds for the purchase of a track spare machine. The club had organised a big summer draw and also a weekly 'Penny on the Drum' scheme, which seems to have been very popular. Even Dr Paget, the track medical officer, is reported to have made a donation towards the fund.

Poole Pirates gave the Falcons a real shock when they came close to pulling off a surprise win at the County Ground on 26 June. Although Exeter took an early lead the Pirates drew level in heat 5 thanks to a 5–1 from Charlie Hayden and Terry Small. The Dorset outfit edged ahead two heats later when Walsh fell leaving Ken Middleditch and Tony Lewis to score a 4–2 over Sargeant. Two further heat advantages in heats 8 and 10 extended the Pirates lead to six points but thanks to Walsh who teamed up first with Sargeant and then Moore for vital 5–1s Exeter regained control and were two points ahead going into the final race. Although Allan Kidd won it for Poole, Sargeant and Bedkober took the minor placings to clinch the match for the Falcons.

Scandinavian champion Olle Nygren was the second half guest star. Although he beat Hardy in the first match race Olle lost out to Sargeant and Middleditch in later races.

The Falcons travelled to Essex on Saturday 30 June where they found the Rayleigh Rockets in unbeatable form and consequently lost heavily 61–23. Back at the County Ground two days later Exeter had no trouble beating Plymouth 54–30.

Poole gained ample revenge for their Exeter defeat when the Falcons visited Dorset the next evening. The Pirates won 53–31 but the scoreline did not reflect the close fast racing in which the track record was equalled four times during the course of the match.

Sargeant was missing from the Exeter line-up due to a knee injury, which ended his world championship hopes, and the Falcons never recovered from Poole's perfect start in which the Pirates took maximum point from the first two races.

Fortunately Johnny Sargeant's knee injury did not prevent him from winning the sack race at the annual supporters sports day at Dawlish Warren. Despite Johnny's brave efforts, Plymouth were the overall winners with Exeter second and Bristol third.

Wolverhampton visited Exeter for the first time on Monday 9 July and were victims of a second massacre, this time by 67–16. Roger and Walsh both scored full maximums for the Falcons, and Hardy collected a paid maximum. Bedkober was the only Exeter rider to finish third but still managed a total of 10 points.

The match was preceded by an international match-race series between Cyril Roger and Edinburgh's Jack Young. Young won the first race and in doing so set a new track record of 73.5 seconds. This was exactly a second faster than the old record set the previous year by Ken Walsh. It was Young's first appearance at the County Ground and his lap times were broken down as follows; lap 1 20.0 seconds, lap 2 17.2 (new flying lap record), lap 3 17.6, and lap 4 18.2. Roger also showed he had not lost his County Ground touch winning the second race and the decider. After such class entertainment the Wolves match proved something of an anti climax.

Exeter enjoyed further success that week when they won 49–35 at Plymouth in the first leg of the Devon Derby. Walsh made up for losing the Exeter track record by breaking the Pennycross record in the opening heat.

The Falcons still clung to the top of the league table but were coming under considerable pressure from Poole. Exeter gained four more valuable league points thanks to home wins over Long Eaton and Rayleigh as July drew to a close and also had high hopes of an away win again the Archers.

Indeed the Falcons started well at Station Road with Goog Hoskin and Ken Walsh taking a 5–1 in the opening heat. But Long Eaton then won the next seven races to establish a 35–15 lead. Undeterred, Exeter fought back gaining two maximums and a 4–2 to reduce the gap to ten points with three races still to go. However Exeter's hopes of snatching a result ended when

Jack Young and Cyril Roger prepare for their match race on Monday 9 July.

Jack Winstanley and Pedlar Palmer teamed up for a 5–1 in heat 12.

Track conditions were not to the Exeter riders' liking at Aldershot 48 hours later where the Shots provided the winners of all 14 heats.

Trevor Redmond was at the County Ground on Monday 30 July for the deciding leg of his Third Division Match Race Championship tie with Plymouth's Alan Smith. Unfortunately this event was cancelled at the last minute. Happily TR's fellow Kiwi Bruce Abernethy was booked in for a second half appearance, so the fans still got some match race action. Abernethy, who rode for the Wembley lions and wore the longest scarf in speedway was beaten by Redmond but in turn defeated Walsh and Roger in other races. In the main event of the evening Exeter beat lowly St. Austell 63–21.

The end of July also saw Poole take over at the top of the league table. Bill Dutton pointed out in his programme notes that the signings of Bill Holden and Roy Craighead from Southampton had greatly strengthened the Pirates who in his view had now become the Falcons most serious rivals for the championship.

August Bank Holiday was a truly gala occasion and saw the first official test match between England and Sweden to be staged in this country take place at the County Ground. As Sweden was still an emerging nation in speedway terms the Swedes would race against England 'C' for whom all the riders would be drawn from the third division. That the series had come about was due in no small way to the efforts of Bill Dutton who at that time was chairman of the Third Division promoters committee. There had been a couple of representative England v Australia matches at the County Ground before the war but those had no official status so this match would also be Exeter's first full international event.

Not surprisingly such an attraction drew a bumper crowd of nearly 11,000. The fans came from all over the West Country and one coach party even travelled down from Blackpool. Three quarters of an hour before the 11.00am start time the queues stretched from the stadium gates a full 400 yards back to the end of Church Road.

The England line-up included Ken Middleditch, George Wall, Jack Unstead, Buster Brown and Terry Small with the Falcons' well represented by Don Hardy, Vic Gent and Bob Roger. The Swedish team consisted of Olle Nygren, Bo Anderson, Eskil Carlsson, Sune Karlsson, Rune Sormander, Olle Segerstrom, Dan Forsberg and Lennart Carlstrom.

The occasion brought out a veritable posse of

England v Sweden – Bill Dutton leads out the teams.

civic dignitaries who were introduced to the riders on the pre-match parade. The civic party included the Deputy Mayor, Alderman J. G. R. Orchard, The Sherriff, Alderman G. J. Greenslade, the Town Clerk, Mr C. J. Newman and the Chief Constable A. R. Rowsell.

Olle Nygren got the meeting off to a sensational start for the Swedes by not only winning the first race but also breaking the track record with a time of 72.8 seconds. Middleditch and Wall finished behind him for a drawn heat.

Don Hardy won heat 2 ahead of Andersson and Karlsson but Sweden took the lead thanks to a Segerstrom/Sormander 5–1 in heat 3. Hardy was out again in the next race but crashed leaving Nygren to notch his second win of the morning. Vic Gent took second place but Carlsson suffered an engine failure so was also a non-finisher.

Bob Roger was given an early reserve ride and led Brown home for a 5–1, which brought England back within a point of Sweden. Middleditch and Wall put the home side ahead for the first time thanks to another maximum in heat 6 and although Sweden took a 4–2 from heat 7 the England opening pair scored their second 5–1 in heat 8 to extend the lead to five points. From then on it was England's match as they stormed away to win 61–46 although nobody could stop the flying Nygren who went on to score a magnificent 18 point maximum. The closest the Swedish No.2 came to defeat was in heat 16 when reserve Jack Unstead, who earlier scored a win and a second place came from last to give Nygren his toughest challenge of the match.

Middleditch and Wall proved to be England's most successful pairing and featured in a thrilling heat 17 during which Bo Andersson's efforts to split them resulted in the Swede hitting the fence fairly hard. Hardy sent the Exeter fans home happy when he won the final race.

After the meeting the riders and officials of both teams were entertained to lunch at the Royal Clarence Hotel by the Exeter directors. Mr L. J. Hallett, the chairman of the directors, toasted the Swedes and praised the efforts of international sport in strengthening the bonds between European nations more than "all the talk you get from the gasometers of politics". In reply Mr P. Ringstrom said that it was a pleasure to race against England.

In the league Exeter had started August with a narrow defeat at Cardiff. The Dragons made a flying start thanks to Kevin Hayden and Gerald Pugh and thereafter held on to win 43–41. The loss of those two vital league points was a blow for Exeter, but at least Johnnie Sargeant made a superb return from injury and only Charlie May prevented him from scoring a maximum in the penultimate heat.

That defeat only encouraged the Falcons to work harder at Swindon a couple of nights later where they reversed the scoreline to win 43–41 and keep their title hopes alive. Exeter followed this up with a home win over Plymouth and victory in a challenge match at Ipswich on what turned out to be an exceptionally wet and greasy track. The slick gating Falcons then completed a hat trick of away wins with yet another victory over the Devils down at Pennycross.

Swindon were duly defeated 53–31 at the County Ground on Monday 20 August, but to the crowd's disappointment the Bronze Helmet match race decider was again postponed at the last minute.

The away successes continued back at Penarth Road when the Falcons made their second visit of the month to Cardiff. This time Exeter came away from Wales as victors by a single point, 42–41.

Trevor Redmond and Alan Smith finally met in the match race championship decider on Monday 27 August. Redmond successfully retained his Bronze Helmet but only managed to score seven points for Aldershot in the league match that followed, the score reading 54–29 to the Falcons.

September proved to be a vital month for both Exeter and Poole as the battle for the championship reached its climax. The Pirates topped the table with 42 points, two ahead of the Falcons who had completed 26 matches compared with Poole's 24.

Morale at the County Ground received a timely boost when the Falcons once again put their name on the Devon Derby trophy by beating Plymouth 53–30. This match was originally scheduled for Monday 3 September but was postponed until the following Friday due to rain.

An even greater boost came the following Monday when Exeter had little difficulty in beating title rivals Poole 55–29. Brim full of confidence the Falcons set off for Cornwall the next afternoon determined to gain more vital points at the expense of St Austell Gulls who were then currently third from bottom.

But luck was not on Exeter's side. In heat 9 Bob Roger was well in front but suffered a puncture on the last bend allowing both Norman Street and Harold Bull to nip through for a Gulls' 5–1. Two heats later Paul Best dropped a valve seventy yards from the finish and lost a safe second place. As a result of these set backs Exeter lost narrowly 43–41.

Bottom of the table Wolverhampton were the next visitors to the County Ground. Exeter showed the struggling Midlands team no mercy notching up ten 5–1s from the 14 heats on the way to a massive 64–19 scoreline. Indeed had not Best suffered further engine trouble in heat 13 while lying second the number of maximum heat wins would have been eleven.

The Falcons were in such good form that their top four scorers, Roger, Hoskin, Hardy and Sargeant, went on to beat second division Bristol Bulldogs 25–11 in a six heat second half mini match.

Monday 24 September was crunch day as far as the third division championship was concerned. That was the day Exeter travelled to Poole desperately needing a win if they were to snatch the title from the Pirates. The Falcons were encouraged by the fact that Poole had lost 47–37 at Cardiff the previous week, but their hopes were to be short lived. Poole won 54–30 and effectively clinched the championship. Such was the interest in the meeting that programmes were completely sold out. The normally calm Hugh Geddes who had just gone along to watch was noted to have become 'extremely excited'.

Exeter had no trouble seeing off Cardiff 60–24 back the County Ground the next night and later in the week notched another good away win, 47–37, at Rayleigh. But there was a high price to pay for that victory over the Rockets.

Disaster struck the Falcons in heat 11 when

Johnny Sargeant practising at the Peamore training track. Note the corrugated iron safety fence.

Jules Benson, replacing Ron Howes in the Rayleigh line-up, made a desperate attempt to overtake Johnnie Sargeant and went into a corner too fast. As a result the Exeter rider was brought down and sustained severe hand injuries including two partly severed fingers. Benson was excluded but in his next race crashed into team mate Jack Unstead and suffered a fractured collarbone.

The accident was to cost Sargeant the index finger of his right hand and brought his until then extremely successful season to a premature end. The injury would also sadly have a long term effect in his highly promising career.

As September came to a close it was apparent that the league championship had slipped from Exeter's grasp but that did not stop the Falcons from ending the campaign on a winning streak.

The final weeks of the season began with a 62–22 thrashing of St. Austell at the County Ground. A bumper pay night for the Exeter riders saw Walsh, Hardy and Roger all score 12 point maximums. But the main attraction for the fans was a return appearance of Jack Young who just a couple of weeks earlier had become the first and only second division rider ever to win the world championship. Youngie was also in fine form at Exeter beating former favourite Cyril Roger 2–0 in a match race and equalling the track record.

The Cornish Gulls gained prompt revenge by again denying the Falcons victory at the Par Moor the next evening where they beat Exeter 44–40 in a closely fought challenge match.

Later in the week the Falcons went up to the Midlands where Wolverhampton gave them their closest run so far at Monmore Green before Exeter eventually came out on top also by 44–40.

Sadly the Exeter injury jinx hit again that night. With Sargeant and Bedkober already sidelined youngster Morris Barnett was give a chance in the reserve berth and scored two points. Unfortunately during a second half race he was flung over the safety fence and suffered a fractured thigh.

For the last away match of the season at Swindon 24 hours later another local junior Colin Selley was drafted in as reserve but failed to score. Nevertheless Exeter won 46–38 with Walsh, Hoskin, Roger and Hardy all chipping in a solid ten points apiece.

Despite the Falcons on track success it had been a frustrating week for the Exeter management. After the home match against St. Austell Bill Dutton had announced that the final home meeting of the year would hopefully be an inter league challenge against first division Harringay Racers depending on whether or not the Speedway Control Board granted the necessary permission. George Kay, the Racers' manager, was present to confirm that his team was willing to visit the County Ground.

The next morning the track office was inundated with calls from away fans wishing to book tickets for the match. On the Wednesday the Control Board gave the meeting the go ahead which would be all ticket with a crowd limit of 14,000. The next day Harringay announced that they would be bringing their full team with the exception of Jack Biggs who had already left for Australia.

By Friday morning extra advertising had been booked and the tickets were already being printed. Then in the afternoon came a major blow. The Racers were no longer keen to come to Exeter or prepared to ride for the money on offer. The agreed basis for payment was for Harringay to ride for second rather than first division pay rates with additional sums depending on the size of the crowd. Suddenly the big match was off.

Exeter concluded their league fixtures in the fog at the County Ground on Monday 8 October where they had no difficulty seeing off the Rayleigh Rockets by 54–29.

It had been a superb season for the Falcons and under normal circumstances Exeter's total of 56 league points would have been sufficient to win the championship, but up the A35 in Dorset Poole had done even better amassing 60 points which had earned the Pirates their league title.

More importantly Exeter's success had been reflected at the turnstiles with increased attendances, so thankfully the serious financial problems, which had brought the track to the brink of closure in 1950 had now been overcome. It was reported that the future of speedway was again safe in the 'Ever Faithful' city.

But the season was not completely over. Following Harringay's last minute withdrawal the ever resourceful Bill Dutton, on the off chance had contacted Wembley.

The all powerful Wembley Lions, who regularly attracted crowds of 80,000 plus to the Empire Stadium on a weekly basis, had just clinched their third successive first division championship but had never appeared on a division three track. To Dutton's amazement Wembley readily agreed to visit Exeter. The date for the great encounter was arranged for Monday 15 October and advance tickets were snapped up as soon as they went on sale.

The ground limit remained at 14,000 and on the morning of the match 13,000 had been sold. The remainder sold out very quickly but one former director firmly believes that the unofficial attendance figure that night was well in excess of 16,000.

To ease the crush at the turnstiles the gates were opened at 5.30pm, an hour earlier than usual. By start time the crowd was packed in like sardines in a tin and my father Ted recalled being hemmed in so tightly that he was unable to fill in his programme.

The Wembley line-up included former world champions Tommy Price and Freddie Williams along with Bruce Abernethy, Bob Oakley, Eric Williams and George Wilks. Skipper Bill Kitchen, who had previously agreed to ride in Denmark, was replaced in the reserve berth by Lions' asset Trevor Redmond who had been recalled along with Jimmy Gooch.

Not surprisingly, in view of the strength of the opposition, the Falcons' top four of Gent, Roger, Hoskin and Hardy had been bolstered by the inclusion of guests George Wall and Hugh Geddes while Jack Unstead joined Ted Moore at reserve.

Exeter made the best possible start with Roger and Gent taking a 5–1 in the opening heat over Abernethy and Price who fell on the second lap. Roger's winning time of 73.1 also proved to be the fastest time of the night.

Wembley provided the winners of the next three heats, all of which were drawn, but Exeter extended their lead with a 4–2 again thanks to Roger and Gent in heat 5. Eric Williams made the start and skilfully held Bob at bay for three laps, but after challenging Williams several times on the inside the Exeter favourite switched to the outside on the last lap and burst around the fence for a narrow win. Exeter thus led 18–12 to the delight of the huge crowd, which remains to this day the post-war County Ground attendance record.

Williams and Trevor Redmond countered with a 5–1 against Hardy and Wall in heat 6, but immediately Hoskin and Geddes retaliated with a maximum for the Falcons. Heat 8 was drawn but Wembley, despite Roger trying everything he knew, took their second 5–1 in the following race thanks this time to Williams and George Wilks.

Abernethy recorded his only win of the match in the tenth heat to hold Exeter to a two point lead. Hoskin notched his second win in the next ahead of Oakley and Eric Williams, while Freddie Williams won heat 12, which was also drawn.

Wembley then levelled the scores at 39–39 when Eric Williams and Redmond took a 4–2 over Geddes and Moore to set up a classic last heat decider.

In the final race Bob Roger and Goog Hoskin

Don Hardy receives the St Thomas Challenge Trophy from Carnival Queen.

lined up against Abernethy and Wilks with every chance of bringing off a shock result. Indeed a shock win for Exeter was very much on the cards as the tapes went up and both Falcons shot out in front. But sadly it was not to last as Hoskin's engine blew leaving Roger to win his last race for Exeter and earn the Falcons a memorable 42–42 draw.

A postscript to this meeting appeared a few days later in the Express & Echo. The local darts correspondent regretted that it was not possible to present an up-to-date league table as the fixture between the Exeter Inn and the Sawyers' Arms had been abandoned due to several players having left early to go to the speedway 'do'.

The curtain fell on Exeter's 1951 season at the County Ground a week later with a charity meeting organised by the St. Thomas (Exeter) Carnival Association for the Invitation Challenge Trophy. The racing followed the crowning of the carnival queen and 'Beating the Retreat' by the Exeter Girls Training Corps. Nine locally based riders and Bert Roger of New Cross contested the meeting, which attracted a crowd of 4,000. The winner was Don Hardy, dropping his only point to Goog Hoskins who suffered another vital engine failure. The evening ended with the traditional firework display.

The Third Division Riders final took place at Cardiff the following evening where the Falcons' representatives Bob Roger and Don Hardy lined up in the opening race against eventual champion Ken Middleditch and Rayleigh's Tom O'Connor. At the first attempt Middleditch and the two Falcons tangled and all three came down. The steward, Mr C. H. King, ordered them back for the rerun. This time Middleditch made the gate while Roger and O'Connor engaged in a three-lap duel, which only ended when the Rockets' rider hit the fence. Hardy was unable to avoid his bike and also crashed. Don injured his hand, which required stitches, and both he and O'Connor withdrew from the meeting. Roger also failed to make it to the rostrum. A five man run-off was required to settle second place. Plymouth's Alan Smith won this, while overall third place went to Jack Unstead.

1952

EXETER
SPEEDWAY
OFFICIAL
PROGRAMME
9D.
Promoted by MOTOR SPORTS (EXETER) LTD.
County Ground Sports Stadium, St. Thomas, Exeter.
MONDAY, 19th MAY, 1952, at 7.30 p.m.
National League (Southern Section)
EXETER v. ST. AUSTELL
SEVENTH MEETING
BETTING STRICTLY PROHIBITED
W. V COLE & SONS, LTD., PRINTERS & STATIONERS, EXETER

HEAT 6

The successful 1951 Falcons' line-up was quickly broken up and Exeter went into the new Elizabethan age with a very different looking outfit. Jack Bedkober had retired and gone home to Australia, while Bob Roger, like his brothers before him, was recalled to New Cross. Ken Walsh had also moved up to the First Division, having been transferred to Harringay. As part of that deal Ron Barrett now joined Exeter from the Racers. Barrett had previously ridden on loan at Plymouth where he became the youngest rider ever to score a maximum for the Devils. Two unknown Australians had also been signed and their names would become synonymous with speedway at Exeter; Jack Geran and Neil Street. Another new addition was an exciting New Zealander called Jack Hart, who came with a reputation as a full throttle rider.

Geran and Street had travelled to England from Australia by boat, a voyage of some six weeks, initially with no definite idea of which track they would join. Geran had already gained plenty of speedway experience riding for the Tracey Tigers team in Melbourne. The ship, SS Orcades, on which his passage to the UK was booked, sailed on the morning of his last meeting so Jack was forced to fly to Adelaide afterwards where he was able to catch up with it further along the coast. His bike had already been loaded so Jack was forced to borrow a machine for his final match. Perhaps it was an omen for the future but the borrowed bike had formerly belonged to Norman Clay.

Before leaving home Jack was warned by Peter

The 1952 Falcons L → R. Back: Jack Geran, Neil Street, Don Hardy, Morris Barnett, Ron Barnett, Colin Selley. Front: Goog Hoskin, Bill Dutton, Vic Gent, Johnny Sargeant, Don Weeks.

Moore, who had ridden in England for Long Eaton the previous year, that "whatever you do don't go to Exeter or marry an English Sheila", the warning was to go unheeded on both counts. During the voyage across the Pacific Ocean Jack received a telegram from Bill Dutton, who, on the recommendation of Ken Walsh, offered not only to pay his fare over but also the return passage at the end of the season if he signed for the Falcons. As the only other offer he had received was for a trial with Birmingham, Jack not surprisingly accepted the Exeter deal.

In Australia Neil Street, a toolmaker by trade, had concentrated on scrambles and road racing and although he had little previous speedway experience, had decided that it was probably the easiest discipline to break into professionally in England.

Geran and Street left the 'Orcades' at Southampton where they were met by Dutton and Don Weekes. Street had planned to head for the Midlands and a trial with Wolverhampton, but Dutton asked Jack if there were any other Aussie prospects on board so Jack naturally recommended his friend.

Their arrival in Exeter was not without incident. Weekes drove them down the coast road in a big Studebaker car. It was a Saturday and Dutton was dropped off in the city centre as he planned to watch Exeter City play at St James Park in the afternoon. One of the first people they saw was Weekes' father, at the wheel of a double-decker bus. The final part of the journey, which had brought them half way across the world, took them along the High Street down Fore Street Hill and across Exe Bridge to St Thomas. Ted Lethbridge recalls seeing them pass his shop in Cowick Street. A little further along, shortly after the railway arch, the big old car broke down and the new arrivals were forced to push it the last few hundred yards into Nelson Road where they would lodge with the Weekes family.

Meanwhile of the previous season's team Don Hardy was promoted to captain, a role he would retain for the next four seasons, while Goog Hoskin took over the No. 1 race jacket. Also back were Vic Gent and Johnny Sargeant now recovered from his Rayleigh accident. Paul Best and Ted Moore had been released, Best having joined Cardiff while Moore moved to Southampton. Morris Barnett was also back on his feet although not yet riding again.

On the league front the 'Third Division' title had become the 'Southern League'. Not surprisingly, Poole had been promoted to Division Two where the Pirates continued their winning ways. Poole's replacement were league debutantes Ipswich Witches. Also back were the Falcons' old south coast rivals, Southampton Saints.

Mrs Weekes with her speedway family. Clockwise – Neil Street, son Don, Ronnie Swaine, Jack Geran.

Several of the Falcons had taken the opportunity to get in some of pre-season practice on the beach at Dawlish Warren where they were able to mark out tracks of different sizes, but with the unique hazard that over enthusiasm could result in an unintentional trip into the sea.

A new programme cover was introduced depicting a drawing of a rider watched by a crowd of Wembley proportions. The design would be used for the next four seasons and would even make an appearance in the sixties.

Prior to the start of the season rumours circulated that the Falcons had made an attempt to buy Bob Roger and Ronnie Genz from New Cross. Dutton later confirmed that the Exeter management were prepared to pay a substantial fee for either of these riders and had also offered a considerable amount to take them both on loan for two years. The deal had fallen through as

Rangers' boss Fred Mockford still intended to persevere with both riders.

The new season commenced at the County Ground on Monday 7 April with an international challenge against Swedish touring side Smerderna. Captained by world finalist Joel Jansson, the Smerderna line-up also included Rune Sormander and Olle Nygren, the joint Exeter track record holder. Nygren had stepped in as a last minute replacement for Ove Fundin, (named as 'Bodin' in the programme), who had been injured at Swindon the previous Saturday.

Unfortunately steady rain had fallen for an hour prior to the start making the track extremely treacherous. Despite the conditions Smerderna looked the stronger side and after six heats were half a dozen points ahead. But a 5–1 by Don Hardy and Vic Gent in heat 7 narrowed the margin to two points. At that stage Jack Hart made his first appearance. Rocketing from the gate the Kiwi led all the way for a comfortable win over Sormander. Johnny Sargeant finished third to level the overall scores.

A ninth heat 4–2 by Goog Hoskin and Jack Geran put Exeter ahead for the first time but the Swedes again drew level thanks to the efforts of Joel Jansson and Bert Lindarw in the following race. Hardy and Gent gained another Falcons 5–1 in heat 11, but again Smerderna matched this in heat 12 when the Anderssons, – Bosse and Lars Erik – relegated Hoskin to third place.

Heat 13 proved to be the race of the night. Hardy and Hart lined up against Nygren and Olle Segerstrom. Before the tapes had reached the top of the gate Hardy was in front, while Nygren was last with Hart ahead of him. Nygren was in no mood to stay at the back, picking off first Hart and then teammate Segerstrom. Although he caught Hardy at the front he could not quite edge ahead and at the flag Hardy won by barely a wheel. Hart in the meantime had also overtaken Segerstrom and Exeter once again held a two point lead. Alas it was not sufficient, as Sven Skoglund beat Geran in the final heat and with Lindarw third the final score was a 42–42 draw.

Sadly Hart's season did not last long as the wet track caught him out during the second half. He crashed and was hit by Lars Erik Anderson. Both were taken to hospital; Andersson with concussion, and Exeter's impressive new Kiwi with a broken leg which would rule him out for the rest of the year.

The first meeting was also a nightmare for Geran and Street, unused as they were both to the concrete starting grid and British wet weather.

Unlucky newcomer Jack Hart.

The Falcons suffered a further setback at Plymouth on Good Friday where they lost their first Southern League match by 57–27 in front of a 14,000 crowd. Unhappily Exeter failed to produce a single race winner. Local youngster Colin Selley was drafted in to replace Hart, and the doubters were already suggesting that the Falcons were too weak.

The rain struck early on Easter Monday and the return fixture against the Devils was postponed.

Exeter's first win of 1952 came when they beat the Wolverhampton Wasps by 73–34 in the first leg of Daily Mail National Trophy at the County Ground a week later. The new Aussies showed that they were quickly learning to adapt to British conditions. Jack Geran included two wins in his nine point tally while Neil Street won both his reserve rides.

This initial success was followed by a 59–49 away victory in the second leg at Monmore Green the following Friday where Goog Hoskin scored an 18 point maximum.

The Falcons were also making an impression off track. The majority of the team now lived locally and tended to socialise as a team, so the management purchased smart green blazers complete with gold braid, which were worn by all the riders when they were around town.

Having disposed of the Wasps by 132–83 on aggregate, the Falcons quickly found themselves facing Plymouth in the semi final of the National Trophy with the first leg being staged at the County Ground on Monday 28 April. Although the Falcons became the first team to beat the Devils that year the 57–51 scoreline would not be enough to earn another aggregate victory.

New faces had also appeared in the second half with 18 year old Wally Monckton and Ron Swaine, another junior from Harringay, making their debuts.

Another good away win was achieved at St. Austell the next night where the Falcons came out on top by an impressive 55–29. Sadly it was not without cost as Johnny Sargeant hit the fence and dislocated his knee. It was put in plaster but Johnny looked likely to be sidelined for at least three weeks. Goog Hoskin once again laid the foundations for Exeter's victory by scoring another maximum.

Exeter were unable to maintain their successful run in the second leg of the National Trophy at Plymouth that Thursday where the Devils won 67–41 to qualify for the Southern League final of the competition by an aggregate score of 118–98. Rain, just before the meeting, made the track fairly heavy and kept the crowd down to just over 5,000. Selley was moved up into the team proper to replace Sargeant while Morris Barnett made his comeback at reserve. Unfortunately neither managed to score but Hoskin upheld Exeter's pride with yet another 18 point maximum and the fastest time of the night.

The wet weather followed the Falcons to Swindon where they rounded off a hectic week with a league match. Exeter lost 48–36 at Blunsdon and Goog Hoskin's chance of notching his third maximum of the week disappeared in heat 7 when his footrest came adrift.

Rapid revenge was gained when the Robins were beaten 49–35 at the County Ground two days later. This time Goog stayed free of mechanical problems and swept to a faultless 12 point maximum. Morris Barnett took over Colin Selley's team place and scored 4 points, but worryingly both the reserves, Street and Selley, failed to score.

It was Vic Gent's turn to score a maximum when Long Eaton visited the County Ground the following week. Skipper Don Hardy notched a paid maximum. He won three races and followed Barnett home in heat 6, but a first-heat mechanical problem cost Hoskin his chance of yet another maximum. Neil Street was unable to ride due to illness so was replaced by Ron Swaine, who included a win in his four point tally. Despite their problems the Falcons still ran out easy winners by 63–20.

In an unusual step all the profits from that night's meeting along with a collection from the public were given to the Exeter Cathedral Restoration Fund. Several local sports organisations had been involved with raising money to meet the cost of rebuilding one of the Cathedral's side chapels, which had been destroyed by an enemy bomb during the Exeter Blitz of May 1942.

Goog Hoskin's maximum chances were again spoilt when he fell in the first race of the Falcons' next home match in which they defeated St. Austell 53–30. Despite the scoreline none of the Exeter riders rode unbeaten, although Swaine impressed with three wins from four rides. The only Gulls' rider to finish ahead of him was the Polish rider, Max Rech who forced the young Falcon into third place in heat 12.

Hoskin's success continued in the second half with a 2–0 victory over Bob Roger in a special match race.

The Falcons took to the road later that week with away matches at Ipswich and Rayleigh. At Foxhall Heath Exeter missed out by a single point, the Witches winning 42–41 despite another superb maximum from Hoskin. Shortly before the meeting, Ipswich lost the services of Alby Smith,who was ruled out on medical advice following a crash at Southampton earlier in the week. His place was taken by 18 year old Dennis Day who scored six from three races. Former Falcon Arthur Pilgrim injured a leg and also had to pull out.

The Falcons fared no better when they moved on to Essex for their Saturday night clash with Rayleigh at the Weir. The Rockets won 49–35 but much more serious for the Falcons was the news that Exeter had suffered a major off-track loss.

The blow fell when Bill Dutton announced that he would be resigning from Exeter to take full control at Cardiff. Dutton had taken over as the

Falcons' team manager in 1949, but since the start of the season he had been dividing his time between Exeter and the Dragons, following the departure of Cardiff's managing director and co-founder Leslie Maidment. Dutton had not wanted to quit Exeter completely so with permission from the County Ground directors he had continued to be involved with both teams. Now Bill had decided that his career prospects were far greater at Cardiff where his aim was to take the Dragons into the First Division.

Dutton had been totally involved at Exeter, even going so far as to become treasurer of the Supporters Club. His efforts had achieved some excellent results and in the words of the management, "Bill leaves the Exeter track with the thanks of all who support this great sport."

The next action at the County Ground was a qualifying round of the World Championship. Goog Hoskin had missed his home track round the previous year as he was riding for England C in Sweden, but he now made up for it by streaking to a 15 point maximum ahead of Edinburgh's Harold Fairhurst and Les Hewitt from Coventry. There were good performances from the other Falcons too. Ron Barrett's 11 points put him in fourth place while Vic Gent and Johnny Sargeant were joint fifth with 9 points apiece. Jack Geran made his world championship trail debut as reserve scoring six points from four outings.

Hoskin's reputation was growing rapidly and the indications were that First Division Birmingham were interested in signing him. Goog was in maximum form again 24 hours later down at St. Austell, this time riding for Devon and Cornwall against an Essex and Wilts Select.

Whit Monday marked Bill Dutton's last match in charge of the Falcons, and by coincidence that morning Exeter beat Cardiff 46–38 in a very wet meeting. The conditions caused several falls and few of the race times were under 80 seconds. Ron Barrett scored his first 12 point maximum for Exeter and Hoskin was again unbeaten, while Geran notched his first double figure score with 10.

Later that evening Dutton received a splendid send off from the riders and supporters at a well attended Supporters Club dance held at Christow.

Dutton's replacement as team manager was a familiar figure to the Exeter public, Bernard 'Broncho' Slade. Slade's connection with speedway

Bernard 'Broncho' Slade takes over as Team Manager from Bill Dutton.

at the County Ground went back to the opening season in 1929 when he had gained free admission by helping to water the track prior to the racing. The following year he had started riding and by the end of the thirties was riding for Hackney. His all action leg trailing style had prompted Frank Buckland to nickname him 'Broncho'. Slade had also raced a Norton in the Manx Grand Prix and was a regular competitor in local grass track events.

Slade's first week as the Falcons' manager was a busy one. Following the home victory over Cardiff, Exeter lost 43–41 in a tight and exciting challenge match at St Austell on the Tuesday evening. Gulls' skipper Norman Street spoilt Hoskin's chance of a third consecutive maximum at the Cornish Stadium when he beat the Exeter star in his first race, but thereafter Goog regained his unbeatable form.

Two nights later the Falcons were in Southern League action at Cardiff where Bill Dutton's Welsh Dragons reigned supreme. In front of a 10,000 crowd Cardiff won convincingly by 58–26.

The new Southern League had cut down the amount of travelling the Falcons had to undertake in 1952, but their second challenge of the week required a long trip up to Lancashire where they rode against the revived Wigan Panthers, who that season were operating on an open licence. The Wigan management had a few problems with their Woodhouse Lane track, but the Falcons seemed happy enough with conditions as they took an early 4 point lead. The Panthers clawed their way back, and despite a battling ride by Don Hardy who snatched second place in heat 11, Wigan held on to win 44–40.

'Broncho' Slade enjoyed his first victory as team manager when Aldershot were defeated 52–29 at the County Ground on 9 June. The visitors arrived one man short and also suffered a variety of machine problems. Ivor Powell and Bert Edwards scored all but nine of the Shots total. Powell even inflicted a surprise defeat on Goog Hoskin in the opening heat after Sargeant was excluded and Archie Windmill fell. There was another 3–2 in the final heat when Powell, the only Aldershot rider in the race, finished ahead of Sargeant after Barrett hit engine trouble while leading.

In the second half, Bradford's Arthur Forrest made a guest appearance beating Hoskin and Hardy in match races and Colin Selley was involved in a spectacular crash. After hitting the fence Selley went down with his machine on top of him, resulting in a stay in hospital.

Goog Hoskin's run of maximums had earned him the nomination as the June challenger for the Bronze Helmet Match Race Championship. Jack Unstead of Rayleigh was the current holder and the two met for the first leg at the County Ground on Monday 16 June. The racing proved so intense that the first leg was not completed. In the first heat, the two aces raced three fantastic laps before crashing on the final circuit. Unfortunately Hoskin injured his wrist and Unstead damaged his machine so badly that the Match Race had to be abandoned.

Even without Hoskin, the Falcons had no problem beating Ipswich 54–30 in the league match that followed. Barrett again topped the score chart but the Falcons' main opposition came from former County Ground favourite Arthur Pilgrim who proved that he had not forgotten his way around by top scoring for the Witches with 9 points. Falcons' Vic Gent however had the satisfaction of clocking the fastest time of the night, 74.0 seconds, which was also his best ever time around the County Ground.

The Falcons did however miss Hoskin for their away league match at Aldershot. Even though the Shots were also without Archie Windmill, Exeter could make little impression on a dusty track upon which intermittent watering had little noticeable effect.

The running of heat 8 proved fairly problematic. At the first attempt Charles Frenzel was excluded after crashing into Neil Street. In the rerun Bert Edwards and Don Hardy were involved in a spill and this time Hardy went out, while Street was complimented by the steward for his sharp avoiding action. At the third time of asking

Goog Hoskin & Jack Unstead crash during the Bronze Helmet match race championship.

Edwards eventually beat Street. The Falcons had to wait until heat 12 for their first success when Barrett and Street claimed a 4–2.

Goog Hoskin's wrist injury had improved sufficiently for him to race Jack Unstead in the Match Race Championship at Rayleigh on Saturday 21 June. Thus what should have been the second leg now became the first.

Unstead won the opening race fair and square, but Hoskin looked set to level the score in the next. He led for three laps and seemed home and dry when Unstead fell, but as the Rocket remounted Goog's chain came off and before he could push his bike across the line, Unstead caught and passed him.

The Exeter leg was restaged at the County Ground 48 hours later and this time Hoskin won in two straight runs. The Falcons followed up by thrashing the struggling Southampton Saints 58–26. Vic Gent led the Exeter scorers with a 12 point maximum.

After a run of big home wins the Falcons were in for a shock when Rayleigh visited the County Ground at the end of June. Hoskin was again missing from the line-up this time suffering from a badly swollen face. Even without him Exeter were 12–6 up after three races but the Rockets snatched the initiative with 4–2s in heats 4 and 5. Then, in heat 7, Maurie McDermott and Jack Unstead gained an important 5–1 and Rayleigh went two points ahead. Following two drawn heats, the same Rockets pairing notched a vital 4–2 in heat 10. Gerald Jackson and Peter Clark extended Rayleigh's lead to six points in the next race. Race wins by Tom O'Connor and Clark in heats 12 and 13 clinched the match for the Rockets, so Geran and Barnett's 4–2 in the final race merely reduced Rayleigh's winning margin to 44–40.

Exeter still without Hoskin, bounced back the next night to gain an exciting away win at Southampton where the Saints crashed to their ninth consecutive Southern League defeat. Vic Gent again headed the Falcons' scorers with another 12 point maximum, while Johnny Sergeant, having fallen in his first race went on to win all his remaining rides. Exeter found the going a lot tougher at Long Eaton a couple of nights later where they went down 53–29 to the Archers with Gent, Hardy and Geran scoring the bulk of Exeter's points.

The Falcons busy week continued with another heavy defeat, this time by 59–25, at revitalised Wolverhampton on Friday 4 July, despite Hoskin's return to the line-up.

The home match against Swindon scheduled for Monday 7 July was rained off but the Falcons were in winning form at Plymouth three days later. Hoskin was again the Falcons star scoring 11 points as Exeter also claimed the extra four heats for the first leg of the Devon Derby, which was run simultaneously with the league match. The Falcons took the Southern League points 44–40 and the Devon Derby 58–50.

The Falcons completed the double over Plymouth the following Monday at the County Ground although the 44–40 scoreline was rather too close for comfort. The scores stood level at 36–36 with two heats to go but the Falcons gained 4–2s in the final two races to ensure victory with Barrett pushing home for a point in heat 14. Although the Falcons had clinched the league points, the four extra Devon Derby races remained but the Falcons successfully completed these to retain the trophy 117–95 on aggregate.

The inter club sports for supporters of Exeter, Bristol and Plymouth were held at Weston-super-Mare that summer. The Bulldogs fans were the victors with the Falcons second and the Devils third.

At that time the Supporters Club provided local fans with an away results service. The County Ground office was staffed up until 10.00pm on away race nights thus enabling Exeter fans to telephone through for the results, details of which were also posted on the front gate. This system did not however always run smoothly. When Hoskin and Unstead met at Plymouth in the match race decider the office could not get through to the Pennycross Stadium so instead contacted the nearby Cherry Tree Inn. The barman said that a customer had just come in and reported that Goog had won. This eagerly awaited news was thus relayed to the fans. Obviously the customer had already had one too many as Unstead was in fact the winner by 2–1.

The system did not operate when the Falcons rode at Plymouth as a team because on those occasions the entire committee travelled down to watch at Pennycross so nobody was left to man the office 'phone.

A switch of fixtures saw St Austell race at the County Ground on 21 July, but the Gulls were outclassed by the all out strength of the Falcons for whom Hardy top scored with a superb maximum.

Exeter proved entertaining opponents at Swindon the next weekend but still lost 49–35.

Chaos reigned in the first race when Bob Wells' engine seized as he led into the first bend. Goog Hoskin was unable to take avoiding action, ran into him and was promptly followed by Bob Jones and Johnny Sargeant. Fortunately nobody was hurt, but the Exeter contingent was angered by the decision to exclude Hoskin even though Wells was the obvious cause of the stoppage.

A tour of Southern League tracks by Sweden promised to be the highlight of the season, but Exeter unfortunately staged the seventh match of the tour. By the time the Swedes, who were in fact the Vargana league team, arrived at the County Ground their machinery was very much the worse for wear and they lost heavily 70–38. The team were also one man short as Dan Forsberg was unavailable to ride due to his commitments with Birmingham.

The Southern League was represented by Falcons: Goog Hoskin and Vic Gent, plus Pete Lansdale, Jack Unstead, Gerald Pugh, Ivor Powell, George Wall and Norman Street, who was making his international debut. Much was expected of track record holder Olle Nygren but he was badly affected by machine problems and could only score 4 points. Sune Karlsson kept the English riders on their toes and scored 17 points, but the match was only completed thanks to the locals lending the Swedes their bikes.

Despite threatening rain a crowd of 5,000 flocked to St. Austell's Cornish Stadium the following evening to see the Falcons win by two points. Exeter took the lead in the fourth heat, but in an evenly contested match it was not until the latter stages that the Falcons consolidated their advantage. A 5–1 seemed to be on the cards for Exeter in heat 12, but on the last lap Lloyd 'Cowboy' Goffe passed Vic Gent down the back straight then took Ronnie Swaine on the last bend. The Gulls needed maximum points in heat 13 to stand a chance of winning. Unfortunately for St. Austell this race was drawn thus effectively ensuring Exeter a useful victory. Harold Bull and George Newton achieved the vital maximum a race too late but reduced the Falcons' overall winning margin to 43–41.

Rayleigh were the August Bank Holiday visitors and enhanced their championship aspirations by repeating their earlier victory, but unfortunately Don Hardy was taken to hospital with an injury to his foot.

A second home meeting was held on the Wednesday of that week to accommodate the restaging of the previously rained off match against Swindon. Once again heavy rain had left the track extremely muddy and the final decision for racing to go ahead was not made until 7.00pm. Even without Hardy the Falcons hoped to make up for Monday's slip, but the Robins showed that they meant business when Bob Jones and Wells won the opening heat 5–1. Geran and Street levelled the scores in heat four, but Swindon went ahead again three races later. As visitors Swindon were entitled to choice of gates in each heat. The Robins continuously chose two and four thus ensuring the driest grids and leaving the Falcons to cope with an exceptionally wet and slick gate one.

Exeter gallantly crept back on level terms but the Jones/Wells partnership again took maximum points in the tenth heat and when Malone and Lambourne registered a 4–2 in the next race Swindon were six points in front. Hoskin and Street hit back with a 5–1 for Exeter and heat 13 was drawn leaving the Falcons needing a maximum in the last race to win. But sadly there was no triumphant finish as Frank Evans and Wells held off Street to ensure victory for Swindon.

After such a terrible week at the County Ground the Falcons were grateful for the consolation of an away win at Ipswich on Saturday 9 August. Bad weather had left the Foxhall Heath track looking decidedly the worse for wear but fortunately the rain had stopped by the time the Falcons arrived. Despite threatening clouds all around the track, racing went ahead and the crowd were rewarded with plenty of exciting action. The Witches led for much of the match but in heat 9 Ron Barrett and Vic Gent combined to put the Falcons into the lead and they went on to win 46–38.

Wolverhampton arrived at the County Ground on Monday 11 August determined to follow in Rayleigh and Swindon's victorious tyre tracks and almost achieved their aim. However the Falcons just managed to hold them off and win narrowly 43–41.

The following week's scheduled visit by Cardiff fell victim to the weather an hour before start time when the ACU Steward declared the track waterlogged and unfit for racing. This was Exeter's fourth rain off of 1952.

If Wolverhampton were disappointed at not winning at the County Ground they must have been shocked when the Falcons returned to Monmore Green that week and took a share of

Vic Gent.

the points. Exeter became the first side to take a league point away from the Midland track when they drew 42–42. Again it was a last heat decider with the Falcons needing a 5–1 to win. Hoskin led from Wasps skipper Benny King with Gent third. King fell at the pits bend during the third lap and the race was stopped. In the rerun Hoskin again made the start and was joined at the front by Vic but on the third lap Jack Cunningham squeezed by Gent along the back straight to avoid a defeat for Wolverhampton.

Ipswich came to the County Ground on 25 August but the big attraction for the fans promised to be an appearance by World Champion and Exeter track record holder Jack Young, who was now riding for First Division West Ham. Alas they were to be disappointed as unfortunately Young was forced to cancel his booking on medical advice. Broncho Slade received a letter from Hammers boss Johnnie S. Hoskins explaining the situation, which was later, reproduced in the programme. Exeter had no difficulty in disposing of the Witches by 55–29. Gent led the way with a 12 point maximum, while Johnny Sargeant made a brilliant comeback and was the second highest scorer with ten points. A new signing, Eric Minall, made his debut as reserve. In the second half New Cross signing Sune Karlsson who rode match races against Sargeant and Gent replaced the absent Jack Young.

Exeter visited their bogey team, Rayleigh, on August 30 and were duly beaten 52–32.

At the end of August the whole of Britain was stunned by the news that the heavy rain had caused a flash flood on Exmoor, which resulted in the North Devon fishing village of Lynmouth being virtually swept away with loss of many lives. A national relief appeal was immediately set up and at the next Exeter meeting on Monday 1 September a collection was held in aid of the fund. The legendary Jack Parker was making a rare appearance at the County Ground that evening and appealed to the crowd to give generously to the collection. £10. 7s. 6d was collected but the total was boosted by donations of 25 guineas each from the management and the supporters club.

That evenings Southern League encounter with Southampton started in a manner that was now becoming only too familiar to Exeter fans with the visitors notching a 5–1 thanks to Brian McKeown and Dudley Smith. On form McKeown led the Saints attack and by heat 10 looked on course to complete his maximum. Up against him was the also unbeaten Goog Hoskin. They rode wheel to wheel for two laps before the Falcons hero pulled away to win. Exeter went on to win 47–36 but the Saints gave the crowd excellent value for money.

The great Jack Parker rode in the second half, only the second time he had raced at the County Ground, his previous experience of the track having been gained in May 1929. In the first of two match races Parker beat Gent before taking second best to Hoskin.

Later that week the Falcons were the unwitting victims of Aldershot's biggest win of the season, a 62–22 massacre. As usual the pear shaped Tongham Stadium track gave the Exeter riders a few problems with only Goog Hoskin and Jack Geran getting the hang of it. In fact Geran was Exeter's only heat winner but even he had problems. Jack still clearly remembers an incident, which took place in the scratch race final.

"Archie Windmill was leading and I went in

> hard under him on the tight third bend. His leg was right across the track in front of me and I had to knock it off so quick that I stalled my engine. The bike was sideways on but I didn't fall off, just stopped. Goog was right behind me and had to lay it down to avoid me. I was excluded even though I hadn't fallen off. Afterwards the referee apologised but said he had no alternative."

This was one of only two exclusions that Geran received in his entire career.

Although no Exeter riders were involved in the forthcoming world final at Wembley it is interesting to note that the Falcons' Supporters Club had arranged an excursion rate with British Railways for fans wishing to travel to London for the big night. The fare would be 22/- (£1.20) return.

Back at the County Ground the Falcons defeated Wolverhampton 51–33 on Monday 8 September. The Wasps put up another good fight and Exeter didn't have everything their own way. An element of farce crept into heat eight when Hoskin broke the tapes. The steward put on the red exclusion light, and all the other riders promptly stopped. Officials encouraged them to carry on but first they had to push start their own machines. The Wasps were quickest away, Eric Irons winning in the time of 124 seconds!

The rain struck again and the Falcons arrived at Southampton the next evening to discover the match had already been called off. The Exeter riders must have wished that it had also been raining in Wales the following Friday. At Cardiff they suffered another defeat as the Dragons stormed to a massive 65–19 victory in a totally one-sided contest during which the Falcons failed to win a single race.

Undeterred the Falcons bounced back to enjoy an equally big win over Aldershot at the County Ground on Monday 15 September. Both Johnny Sargeant and Goog Hoskin scored 12 point maximums as the Falcons thrashed the Shots 63–21, while Barrett's hopes of a full house were only spoilt by Ivor Powell, who along with Bill Grimes, provided what little entertainment there was.

The penultimate home league match at the County Ground saw Plymouth almost pull off a surprise victory. The Devils led by a single point after seven races but the Falcons produced a strong finish to win 48–35. Plymouth's hopes of success dwindled after George Wall and Roy Moreton took heavy falls.

The Falcons' final home fixture on 29 September was also a tough one, as they were pushed all the way by highflying Cardiff, who were desperately attempting to catch Rayleigh in the race for the league championship. The Falcons eventually won 45–39 but the Dragons were unlucky to lose Frankie Johnson in heat ten. After hitting the fence very hard, the all action Johnson was hurled across the track and as a result was taken to hospital with a suspected broken shoulder.

Exeter's victory proved to be the ideal present for Broncho Slade who was celebrating his birthday. The Falcons' achievement was highlighted by the fact that they were still without the injured Don Hardy and Jack Geran who had already returned home to Australia. The meeting ended with the traditional close of season fireworks display.

The depleted Falcons ended their Southern League campaign with the restaging of the Southampton match where, with several juniors in their line-up, they suffered yet another heavy away defeat this time going down to the Saints by 62–21. Ron Barrett was the only Exeter rider to win a race.

Barrett also won the final County Ground meeting, the St. Thomas Carnival Challenge Trophy. Exeter riders, and local riders contested the ten heat individual event, which was won by Barrett with a 12 point maximum with Herbie Plain winning the junior event. Goog Hoskin missed the meeting as he had joined the Bristol Bulldogs for a three-week tour of Sweden.

The successful meeting and season drew to a close with the crowning of the Carnival Queen and a fireworks display.

1953

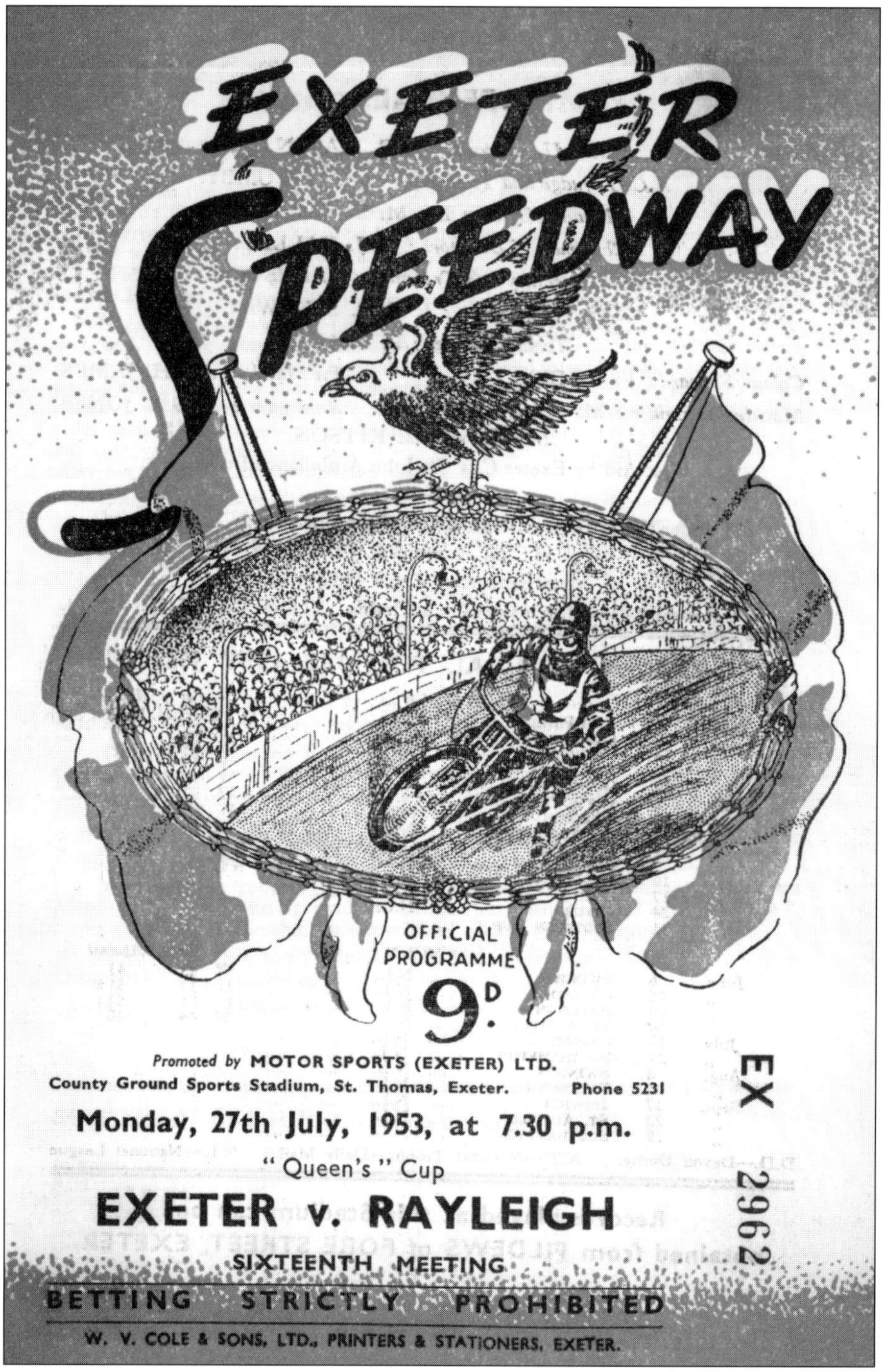
EXETER
SPEEDWAY
OFFICIAL
PROGRAMME
9D.
Promoted by MOTOR SPORTS (EXETER) LTD.
County Ground Sports Stadium, St. Thomas, Exeter. Phone 5231
Monday, 27th July, 1953, at 7.30 p.m.
"Queen's" Cup
EXETER v. RAYLEIGH
SIXTEENTH MEETING
BETTING STRICTLY PROHIBITED
W. V. COLE & SONS, LTD., PRINTERS & STATIONERS, EXETER.
EX 2962

HEAT 7

The Coronation of Queen Elizabeth II dominated the summer of 1953. The great occasion coupled with several weeks of bad weather would have a detrimental effect on speedway generally that year, and as a result three tracks, New Cross, Liverpool, and Cardiff, ironically one from each division, would close during the campaign. The lasting effect of the Coronation would be the huge increase in the popularity of television. Up until then very few homes possessed a TV set, but sales rocketed when it was announced that the ceremony on Tuesday 2 June would be televised for the first time. Few anticipated at the time the disastrous effect this would have on speedway audiences.

At Exeter there were high hopes for the Falcons in the Southern League. The majority of the 1952 line-up was retained, with the addition of another promising Australian, Bob Meyer. Meyer had tried his luck in England before but had been unable to secure a regular team place anywhere, so instead worked as a mechanic with the Wembley Lions. He had recently won the Australian junior championship at Sydney and was keen to make another attempt to break into British speedway. Jack Hart, the New Zealander who had broken his leg in the opening meeting of 1952, was back again while another young hopeful was Eric Minall who had previously ridden for Long Eaton.

Neil Street spent the winter in England, as he was unable to afford the return fare to Australia. Instead he determined to make his mark in 1953 and spent as much time as possible practising on the beach at Dawlish Warren prior to the start of the season. Johnny Sargeant had also been keeping fit playing for the Lympstone football team.

The 1953 Falcons L → R. Back: Jack Hart, Neil Street, Eric Minall, Jack Geran, Bob Meyer. Front: Vic Gent, Charlie May, Bernard Slade, Don Hardy, Gordon Gray (mascot), Goog Hoskin.

The Southern League had lost Aldershot and Wolverhampton but had regained Oxford. Cardiff had applied for promotion to the second division but had been turned down, possibly because the Scottish tracks did not relish the long trip down to Wales.

Tragedy struck at the County Ground even before the first meeting. At that time all but the top Australians still travelled to England by ship and invariably newcomers found a number of promoters waiting with offers of contracts on the quayside when they disembarked. Such was the case of Roy Ether, who with two seasons experience of Australian racing behind him, was signed on an extended trial agreement by Bernard Slade on the dockside at Tilbury following an introduction by Arthur Malm of White City.

When Ether reached Exeter he was so keen to see his new track that he headed straight for the County Ground rather than find himself accommodation and as a result was forced to sleep on the dressing room floor. He was equally keen to start practicing but on 12 March he crashed when his chain broke, and was taken to hospital where he was detained with concussion. Ether was passed fit to ride again a fortnight later, and immediately returned to the track for a private practice. The same day (26 March) Ether crashed again coming out of the second turn and was thrown over the handlebars into the fence, hitting his head on a lighting pole. He was taken to the RD&E Hospital, this time with a fractured skull, and sadly died at 2.30pm that afternoon.

Royal Hubert Ether, his name also appeared spelt Eather, came from Hamilton, New South Wales, and was the first rider to lose his life on the Exeter track. Something of a mystery surrounded his age. At the inquest Dr D. T. L Nash, who had treated him in hospital, expressed the view that Ether's age was 'about 40', but the rider had told him on the first occasion that he was 26. Reg Anstead, the general secretary of Motor Sports (Exeter) Ltd, the promoting company told the court that Ether had given his age as 24, but the police produced his passport, which stated his age as 32.

The funeral took place at St Thomas Church close to the stadium and following cremation his ashes were returned to Australia. In an interview with the Sunday Independent Bernard Slade recalled that he ran to Ether's aid after the crash and helped carry him into the pits.

> "He crashed the first time because he was going too fast, the second and last time because he was going too slow."

The tragedy overshadowed the start of the new season that opened on Easter Saturday at St Austell where the Falcons were beaten 46–38 in a challenge match. Exeter were without Jack Geran, who had not yet returned after spending the winter back home in Australia, but Goog Hoskin got off to a perfect start with a faultless maximum. It was his second unbeaten score in 24 hours as the previous afternoon Goog had won the John A. Chapman Trophy at Plymouth with a 15 point tally heralding what would be the most successful season of his career. Ron Barrett also had a good afternoon finishing third and equalling the Pennycross track record to become the fifth joint holder!

The traditional Easter Monday opener at the County Ground saw the Falcons entertain Swedish touring side Filbyterna on a rain soaked track in front of a near 10,000 crowd. It very nearly turned into a non-event, as the visitors had not been informed that it was a morning meeting. Fortunately they were woken at their hotel and reached the track in time.

The Swedish line-up included an up and coming 20 year old, Ove Fundin. Fundin top scored for the visitors with 8 points but could not prevent Exeter from winning 47–37. The future five times world champion featured in the most exciting race of the morning during which he chased Sargeant for the whole four laps but despite some determined challenges failed to force the Exeter man off his line. Fundin was also on course to win the second half final until his machine failed near the finish.

Hoskins recorded two more wins and a second place behind Morris Barnett before being replaced by reserve Eric Minall in heat 12.

Exeter started the league campaign proper a week later with a 56–28 win over the St Austell Gulls at the County Ground which saw Ron Barrett, Don Hardy, and naturally Goog Hoskin score maximums. Jack Geran and Jack Hart arrived back in Exeter later that week and Geran was immediately drafted in as reserve for the Falcons' trip to Rayleigh on Saturday 18 April. Little did anyone realise what effect this move would have later in the season.

The Rayleigh Rockets were the reigning Southern League Champions and judging by Exeter's previous unsuccessful efforts at the Weir there seemed little danger of the Falcons damaging Rayleigh's proud home record, especially when the Rockets gained a 10 point lead from the first four races.

At this stage the Falcons switched their choice of gate positions from one and three to two and four. The effect was extraordinary and immediate. The Falcons were faster away from the starts and rapidly began to pull back the Rockets lead. By heat 10 the scores were level at 30–30. Exeter went ahead thanks to a 5–1 by Hardy and Barnett, but Rayleigh immediately countered this by gaining a maximum of their own to once again level the scores.

Geran and Barnett came out in heat 13 determined to put Exeter back in front. The Falcons' pair led around the first bend but McGillivray caught Barnett and after a terrific battle passed him before going on to overhaul Geran. However, the Falcon fought back and drove under McGillivray in superb fashion to retake the lead.

Exeter went into the last race two points up. Hoskin and Barrett lined up for the Falcons against Tom O'Connor and Frank Bettis. Bettis looped at the gate leaving O'Connor to chase fruitlessly after the flying Falcons. Despite losing their home record many Rayleigh fans considered this the most exciting match ever seen at the Weir. However not everyone was happy with the result and the Rockets' management protested that under rule 506 Jack Geran should not have ridden at reserve as he had scored more than 50% of his possible points in his previous six matches. The Speedway Control Board later upheld the protest and ordered that the result be expunged from the records. It seems extraordinary that at such an early stage of the season no provision was made for the match to be rerun.

Back at the County Ground the Falcons beat Swindon 60–48 in the first leg of the Daily Mail National Trophy. Goog Hoskin notched an unbeaten 15 while Barrett collected a similar score from six starts, having suffered an engine failure while in second place behind Hoskin in heat 7. He was not the gremlins only victim and sadly a spate of mechanical troubles prevented the Falcons from running up the big lead they wanted. A twelve point lead would not prove sufficient for Exeter, as later in the week the Robins gained revenge with a 68–40 victory at Blunsdon which took them through to the second round 116–100 on aggregate.

Goog Hoskin, Morris Barnett and Jack Geran were all unbeaten from four starts as the Falcons tore Ipswich apart, 69–15 at a very wet and muddy County Ground on Monday 27 April. The Witches didn't like the conditions at all but local man Barnett was delighted to record his first ever maximum. Neil Street moved up from reserve to replace Vic Gent in the team as a result of the latter's loss of form.

The continual wet weather meant a wasted trip to Oxford for the Falcons later that week where their league match was rained off, but a narrow two point win at Plymouth the next night provided ample compensation. The scoring power of Exeter's second strings proved all-important on this occasion, with Barnett and Street giving vital backing to Hoskin and Barrett.

Goog Hoskin accompanied by Broncho Slade spent Saturday travelling to Rayleigh where he had been nominated to challenge Gerald Jackson for the Southern League match race championship. Goog won the first leg at the Weir 2–1, and then returned to the County Ground where he clinched the title again by 2–1. Hoskin then joint top scored with Don Hardy as the Falcons convincingly beat Cardiff by 55–29 in a match which marked the last appearance of Ron Barrett in Exeter colours before being transferred to First Division Birmingham. This was another blow to Exeter's increasing championship hopes as Ron had already notched three maximums so far. Jack Hart was also beginning to make his mark by winning both his reserve outings.

The Falcons took a break from league racing on Monday 11 May when they entertained First Division Harringay 'Stars' in a challenge match. The visitors' line up included regular Harringay team men Split Waterman, Jeff Lloyd, and former Falcon Ken Walsh, along with Bill Longley of New Cross and another former Exeter favourite Hugh Geddes, while local riders Bob Meyer and Wally Monckton filled the reserve berths. This medley of talent proved just too strong for the Falcons who were beaten 40–44. Gent came back into the Exeter line-up for this match but failed to score.

Encounters with Oxford seemed doomed that summer as the Cheetahs' visit to the County Ground seven days later also fell victim to the apparently never ending bad weather, but the Falcons' final appearance at doomed Cardiff went ahead. This match proved to be the best ever seen at the Penarth Road Stadium, with plenty of superb racing. Sadly only 5,000 fans were present to witness the action. Barnett and Hardy put Exeter ahead in the second race and the Falcons retained their lead until heat 7. The turning point came when Hardy was hit by engine trouble while leading heat 11, and the resulting 4–2 put the Dragons ahead. Cardiff held on to win 45–39.

Whit Monday saw the Falcons challenge their old rivals Plymouth in the first leg of the Devon Derby. A 12 point maximum from Goog Hoskin helped the Falcons to victory by 53–31. Hoskin also gave the Bank holiday crowd plenty to talk about in heat 1 when he lowered the Exeter track record to 72.6 seconds. Not everything went Goog's way as he crashed in the second half and suffered a head injury. After treatment he was advised not to ride in the second leg at Plymouth that same evening, where the Devils took full advantage of Goog's absence to not only win the match but also take the Trophy on aggregate.

The Falcons returned to league action with a vengeance, winning 43–41 at Ipswich in another thrilling last heat decider. Hoskin had recovered sufficiently to score another maximum and equalled the Foxhall Heath track record for a second time. Eight points for Neil Street's marked his best away score so far.

The build up to the Coronation was reaching fever pitch and the local celebrations got off to a splendid start on Monday 1 June when the Exeter round of the Coronation Best Pairs, staged on the eve of the ceremony, was won convincingly by Goog Hoskin and Don Hardy with a maximum of 20 points. Goog won all four of his races with Don second each time. Three days later the Falcons duo scored 23 out of a possible of 25 to win the Ipswich round.

The Falcons acquired a further two league points at top of the table Swindon at the end of the week where Hoskin collected yet another maximum as Exeter ended the Robins unbeaten home run. A 4–2 and a 5–1 got the Falcons off to a good start. Heat 4 saw the Robins level the scores but further 4–2s to the Falcons in heats 5 and 6 put them back into the lead. Although Frank Evans and Bob Wells gained a 4–2 for Swindon in heat 9 the remaining races were drawn giving Exeter a narrow 43–41 victory.

Charlie May made his Falcons' debut at Blunsdon that night. He was programmed at No. 1 but could only manage a meagre two points. Earlier in the week May had scored 10 points as one of Cardiff's representative in the Coronation Cup meeting at Exeter and it would seem likely that the Dragons sold him to the Falcons in bid to raise some urgently needed cash. The Welsh club was already in serious trouble and would close down a fortnight later. The situation seems ironically similar to that in which the Falcons' had transferred Hugh Geddes to Swindon in 1950.

Oxford made an excellent start at the County Ground on Monday 8 June, with Jim Gregory beating Hoskin in the opening heat before going on to score a maximum. The Cheetahs drew heat 2, but then the Exeter points machine slipped into gear and the Falcons ran out easy winners by 54–30. May scored 8 points in his first home appearance but the evening was overshadowed by a serious accident in heat 10, which was to end the career of local rider Morris Barnett.

Barnett had made a big impact at Exeter, only a few weeks before scoring his first maximum. The accident occurred when he clipped Oxford reserve Bill Kemp's back wheel on the last bend and was catapulted into the safety fence, resulting in him being taken to hospital with concussion and serious head injuries.

The loss of Barnett from the team was a serious blow to the Falcons' championship hopes, especially as three important fixtures were scheduled for the following week. Leaders Swindon were due at the County Ground on Monday 15 June while the Falcons were due to visit Oxford and Rayleigh later in the week.

Before that no less than six Falcons were back at Blunsdon on Saturday 13 June. A team of Young Danes was due to visit but the tour had been cancelled and instead Swindon manager Bill Dutton decided to stage an unofficial test match between Young England and Young Overseas. Hoskin, Hardy and May all rode for England while Geran, Street and Hart lined up for the Overseas team captained by ex Falcon Ken Walsh. The Colonials won 47–36 but Hoskin top scored for England with 9 and went on to defeat both Walsh and Johnny Chamberlain in a second half match race series.

Immediately before the eagerly anticipated league match between Exeter and Swindon at the County Ground two days later Goog Hoskin faced a new challenger in Alan Smith of Plymouth for the match race championship. On a wet and difficult track Goog won the first race from the gate, then passed Smith after one lap to win the first leg 2–0.

The Falcons then demolished Swindon 58–26 with both Hoskin and Geran scoring paid maximums. Unfortunately it would be Exeter's only success of the week. They were defeated 51–33 at Oxford's Sandy Lane while Rayleigh eagerly made up for that controversial early season defeat with a 53–31 win. During the early stages it looked as though the Falcons would repeat their win when Hart and Hoskin opened with a 5–1 maximum but the Rockets rapidly hit back with three 5–1s and a 4–2 to gain a substantial lead that Exeter could not overcome.

On the way home from Rayleigh the supporters' club coach made a detour through the centre of London to enable the fans to see the Coronation illuminations.

The Falcons returned to winning ways in thrilling fashion forty-eight hours later, when in the return at the County Ground they beat the Rockets 49–35. The match opened with a superb race in which Rayleigh's Gerald Jackson outgated Hoskin and held him off almost to the end when Goog slipped through in the last few yards to snatch victory. All the Exeter riders were determined to win this match and although the Rockets were only two points down after eight races the Falcons took three 5–1s from the last four heats to ensure victory. Jack Geran capped a fine evening's racing by completing a full maximum in the last heat while Hoskin scored another paid maximum. Bob Meyer unfortunately took a nasty fall in heat 8, which put him out of the meeting with facial cuts and a swollen knee.

The Falcons victory put them joint top of the table with Rayleigh. Both teams had won nine of the twelve matches that they had ridden, giving them 18 points each. The win also launched a run of successes, which put Exeter on course for the league championship. Lowly St Austell gave the Falcons' chances an enormous boost the following evening, by sensationally beating Rayleigh at the Cornish Stadium.

Goog Hoskin was off to London for a second half booking at Wembley later that week, before dashing back down to Plymouth to contest the second leg of the Match Race Championship. He won the first race but Alan Smith fought back to take the honours in both the second and the decider forcing a run-off which would be staged at neutral St Austell.

Concern was being voiced around the country as attendance figures were again declining. Those worries were also being echoed in the Exeter programme where disappointment was being expressed that crowd numbers were not adequately reflecting the Falcons' on track success.

Second Division Stoke Potters came to the County Ground on Monday 29 June for the first round of a new knockout cup competition, the Queen's Cup, and were soundly beaten 72–36 over 18 heats. Hoskin was again in immaculate form returning an 18 point maximum, while Jack Hart came within a second of the track record and notched 12 points from five rides.

Two more vital league points were gained at St Austell the next evening. The teams were level at 39–39 with one race to go but Hoskin and Geran duly sewed the win up with a heat 14 5–1. Hoskin's chances of another maximum were spoilt by a first race fall, so Geran top scored with 10.

Meyer's knee was now in plaster and he had been replaced first by Wally Monckton, and then Dick Howard. Charlie May was also sidelined with tonsillitis, which allowed Eric Minall a further opportunity at reserve.

The Exeter management may have been concerned about attendance figures, but the regular fans were still showing plenty of interest. After the St Austell match supporters club officials who ran an away results service reported that over 70 fans had telephoned the Speedway Office at the County Ground to hear the score. The system had become so popular that the officials appealed for interested supporters not to ring too early as they frequently blocked the line and prevented the important results call from the away track being connected.

On Thursday 2 July Hoskin and Hardy clinched the Coronation Pairs title at Cardiff with a total of 60 points from a possible 70.

Plymouth Devils gave the Falcons a hard time over the first few races at the County Ground on Monday 6 July. Pete Lansdale beat Hoskin in the opening heat and Alan Smith pushed Hardy all the way in heat 2. But 5–1s by Exeter in heats 5 and 6, despite a two-minute exclusion for Hoskin, established a lead they would not lose.

A BBC recording car was present at this meeting covering the action for that week's Sport in the West radio programme.

Exeter's injury list grew at St Austell the next evening when Jack Geran collided with his fallen partner Jack Hart in the Coronation Pairs round at the Cornish Stadium. Geran was ambulanced to hospital with severe concussion and facial injuries, but Hart managed to stagger out and win the rerun. He later outpaced Norman Street and Bob Duckworth but then reared at the start of the last

Jack Hart.

race, landed on his already damaged knee and suffered torn ligaments.

Cardiff Speedway fell victim to the declining crowds and the Dragons closed that week, never to reopen.

Geran was missing from the Falcons' line-up which beat Swindon at the County Ground the following Monday but Hart continued to ride. Robins' Danny Malone, Ian Williams and Bob Wells made the home riders work hard for their points, but could not prevent Hoskin from scoring a maximum. Vic Gent unluckily missed out on a full score thanks to a flat tyre in his fourth outing after chalking up three wins.

Hoskin was in winning form again at St. Austell twenty-four hours later when he beat Alan Smith 2–0 to retain his match race championship. The Exeter star won the first race comfortably while Smith took the lead in the second and seemed on course to force a decider until his engine blew up.

Exeter's next league opponents at the County Ground on 20 July were Southampton Saints. After an uneasy start the Falcons stormed ahead and had the points in the bag by heat 10. Jack Geran returned to action scoring 7 points while Dick Howard won both his reserve races. Guest of honour was film star Honor Blackman who had come along to present the 'Corvette' Trophy to Coronation Best Pairs winners Goog Hoskin and Don Hardy. The Exeter Speedway Supporters Club also presented the riders with £5 each.

In the second half first division stars Aub Lawson and Billy Bales rode against the Falcons. Lawson won two of his races but missed out to Geran in the third.

Film star Honor Blackman presents the Coronation Cup to Don Hardy and Goog Hoskin.

The Supporters Club sports at Dawlish Warren.

For once even the annual supporters clubs sports day was effected by the weather. That summer the sports took place at Dawlish Warren but had to be abandoned halfway through due to the heavy rain. Bristol SSC were well ahead at time of the stoppage as their girl fans had been practising for several weeks. It was agreed that the Bulldogs fans should be allowed to retain the trophy.

The Falcons' championship hopes suffered a set-back at Oxford where they lost 46–38 to the fourth placed Cheetahs, but a psychological boost was gained when Exeter easily defeated arch rivals Rayleigh 69–39 in the quarter final of the Queen's Cup at the County Ground the following week. Plenty of excitement surrounded the Falcons' visit to Southampton the next evening. In a terrific match Exeter tightened their grip on the championship with a superb 45–39 win over the Saints. Once again victory was clinched in a last heat decider after the lead had changed several times during the match.

Southampton were four points ahead after the first two races, but Exeter levelled the scores in heat 3 then went ahead for the first time thanks to a May/Hart 4–2 in the fourth heat. Saints' Ernie Brecknell rode around Geran in brilliant fashion on the last lap of heat six to put the scores level at 18–18. Brian McKeown came from the back in the next race to pass Hoskin but Hart won to nose Exeter back in front. Heats 8 and 9 were drawn, but the Hoskin /Hart pairing increased the Falcons lead to 32–28 in heat 10.

Neil Street just failed to hold off the challenge of McKeown with a lap to go in heat 11, after which McKeown and partner Brian Hanham brought the Southampton fans to their feet with a 5–1, levelling the scores once again at 36–36. But Exeter's hopes rose again when May held off Hugh Geddes and Hardy claimed the all-important third place in heat 13. To the huge relief of the Falcons' camp Hoskin and Geran raced from the gate in the final heat and with a splendid display of team riding held McKeown at bay for the entire four laps to ensure a vital win.

Exeter tracked yet another new reserve, Johnny Applegate, in this match but he failed to score. Unfortunately Applegate's career as a Falcon did not last long. In the very next meeting, the August Bank Holiday clash with Plymouth at the County Ground, he crashed on the second bend during heat 11 and broke his wrist. By that time the

Falcons were ten points in front and despite some hard riding by Alan Smith, Pete Lansdale and George Wall Exeter went on to win comfortably 51–33.

As always with morning meetings dust proved to be a problem in the later races. Although the track had been thoroughly watered prior to the meeting the hot sunshine quickly dried it out and in his programme notes the following week team manager Broncho Slade expressed the view that a water cart or fire service pump would in future be the only solution to the problem.

The Falcons returned to Swindon the following Saturday where they again won 43–41. Pride was very much at stake in this meeting as former Falcons' officials, Bill Dutton and Don Weekes managed the Robins. As Neil Street and Jack Geran were still lodging with Weekes' parents back in Exeter rivalry was naturally intense.

Once again the Falcons' dynamic last heat pairing of Hoskin and Geran clinched the match for Exeter after yet another thrilling meeting. Heat 10 saw Swindon's Ian Williams the unlucky victim of an unusual incident. Williams was well in front and heading for a vital win over Hoskin and Hart, when the tread broke away from his rear tyre and struck him violently on the back of his crash helmet. Ian earned a commendation from the ACU steward for keeping his machine under control but unfortunately for the Robins he was out of the race.

The Falcons secured two more league points with a convincing 53–31 victory over the Ipswich Witches in an uninspiring match at the County Ground on 10 August. However there was disappointment for Goog Hoskin who was beaten in two straight races by Rayleigh's Gerald Jackson in the first leg of the Match Race Championship. Later Goog gained a certain amount of compensation by beating special guests, former world champion Freddie Williams and his brother and Wembley teammate Eric from the back in the second half final.

Unfortunately for Goog, Jackson also went on to win the second leg at Rayleigh later that week by the same score of 2–0, and thus regained the Match Race Championship and the Bromley Bowl that went with it. While the Falcons' No. 1 may not have enjoyed the best of fortune at the Weir that night four of his team mates, (Geran, Hart, Hardy and Gent) won a four-team tournament by beating Oxford and two quartets representing the Rockets.

Glasgow (White City) were due to be the Falcons next opponents at the County Ground in the Queen's Cup but as their No. 1 Tommy Miller had been picked to ride for England the same evening the match was put back until later in the month and instead Exeter enjoyed a walkover against bottom of the table St. Austell in a hastily rescheduled league fixture. The Gulls were hammered 61–23 with former Falcon Johnny Sargeant, who had recently been transferred to the Cornish club, their top scorer with 8 points.

The weather forced an early cancellation of the Falcons' match at Plymouth on Thursday 20 August. The rain-off came as a big disappointment to the many Exeter fans who had made a wasted journey down the A38.

Oxford were the next side to taste defeat at what had become fortress County Ground. The Cheetahs went down 57–27 despite Jim Gregory and Jim Boyd giving the locals a run for their money. The second half attraction on this occasion was a display of Australian sidecar speedway in which Jim Davies and his passenger Johnny Glassbrenner, mounted on a 1,000cc JAP powered outfit defeated Peter Sperrin and his passenger Wilf Wilstead, 2–1.

On Saturday 29 August Jack Geran became the first Southern League rider to gain a full international cap when he partnered reigning world champion Jack Young for Australia against England in the third test at Birmingham. England won 61–47 with Jack scoring 2 points while Young netted 15.

The visit of second division Glasgow (White City) was rearranged for Monday 31 August and saw the on form Falcons beat the Scots 69–39 in the first leg of the Queen's Cup semi final. Tigers' No. 1 Tommy Miller won the opening heat in the fast time of 73.0 seconds, but was later to be beaten by both Hoskin and Geran. The Scots other top rider, Ken McKinlay, fell in heat 17 but still scored 11 points. The Falcons' 30-point winning margin could have been even greater had they not been beset by a spate of engine problems. Not surprisingly this important match attracted a near record crowd, but ultimately those machine failures would cost the Falcons dear.

Goog Hoskin became the holder of three track records when he clocked 71.0 seconds around Plymouth's Pennycross Stadium in the opening heat when the previously rained off Southern League encounter between the Devils and the Falcons finally took place on Thursday 3 September. Goog

Track record holder Goog Hoskin in action.

went on to score another full maximum as the Falcons won 48–36 and also featured in what was later described as the best race ever seen at Pennycross. This classic came in heat 10 and also involved Jack Hart and the Devils pairing of Alan Smith and Bill Thatcher. All four riders battled it out in close company over the entire fours laps and afterwards received the commendation of the ACU steward for an excellent race. Hoskin won by half a length from Smith.

Exeter now had 38 league points from 22 matches while Rayleigh, who had also ridden 22, were on 35.

The unfortunate demise of Cardiff meant that a filler meeting was required for Monday 7 September. The Falcons took on and beat a Southern Select side, which included Jim Gregory and Danny Malone, who jointly top scored with 9 each. The final score was 48–36 and Goog Hoskin chalked up yet another 12 point maximum. The most important aspect of this challenge match would turn out to be Hoskin's winning time in heat 1. In beating Gregory, Goog set a new County Ground track record of 72.0 seconds, That legendary record would stand until 1965 when it was finally bettered by Igor Plechanov of the USSR, but remains for ever the fastest time achieved by a JAP engine.

To maintain the Falcons' in depth strength more second half events were being staged for novices. Eric Minall and Bill Albertson had proved the best of the current crop of juniors, which also included Ivan Sparkes and Bob Emery. Although by this stage of the season the promising Albertson had already returned to Australia, two local newcomers, Cyril Lock from Bradninch, and Tedburn St. Mary based Francis Cann, who made his County Ground debut at the end of August, were beginning to be noticed.

The next evening the Falcons travelled across the Tamar to St Austell where victory would almost certainly settle the championship race in their favour. But amazingly the lowly Gulls produced the shock of the season and ended the Falcons' long run of away wins with a narrow 43–40 victory.

Manager Broncho Slade afterwards expressed the view that some of the Falcons were over eager, while one reporter described the Exeter tactics as 'aggressive and at times ruthless'. Hoskin's brilliant form continued with a faultless maximum and he also came within a fifth of a second of the Par Moor track record. Hardy and Geran provided able support but the Exeter reserves were not strong enough to cover for those riders who were off form.

Had Hoskin broken the St Austell track record he would have completed a hatrick of Westcountry tracks within six days. Nevertheless he had still scored maximums at all three tracks, a truly remarkable achievement.

The league championship was now building up to a thrilling climax. Exeter added two more points to their tally by beating Southampton 60–24 at the County Ground but suffered another unexpected set back when they finished on the wrong end of a 59–25 whipping at Ipswich. Goog Hoskin was actually beaten for the first time at Foxhall Heath when Bert Edwards nipped by on the outside in heat 7.

The race for the championship was now expected to reach its climax at the County Ground on Monday 21 September when Exeter would appropriately face their closest rivals for the title, the Rayleigh Rockets, in the last home league match. Once again the rain made itself felt and the match was called off well before start time and rescheduled for the following week.

But before the championship race could be decided the Falcons travelled north to Scotland in a brave bid to reach the final of the Queen's Cup. The second leg of the semi final against Glasgow, (White City) was scheduled for Wednesday 23 September at Ibrox. Despite defending a healthy thirty point lead the Falcons soon found the going tough, and it took most of the first half of the match for the Exeter riders to master the long straights and narrow tricky bends of the White City track.

The luck did not go Exeter's way either. Both Hardy and Hart fell in the early heats while Tigers' Junior Bainbridge tantalisingly just managed to cross the finish line before his engine blew after being harassed all the way by Geran. Tension among the Falcons led to further mistakes and their lead was rapidly whittled away. Fortunately Exeter were quick to learn. Hart won heat 6 from Peter Dykes and Bob Sharp then joined Geran to hold off Bainbridge for a share of the points in heat 10.

By heat 12 the Tigers' scoring rate had slowed and Exeter still held a six point aggregate lead. But Westcountry hopes faded in heat 13 when Glasgow notched another 5–1. The Falcons hit back with a 4–2 thanks to some brilliant riding by Vic Gent and Charlie May, but the Tigers maintained the pressure and with two heats to go the aggregate scores were level on 102–102.

The Exeter riders desperately tried to hold on but by now there was no stopping the rampant Tigers who eventually won 72–36 on the night and 111–105 on aggregate. In the final Glasgow met Scottish rivals Edinburgh Monarchs who won 117–99 over two legs.

The Falcons returned south determined to beat Rayleigh and claim the Southern League championship, but controversy arose even before the match got underway. During the previous Saturday's home match at the Weir Rayleigh's Les McGillivray had been injured and was not fit to take his place in the line-up at the County Ground. He had been named in the team which the Rayleigh management had given to Exeter five days previously but now Mrs Tippy Atkinson, the Rockets' team manager, asked the ACU Steward, F.E.G. Vigers, for permission to rearrange the pairings to cover for McGillivray's absence. Mr Vigers refused to sanction the switch of pairing and Rayleigh rode under protest.

The actual match proved to be a disappointing anti-climax.

The first four races were all drawn but in heat 5 Goog Hoskin and Dick Howard recorded the first Exeter 5–1 of the evening. Don Hardy and Jack Hart produced the second in the next race after skipper Hardy had fought a tremendous duel with Peter Clark. Rayleigh sustained a further set back in heat 7. Gerald Jackson and Tom O'Connor were well in front when Jackson's chain snapped and he fell. O'Connor crashed into his teammate and was taken to hospital with suspected stomach injuries. With Jackson excluded and reserve Ron Howes replacing the unfortunate O'Connor Street and Geran exploited the situation to the full and raced to Exeter's third consecutive maximum heat advantage. The Falcons totally dominated the remainder of the match and only Maurice McDermott's win in heat 12 interrupted a veritable avalanche of Exeter 5–1s. The final score was 60–24 and the championship was within the Falcons grasp.

Controversial ACU steward Mr F. E. G. Vigers photographed in the County Ground referee's box in the late eighties.

While the Rayleigh protest was being processed by officialdom Exeter travelled to Southampton the next day determined to round off the season in style and clinch the title with a final away win. That seemed far from certain as the Saints kicked off with three 5–1s and a 4–2 to go 19–5 in front, but a short sharp shower of rain altered the complexion of the match completely. The Exeter riders quickly adapted to the wet conditions and with the championship almost within their grasp the Falcons were prepared to take a risk or two.

Don Hardy set the ball rolling by winning heat 5. In the next race Charlie May replaced Neil Street and partnered Jack Geran to the Falcons' first 5–1 of the evening. May and Jack Hart gained a second maximum in heat 8 which reduced the arrears to six points. The Saints again extended their lead with a heat 9 4–2, but May, replaced Howard, and together with Hoskin roared to a third success. Hardy and Hart produced a 4–2 in heat 11 which brought the Falcons to within two points of Southampton, 34–32. The Saints narrowly maintained their lead thanks to a 4–2 in heat 12, but Hardy won heat 13 from Geddes and Gleed, which left the Falcons needing a 5–1 in the final race to draw.

The tension was electric as the riders came to the start, and when the tapes flew up it was Geran and Hoskin who made their now traditional lightning start. As they had done so many times during that royal summer the Falcons' top two stormed home together for the vital 5–1 which now levelled the scores at 42–42 and clinched the Southern League championship for Exeter.

Exeter's elation was short lived. Three days later on Friday 2 October the Speedway Control Board upheld Rayleigh's protest having decided that ACU steward Freddie Vigers had misinterpreted the rules and should have allowed the Rockets' management to change their pairings. As a result of the SCB's decision the league match at Exeter on 28 September was declared null and void. The loss of the two match points meant that the Falcons had lost the championship through no fault of their own. The Exeter management, who had not been invited to the hearing, immediately appealed to the Stewards of the RAC. Their appeal was heard in London on 29 November. The RAC Stewards in their wisdom decided that the SCB should have heard Rayleigh's protest with Exeter represented, and the title returned to the County Ground. But Rayleigh would not let the matter drop and the debate continued into 1954 when in January a further protest by the Rockets succeeded in getting the match struck from the records, and the whole sorry situation petered out without any official decision ever being made.

In the light of Falcons' 36 point winning margin, even if Vigers had allowed the Rockets to switch their pairings, would it have made that much difference to the score line? I very much doubt it. Now nearly fifty years on I consider that Exeter, having won that vital match fair and square where it really mattered out on the track, were morally the 1953 Southern League Champions.

LEAGUE TABLES 1947–1953

1947 – Third Division	P	W	D	L	Pts
Eastbourne	28	18	0	10	**36**
Cradley Heath	28	18	0	10	**36**
Southampton	28	17	1	10	**35**
Exeter	28	15	0	13	**30**
Tamworth	28	12	0	16	**24**
Hanley	28	12	0	16	**24**
Wombwell	28	12	0	16	**24**
Plymouth	28	7	1	20	**15**

1948 – Third Division	P	W	D	L	Pts
Exeter	44	32	1	11	**65**
Cradley Heath	44	29	2	13	**60**
Southampton	44	29	0	1	**58**
Tamworth	44	23	4	17	**50**
Hanley	44	24	1	19	**49**
Hastings	44	22	0	22	**44**
Plymouth	44	21	1	22	**43**
Coventry	44	19	1	23	**39**
Hull	44	19	0	25	**38**
Poole	44	17	0	27	**34**
Yarmouth	44	13	1	30	**27**
Wombwell	44	10	1	33	**21**

1949 – Third Division	P	W	D	L	Pts
Hanley	48	35	1	12	**71**
Yarmouth	48	35	1	12	**71**
Tamworth	48	33	0	15	**66**
Halifax	48	28	2	18	**58**
Plymouth	48	28	2	18	**58**
Poole	48	2	0	21	**54**
Exeter	48	24	0	24	**48**
Hastings	48	21	1	26	**43**
Liverpool	48	19	0	29	**38**
Leicester	48	17	1	30	**35**
Swindon	48	15	1	32	**31**
Rayleigh	48	14	0	34	**28**
Oxford	48	11	1	36	**23**

1950 – Third Division	P	W	D	L	Pts
Oxford	36	26	2	8	**54**
Poole	36	23	3	10	**49**
Leicester	36	21	0	15	**42**
Swindon	36	19	1	16	**39**
Aldershot	36	18	1	17	**37**
Tamworth	36	17	0	19	**34**
Exeter	36	16	1	19	**33**
Liverpool	36	14	1	21	**29**
Rayleigh	36	12	0	24	**24**
St Austell	36	9	1	26	**19**

1951 – Third Division	P	W	D	L	Pts
Poole	36	30	0	6	**60**
Exeter	36	28	0	8	**56**
Aldershot	36	21	1	14	**43**
Rayleigh	36	21	0	15	**42**
Swindon	36	16	2	18	**34**
Plymouth	36	16	1	19	**33**
Cardiff	36	13	3	20	**29**
St Austell	36	13	0	23	**26**
Long Eaton	36	13	0	23	**26**
Wolverhampton	36	5	0	30	**11**

1952 – Southern League	P	W	D	L	Pts
Rayleigh	36	28	0	8	**56**
Cardiff	36	23	0	13	**46**
Plymouth	36	20	1	15	**41**
Wolverhampton	36	20	1	15	**41**
Exeter	36	20	1	15	**41**
Swindon	36	18	0	18	**36**
Aldershot	36	15	1	20	**31**
Ipswich	36	12	0	24	**24**
Southampton	36	11	0	25	**22**
St Austell	36	11	0	25	**22**

1953 – Southern League	P	W	D	L	Pts
Exeter	27	21	1	5	**43**
Rayleigh	27	21	1	5	**43**
Ipswich	28	13	2	13	**28**
Swindon	28	13	2	13	**28**
Southampton	28	12	2	14	**26**
Oxford	28	9	1	18	**19**
St Austell	28	9	0	19	**18**
Plymouth	28	8	1	19	**17**

STATISTICS 1947

14 April
BATTLE FOR TEAM PLACES

Charlie Hayden	11	Dink Philpotts	7	Gordon Taylor	4	Ted Golding	3
Sid Hazzard	10	Herbert Hayden	6	Les Tredgett	3	Bill Sale	2
Allan Chambers	10	Cyril Roger	6	Tom Crutcher	3	Dick Shepherd	2
Broncho Slade	9	Don Hardy	5	Reg Beer	3	Howard Davies	1
Ted Moore	9	John Nailor	5	Ron Wickwar	3	Les Trim	0
Bill Williams	8	Bill Keen	5	Al Collins	3		

22 April
POSSIBLES v PROBABLES

POSSIBLES 44				PROBABLES 37			
Cyril Roger	12	Dick Shepherd	2	Allan Chambers	11	Bill Williams	3
Les Trim	11	Bill Sale	2	Broncho Slade	8	Sid Hazzard	2
Don Hardy	8	Reg Beer	1	Ted Moore	7	Herbert Hayden	2
Tom Crutcher	5	Charley Hayden	0	Dink Philpotts	3	John Naylor	1
Gordon Taylor	3						

26 April
CHALLENGE MATCH

EASTBOURNE 63				EXETER 20			
Jim Coy	12	Basil Harris	9	Cyril Roger	4	Don Hardy	3
Dennis Gray	11	Jock Grierson	6	Allan Chambers	4	Broncho Slade	2
Harry Saunders	11	Bob Sivyer	4	Ted Moore	3	Sid Hazzard	1
Ken Tidbury	9	Mike Tams	1	Les Trim	3	Tom Crutcher	0

28 April
CHALLENGE MATCH

EXETER 52				EASTBOURNE 32			
Chambers	11	Moore	5	Ken Tidbury	9	Basil Harris	3
Slade	10	Hardy	5	Dennis Gray	7	Ron Clarke	2
Trim	8	Crutcher	5	Jim Coy	5	Jock Grierson	1
Roger	6	Hazzard	2	Harry Saunders	4	Dick Angel	1

1 May
CHALLENGE MATCH

PLYMOUTH 33				EXETER 48			
Ivan Kessell	7	Jim Cashmore	6	Chambers	11	Moore	6
Billy Newell	7	Vic Bernard	1	Hardy	9	Crutcher	4
Bill Deegan	6	Len Covell	0	Roger	7	Hayden	3
Des Tamblin	6	Ralph Westwood	0	Slade	6	Philpotts	2

5 May
CHALLENGE MATCH

EXETER 47				PLYMOUTH 34			
Slade	10	Roger	7	Ivan Kessell	9	Bill Deegan	3
Chambers	9	Hardy	4	Billy Newell	8	Jim Cashmore	3
Hayden	9	Bill Williams	1	Les Tamblyn	4	Mike Collings	1
Crutcher	7	Ted Moore	0	Len Covell	5	Alf Simpson	1

12 May
NATIONAL LEAGUE DIVISION 3

EXETER 62				HANLEY 20			
Les Trim	11	Don Hardy	9	Cyril Page	7	Bert Danner	1
Allan Chambers	10	Dink Philpotts	6	Reg Gregory	7	George Fisher	0
Charlie Hayden	9	Bill Williams	5	Gil Blake	3	Les Jenkins	0
Cyril Roger	9	Broncho Slade	3	Dave Anderson	2		

15 May
NATIONAL LEAGUE DIVISION 3

HANLEY 49				EXETER 33			
George Fisher	12	Dick Howard	5	Allan Chambers	9	Broncho Slade	3
Cyril Page	10	Dave Anderson	5	Les Trim	6	Charlie Hayden	2
Reg Gregory	10	Les Jenkins	1	Cyril Roger	6	Bill Williams	2
Bert Danner	6	Gil Blake	0	Don Hardy	3	Tom Crutcher	2

16 May
NATIONAL LEAGUE DIVISION 3

WOMBWELL 48				EXETER 35			
Stan Hodson	12	Gerry Williams	4	Cyril Roger	10	Les Trim	4
Harwood Pike	11	Ralph Horne	3	Sid Hazzard	8	Don Hardy	1
Len Tupling	10	Bert Thomas	3	Broncho Slade	5	Allan Chambers	1
Ken Allick	5	Jan Yates	0	Charlie Hayden	5	Dink Philpotts	1

19 May
TRACK CHAMPIONSHIP

C. Roger	12	Taylor	7	Hardy	4	Hayden	3
Slade	8	Williams	7	Crutcher	4	Nailor	3
Chambers	8	Hazzard	5	Philpotts	4	Bill Sale	3

26 May
RIDERS CHAMPIONSHIP

Cyril Roger	15	Steve Langton	10	Peter Robinson	7	Basil Harris	4
Len Tuplin	14	Don Hardy	9	Cyril Page	6	Ken Allick	2
Vic Pitcher	12	Dave Anderson	9	Gordon Taylor	6	Jim Cashmore	1
Broncho Slade	11	Ivan Kessell	8	Sid Hazzard	4	Reg Gregory	1

2 June
NATIONAL LEAGUE DIVISION 3

EXETER 50				WOMBWELL 31			
Slade	12	Hazzard	5	Len Tuplin	8	Jim Schofield	3
Roger	12	Crutcher	5	Harwood Pike	6	Gerry Williams	2
Chambers	9	Hayden	1	Ken Allick	4	Jeff Bishop	2
Hardy	6	Williams	0	Sam Marsland	4	Bernard Thomas	2

9 June
NATIONAL LEAGUE DIVISION 3

EXETER 56				TAMWORTH 28			
Roger	11	Hazzard	7	Steve Langton	9	Vic Pitcher	3
Chambers	11	Slade	6	Arthur Payne	4	Jack Ladd	3
Crutcher	9	Bill Williams	3	Bill Harris	4	Jack Kidd	1
Hardy	8	Taylor	1	Ted Gibson	3	Reg Challenger	1

16 June
NATIONAL LEAGUE DIVISION 3

EXETER 57				CRADLEY HEATH 26			
Roger	12	Hazzard	8	Geoff Bennett	9	Stan Crouch	2
Slade	10	Crutcher	5	Ray Beaumont	6	Eric Irons	2
Hardy	8	Williams	3	Jimmy Wright	3	Alan Hunt	1
Chambers	8	Trim	3	Les Beaumont	2	Alan Briggs	1

23 June
NATIONAL LEAGUE DIVISION 3

EXETER 43				SOUTHAMPTON 41			
Roger	11	Slade	4	Peter Robinson	10	Bert Croucher	4
Chambers	9	Trim	4	Bob Oakley	9	George Bason	3
Hardy	7	Hazzard	2	Jimmy Squibb	7	Vic Collins	2
Crutcher	5	Charley Hayden	1	Alf Kaines	5	Pete Lansdale	1

24 June
NATIONAL LEAGUE DIVISION 3

SOUTHAMPTON 47½				EXETER 36½			
Peter Robinson	12	Vic Collins	4	Hardy	11	Slade	3½
Bob Oakley	8	Jimmy Squibb	3½	Roger	10	Chambers	2
Alf Kaines	8	Pete Lansdale	2	Trim	5	Philpotts	1
George Bason	8	Bert Croucher	2	Hazzard	4	Crutcher	0

30 June
PAIRS CHAMPIONSHIP

SOUTHAMPTON 21		PLYMOUTH 17		TAMWORTH 16		EXETER 15	
Peter Robinson	15	Ivan Kessell	9	Steve Langton	12	Cyril Roger	8
George Bason	6	Stan Lanfear	8	Vic Pitcher	4	Allan Chambers	7
WOMBWELL 14		**HANLEY 7**					
Len Tuplin	12	Dick Howard	3				
B. Slade (res)	2	Dave Anderson	4				

5 July
NATIONAL LEAGUE DIVISION 3

CRADLEY HEATH 50				EXETER 34			
Geoff Bennett	11	Bob Fletcher	5	Roger	11	Chambers	2
Jimmy Wright	11	Ray Beaumont	5	Hardy	7	Crutcher	2
Phil Malpass	8	Alan Hunt	3	Trim	7	Myson	1
Les Beaumont	7	George Scrivens	0	Slade	4	Hazzard	0

7 July
NATIONAL LEAGUE DIVISION 3

EXETER 55				PLYMOUTH 28			
Hardy	10	Trim	8	Charlie Challis	10	Harold Sharpe	2
Crutcher	10	Myson	6	Ivan Kessell	8	Stan Lanfear	0
Chambers	9	Hazzard	3	Doug Bell	5	Alex Gray	0
Roger	9	Slade	0	Vic Gent	3	Bill Williams	0

10 July
NATIONAL LEAGUE DIVISION 3

PLYMOUTH 40				EXETER 43			
Charlie Challis	12	Harold Sharpe	3	Myson	10	Slade	4
Ivan Kessell	9	Vic Gent	1	Roger	9	Chambers	4
Alex Gray	8	Ralph Westwood	0	Hardy	7	Crutcher	2
Doug Bell	7	Mal Hogan	0	Trim	6	Hazzard	1

14 July NATIONAL LEAGUE DIVISION 3	EXETER 50				EASTBOURNE 32			
	Roger	12	Crutcher	5	Ken Tidbury	9	Jim Coy	1
	Hardy	10	Trim	5	Wally Green	8	Basil Harris	1
	Myson	6	Hazzard	3	Jock Grierson	7	Ron Clarke	0
	Chambers	6	Slade	3	Harry Saunders	6	Basil Bumstead	0

16 July NATIONAL LEAGUE DIVISION 3	TAMWORTH 48				EXETER 36			
	Steve Langton	12	Ted Gibson	6	Hardy	8	Myson	4
	Arthur Payne	8	Jack Ladd	4	Trim	8	Crutcher	2
	Bill Harris	7	Jack Baxter	4	Slade	7	Chambers	1
	Charlie Oates	7	Jack Kidd	0	Roger	5	Hazzard	1

21 July NATIONAL LEAGUE DIVISION 3	EXETER 52				HANLEY 31			
	Roger	11	Myson	7	Gill Blake	9	Les Jenkins	2
	Hardy	9	Crutcher	4	Dick Howard	8	George Fisher	2
	Chambers	9	Hazzard	3	Reg Gregory	6	Jack Dorey	0
	Slade	8	Trim	1	Ray Harris	4	Brian Gorman	0

24 July NORTH v SOUTH CUP	PLYMOUTH 48				EXETER 47			
	Ivan Kessell	12	Billy Newell	6	Roger	11	Hazzard	6
	Alex Gray	11	Harold Sharpe	4	Chambers	9	Slade	4
	Charlie Challis	8	Vic Gent	1	Myson	7	Crutcher	2
	Doug Bell	6	Jack Milross	0	Hardy	6	Trim	2

26 July NATIONAL LEAGUE DIVISION 3	EASTBOURNE 49				EXETER 32			
	Wally Green	12	Jock Grierson	4	Roger	9	Slade	3
	Ken Tidbury	10	Harry Saunders	4	Hardy	6	Chambers	2
	Basil Harris	10	Ron Clark	1	Trim	5	Hazzard	2
	Jim Coy	7	Bob Sivyer	1	Myson	5	Williams	0

28 July NATIONAL LEAGUE DIVISION 3	EXETER 43				WOMBWELL 41			
	Roger	12	Trim	4	Harwood Pike	11	Len Tuplin	2
	Slade	9	Nailor	3	Stan Hodson	11	Jeff Bishop	2
	Chambers	7	Myson	2	Alf Elliott	8	Harry Modral	1
	Hardy	5	Crutcher	1	Gerry Williams	6	Reg Challenger	0

1 August NATIONAL LEAGUE DIVISION 3	WOMBWELL 51				EXETER 33			
	Harwood Pike	10	Jeff Bishop	6	Roger	11	Crutcher	2
	Harry Modral	9	Gerrry Williams	5	Hardy	8	B Williams	2
	Stan Hodson	8	Ken Allick	3	Myson	5	Slade	1
	Alf Elliott	8	Red Hamley	2	Chambers	4	Naylor	0

2 August NATIONAL LEAGUE DIVISION 3	CRADLEY HEATH 61				EXETER 22			
	Geoff Bennett	12	Ray Beaumont	8	C Roger	7	Slade	1
	Les Beaumont	11	Frank Evans	7	Chambers	6	Naylor	1
	Jimmy Wright	10	Phil Malpass	3	Hardy	5	Crutcher	0
	Eric Irons	9	Alan Hunt	1	Myson	2	Williams	0

4 August NORTH v SOUTH CUP	EXETER 51				PLYMOUTH 45			
	Roger	15	Hazzard	6	Ivan Kessell	12	Harold Sharpe	5
	Hardy	9	Nailor	4	Charlie Challis	8	Stan Lanfear	4
	Chambers	7	Crutcher	2	Billy Newell	8	Doug Bell	2
	Myson	7	Slade	1	Alex Gray	5	Bill Sale	1

7 August NATIONAL LEAGUE DIVISION 3	HANLEY 54				EXETER 23			
	Les Jenkins	12	George Fisher	5	C Roger	6	Chambers	3
	Vic Pitcher	12	Ray Harris	4	Myson	4	Trim	2
	Dick Howard	10	Gil Blake	2	Hazzard	4	Nailor	1
	Dave Anderson	9	Reg Gregory	0	Hardy	3	Tamblyn	0

11 August NATIONAL LEAGUE DIVISION 3	EXETER 47				TAMWORTH 37			
	C Rogers	12	Hazzard	7	Steve Langton	8	Fred Yates	4
	Myson	8	Crutcher	5	Bill Harris	8	Ted Gibson	3
	Chambers	8	Trim	0	Arthur Payne	8	Charlie Oates	2
	Hardy	7	Williams	0	Jack Baxter	4	Cyril Page	0

13 August NATIONAL LEAGUE DIVISION 3

TAMWORTH 50				EXETER 34			
Charlie Oates	9	Arthur Payne	7	C Roger	12	Pilgrim	3
Ted Gibson	9	Jack Baxter	6	Hardy	10	Crutcher	1
Bill Harris	8	Steve Langton	3	Chambers	4	Davey	0
Cyril Page	7	Jack Ladd	1	Myson	4	Hazzard	0

18 August NORTH v SOUTH CUP

EXETER 45				EASTBOURNE 51			
Roger	15	Hardy	3	Wally Green	13	Basil Harris	6
Hazzard	9	Pilgrim	3	Jim Coy	9	Harry Saunders	5
Myson	7	Chambers	2	Jock Grierson	7	Ron Clark	3
Slade	5	Williams	1	Ken Tidbury	6	Bob Sivyer	2

25 August NATIONAL LEAGUE DIVISION 3

EXETER 53				SOUTHAMPTON 31			
Hardy	11	Hodson	6	Peter Robinson	8	Pete Lansdale	3
C Roger	10	Slade	4	Bob Oakley	8	George Bason	2
Hazzard	8	Chambers	3	Jimmy Squibb	6	Vic Collins	0
Myson	8	Crutcher	3	Alf Kaines	4	Bert Croucher	0

26 August NATIONAL LEAGUE DIVISION 3

SOUTHAMPTON 55				EXETER 29			
Alf Kaines	11	George Bason	8	Roger	9	Hazzard	3
Jimmy Squibb	10	Peter Robinson	3	Hardy	5	Myson	2
Bob Oakley	10	Tony Buxey	3	Hodson	5	Pilgrim	1
Pete Lansdale	8	Vic Collins	2	Chambers	4	Slade	0

1 September NATIONAL LEAGUE DIVISION 3

EXETER 62				CRADLEY HEATH 22			
Hodson	12	Hazzard	7	Geoff Bennett	9	Les Beaumont	1
C Rogers	12	Myson	6	Bob Fletcher	5	Jimmy Wright	1
Hardy	11	Slade	3	Eric Irons	3	Frank Evans	0
Chambers	8	Pilgrim	3	Alan Hunt	3	Wilf Wilstead	0

8 September NATIONAL LEAGUE DIVISION 3

EXETER 53				PLYMOUTH 30			
Hazzard	10	C Roger	6	Stan Lanfear	12	Harold Sharpe	2
Chambers	9	Slade	6	Ivan Kessell	7	Vic Gent	1
Hardy	7	Pilgrim	5	Billy Newell	5	Charlie Challis	0
Myson	7	Hodson	3	Len Read	3	Phil Day	0

11 September NATIONAL LEAGUE DIVISION 3

PLYMOUTH 44				EXETER 40			
Charlie Challis	10	Len Read	5	C Roger	12	Slade	5
Stan Lanfear	8	Ivan Kessell	5	Hodson	7	Pilgrim	4
Billy Newell	7	Harold Sharpe	2	Myson	6	Hazzard	1
Alex Gray	6	Vic Gent	1	Hardy	5	Chambers	0

15 September NATIONAL LEAGUE DIVISION 3

EXETER 47				EASTBOURNE 37			
C Roger	12	Chambers	4	Jim Coy	8	Jock Grierson	7
Hazzard	8	Slade	3	Ken Tidbury	7	Ron Clarke	1
Myson	8	Hodson	3	Wally Green	7	Harry Saunders	0
Hardy	6	Pilgrim	3	Basil Harris	7	Eric Dunn	0

22 September CHALLENGE

EXETER 62				THE REST 21			
Roger	11	Hardy	8	Wally Green	10	Charlie Hayden	1
Hazzard	9	Slade	8	Jim Squibb	5	Dave Anderson	1
Hodson	9	Chambers	5	Ivan Kessell	3	Geoff Bennett	0
Myson	9	Pilgrim	3	Steve Langton	1	Harold Sharpe	0

23 September NORTH v SOUTH CUP

SOUTHAMPTON 61				EXETER 34			
Bert Croucher	13	Jim Squibb	8	Hardy	9	Myson	3
Pete Lansdale	12	Alf Kaines	7	Roger	7	Hazzard	2
Bob Oakley	9	Ernie Rawlins	2	Chambers	6	Pilgrim	2
George Bason	8	Vic Collins	2	Hodson	5	Slade	0

27 September NATIONAL LEAGUE DIVISION 3

EASTBOURNE 50				EXETER 33			
Basil Harris	11	Ron Clark	4	Roger	11	Chambers	4
Wally Green	10	Harry Saunders	4	Hardy	7	Slade	1
Jock Grierson	10	Alan Briggs	2	Pilgrim	5	Myson	0
Ken Tidbury	8	Jim Coy	1	Hodson	5	Hazzard	0

29 September NORTH v SOUTH CUP	EXETER 69				SOUTHAMPTON 27			
	Roger	15	Myson	8	Alf Kaines	6	Tony Buxey	3
	Hodson	11	Hardy	6	Bob Oakley	6	Bert Croucher	2
	Slade	9	Pilgrim	6	Pete Lansdale	5	Gordon Taylor	2
	Hazzard	8	Chambers	6	Jim Squibb	3	Bill Griffiths	0

6 October TRACK CHAMPIONSHIP								
	C Roger	15	Chambers	11	Sid 'Dingo' Davey	6	Des Tamblyn	3
	Hodson	14	Myson	10	Hayden	5	Ted Moore	2
	Hardy	12	Slade	9	Taylor	4		
	Hazzard	12	Pilgrim	8	Philpotts	3		

15 October NORTH v SOUTH CUP	EXETER 62				EASTBOURNE 34			
	Roger	11	Chambers	7	Ken Tidbury	12	Harry Saunders	3
	Myson	10	Pilgrim	7	Jock Grierson	6	Jim Coy	2
	Hodson	9	Slade	5	Wally Green	5	Ernie Pawson	1
	Hazzard	8	Hardy	4	Ron Clarke	5	Basil Harris	0

23 October DEVON DERBY	PLYMOUTH 47				EXETER 36			
	Charlie Challis	9	Len Read	6	Roger	9	Hardy	3
	Alex Gray	9	Stan Lanfear	5	Hodson	9	Pilgrim	3
	Billy Newell	7	Harold Sharpe	3	Slade	5	Chambers	1
	Vic Gent	7	Ivan Kessell	1	Myson	5	Hazzard	1

STATISTICS 1948

29 March TOM CRUTCHER MEMORIAL TROPHY								
	Cyril Roger	15	Norman Clay	9	Dingo Davey	5	Bill Elliott	3
	Johnny Myson	12	Don Hardy	7	Hugh Geddes	5	Billy Newell	1
	Bert Roger	12	Gordon Taylor	7	Broncho Slade	4	John Hancox	1
	Arthur Pilgrim	11	Keith Gurtner	7	Art Hood	4	Herbie Plain	0
	Pete Lansdale	11	Reg Robins	6				

5 April DEVON DERBY	EXETER 68				PLYMOUTH 28			
	Cyril Roger	15	Hugh Geddes	7	Pete Lansdale	9	Alex Gray	2
	Broncho Slade	14	Arthur Pilgrim	7	Ivan Kessell	7	Charlie Challis	2
	Norman Clay	8	Johnny Myson	5	Billy Newell	4	Len Read	1
	Bert Roger	8	Keith Gurtner	4	Ted Gibson	2	Harold Sharp	1

6 April NATIONAL LEAGUE DIVISION 3	SOUTHAMPTON 57				EXETER 27			
	Alf Bottoms	12	Alf Kaines	7	C Roger	10	Clay	3
	Jim Squibb	9	George Bason	6	Pilgrim	4	Slade	2
	Bob Oakley	8	Tom Oakley	5	Myson	3	Hardy	1
	Bert Croucher	8	Tony Buxey	2	Geddes	3	B Roger	1

7 April NATIONAL TROPHY	TAMWORTH 82				EXETER 26			
	Steve Langton	17	Cyril Page	11	C Roger	11	B Roger	3
	Basil Harris	13	Arthur Payne	6	Pilgrim	4	Myson	2
	Bill Dalton	13	Peter Orpwood	6	Clay	3	Hardy	0
	Charlie Oates	11	Harry Saunders	5	Geddes	3	Slade	0

12 April NATIONAL TROPHY

EXETER 81				TAMWORTH 27			
Slade	14	Hardy	9	Steve Langton	8	Charlie Oates	2
Hodson	14	Geddes	7	Basil Harris	7	Arthur Payne	1
B Roger	13	Clay	7	Bill Dalton	5	Cyril Page	0
C Roger	12	Myson	5	Peter Orpwood	4	Harry Saunders	0

15 April DEVON DERBY

PLYMOUTH 44				EXETER 52			
Alex Gray	10	Charlie Challis	5	C Roger	14	Clay	6
Billy Newell	8	Ivan Kessell	4	Hodson	12	Slade	5
Ted Gibson	6	Vic Gent	4	Geddes	7	Myson	2
Pete Lansdale	5	Dave Hynes	2	Pilgrim	6	Keith Gurtner	0

19 April NATIONAL LEAGUE DIVISION 3

EXETER 57				HASTINGS 27			
Slade	11	Pilgrim	7	Jock Grierson	7	Ron Clark	4
C Roger	10	Hardy	5	Ken Tidbury	5	Dave English	1
B Roger	9	Clay	4	Wally Green	5	Ken Middleditch	1
Geddes	8	Hodson	3	Eric Dunn	4	Hal Collins	0

26 April NATIONAL LEAGUE DIVISION 3

EXETER 60				HULL 23			
Bert Roger	12	Norman Clay	8	Mick Mitchell	7	Norman Johnson	2
Arthur Pilgrim	9	Stan Hodson	6	George Craig	4	Derek Glover	2
Cyril Roger	8	Broncho Slade	6	John White	4	Rae Muir	2
Hugh Geddes	8	Don Hardy	3	Allan Nicholson	2	Brian Gorman	0

28 April NATIONAL LEAGUE DIVISION 3

HASTINGS 40				EXETER 44			
Wally Green	12	Hal Collins	2	C Roger	11	Pilgrim	5
Jock Grierson	10	Jack Scott	2	Geddes	10	Hodson	4
Eric Dunn	7	Ron Clark	1	Bert Roger	6	Hardy	3
Ken Tidbury	5	Bill Osborne	1	Slade	5	Clay	0

3 May SPEEDWAY RIDERS CHAMPIONSHIP

Bert Roger	13	Bronco Slade	11	Ken Tidbury	6	Steve Langton	4
Wally Green	13	Stan Hodson	10	Junior Bainbridge	5	Bill Dalton	4
Jock Grierson	12	Alf Kaines	10	Eric Dunn	5	Ray Harris	2
Cyril Roger	11	Bert Baird	6	Gil Blake	5	John Myson	2

10 May NATIONAL LEAGUE DIVISION 3

EXETER 65				CRADLEY HEATH 18			
C Roger	12	Slade	8	Les Beaumont	4	Phil Malpass	2
B Roger	11	Geddes	6	Jimmy Wright	4	Ted Moore	2
Hodson	10	Myson	5	Alan Hunt	3	Bill Clifton	1
Pilgrim	10	Hardy	3	Eric Irons	2	Jim Coy	0

13 May NORTH v SOUTH CUP

PLYMOUTH 38				EXETER 57			
Pete Lansdale	9	Ivan Kessell	5	Bert Roger	15	Pilgrim	5
Ted Gibson	8	Charlie Challis	2	Hodson	14	Myson	4
Peter Robinson	7	Len Read	2	Hardy	7	Slade	3
Alex Gray	5	Billy Newell	0	Clay	6	Geddes	3

17 May CHALLENGE

EXETER 51				NORWICH 33			
C Roger	11	Pilgrim	6	Ted Bravery	9	Howdy Byford	3
B Roger	10	Hardy	6	Aussie Powell	8	Paddy Hammond	3
Hodson	7	Clay	4	Paddy Mills	6	Sid Hipperson	1
Slade	6	Myson	1	Phil Clarke	3	Roy Duke	0

24 May NORTH v SOUTH 21 ANNIVERSARY CUP

EXETER 65				PLYMOUTH 31			
C Roger	14	Myson	7	Vic Gent	7	Len Read	2
B Roger	12	Hardy	5	Ted Gibson	6	Charlie Challis	2
Slade	11	Hodson	5	Ivan Kessell	6	Pete Lansdale	1
Pilgrim	8	Geddes	3	Pete Robinson	6	Alex Gray	1

31 May NATIONAL LEAGUE DIVISION 3

EXETER 65				POOLE 19			
C Roger	10	Slade	9	Alf Elliott	5	Sid Clark	2
B Roger	10	Pilgrim	9	Joe Bowkiss	4	George Butler	2
Myson	10	Geddes	5	Allan Chambers	2	Fred Pawson	1
Hodson	9	Clay	3	George Gower	3	Bingley Cree	0

7 June NATIONAL LEAGUE DIVISION 3

EXETER 66				HANLEY (STOKE) 18			
Cyril Roger	11	Geddes	8	Gil Blake	6	Ray Harris	2
Bert Roger	11	Hodson	7	Dick Howard	3	Les Jenkins	1
Slade	11	Clay	5	Bert Danner	3	Vic Pitcher	0
Pilgrim	9	Hardy	4	Ken Adams	3	Frank Evans	0

14 June NATIONAL LEAGUE DIVISION 3

EXETER 57				COVENTRY 27			
B Roger	12	Hodson	6	Vic Emms	10	Bernard Tennant	3
Slade	9	C Roger	5	Lionel Levy	5	John Yates	1
Clay	9	Hardy	4	Fred Yates	4	Bob Graves	0
Pilgrim	8	Myson	4	George Smith	4	Bert Lacey	0

15 June NATIONAL LEAGUE DIVISION 3

YARMOUTH 35				EXETER 45			
Billy Bales	9	Paddy Hammond	3	Cyril Roger	12	Hardy	4
Reg Morgan	9	Bert Rawlinson	2	Bert Roger	11	Clay	4
Sid Hipperson	6	Ted Rawlinson	2	Hodson	6	Pilgrim	3
Roy Duke	4			Geddes	4	Myson	1

19 June NATIONAL LEAGUE DIVISION 3

COVENTRY 26				EXETER 56			
Vic Emms	6	John Yates	2	Bert Roger	12	Clay	6
Bernard Tennant	6	Lionel Levy	1	Cyril Roger	12	Geddes	5
Bob Fletcher	5	Fred Yates	1	Hodson	10	Slade	2
George Smith	5	Bert Lacey	0	Pilgrim	9	Hardy	0

21 June NATIONAL LEAGUE DIVISION 3

EXETER 69				WOMBWELL 15			
Bert Roger	12	Hodson	9	Harry Welch	3	Jeff Bishop	2
Slade	11	Hardy	7	Len Tupling	3	Red Hamley	1
Cyril Roger	11	Geddes	6	Stan Beardsall	3	Harry Saunders	1
Pilgrim	9	Clay	4	Harwood Pike	2	Harry Modral	0

28 June NATIONAL LEAGUE DIVISION 3

EXETER 67				CRADLEY HEATH 16			
Bert Roger	12	Hodson	9	Gil Craven	5	Jimmy Wright	1
Cyril Roger	11	Hardy	8	Bill Clifton	4	Eric Irons	1
Pilgrim	10	Geddes	6	Alan Hunt	3	Ray Beaumont	0
Clay	9	Slade	2	Phil Malpass	2	Les Beaumont	0

29 June NATIONAL LEAGUE DIVISION 3

YARMOUTH 42				EXETER 41			
Billy Bales	10	Bert Rawlinson	5	B Roger	12	Hodson	5
Paddy Hammond	8	Roy Duke	3	C Roger	8	Hardy	4
Sid Hipperson	7	Ted Rawlinson	2	Clay	5	Geddes	2
Reg Morgan	6	Bill Carruthers	1	Pilgrim	5	John Hancox	0

1 July NATIONAL LEAGUE DIVISION 3

PLYMOUTH 32				EXETER 51			
Pete Lansdale	8	Billy Newell	3	C Roger	11	Hodson	5
Alex Gray	6	Ivan Kessell	2	B Roger	11	Clay	5
Peter Robinson	6	Charlie Challis	1	Hardy	7	Geddes	3
Len Read	6	Vic Gent	0	Pilgrim	6	Gordon Taylor	3

5 July NATIONAL LEAGUE DIVISION 3

EXETER 58				HASTINGS 26			
B Roger	11	Hodson	6	Jock Grierson	8	Ken Middleditch	2
C Roger	11	Geddes	4	Bill Osborne	5	Dave English	1
Clay	10	Hardy	3	Buddy Fuller	4	Ron Clark	1
Pilgrim	10	Taylor	3	Ken Tidbury	4	Ken Mold	1

10 July NATIONAL LEAGUE DIVISION 3

COVENTRY 47				EXETER 35			
Lionel Levy	12	Ralph Horne	6	C Roger	8	Hardy	4
Bob Fletcher	8	John Yates	3	Hodson	8	Taylor	3
Vic Emms	8	Fred Yates	2	Geddes	5	Clay	3
Bert Lacey	7	George Smith	1	Pilgrim	4	Hancox	0

12 July NATIONAL LEAGUE DIVISION 3

EXETER 48				SOUTHAMPTON 36			
C Roger	11	Hodson	4	Alf Bottoms	10	Tom Oakley	3
B Roger	10	Pilgrim	4	Jimmy Squibb	7	Cecil Bailey	2
Clay	8	Hancox	2	Bob Oakley	7	George Bason	1
Hardy	8	Geddes	1	Alf Kaines	6	Bill Griffiths	0

16 July NATIONAL LEAGUE DIVISION 3

CRADLEY HEATH 50				EXETER 33			
Gil Craven	12	Alan Hunt	6	Hodson	11	Hardy	3
Eric Irons	10	Phil Malpass	4	B Roger	7	Slade	3
Bill Clifton	9	Ray Beaumont	1	C Roger	5	Clay	1
Les Beaumont	8	Roy Moreton	0	Geddes	4	Pilgrim	1

17 July NATIONAL LEAGUE DIVISION 3

HULL 63				EXETER 21			
Mick Mitchell	11	Bob Baker	8	Hodson	7	Pilgrim	2
Norman Johnson	10	Dick Shepherd	7	B Roger	5	Hardy	1
George Craig	10	Derek Glover	5	C Roger	3	Geddes	1
John White	9	Al Allison	3	Clay	2	Slade	0

19 July NATIONAL LEAGUE DIVISION 3

EXETER 58				PLYMOUTH 25			
C Roger	11	Slade	9	Bonny Waddell	5	Vic Gent	3
Clay	10	Hardy	8	Len Read	5	Ken Slee	2
Pilgrim	10	Geddes	1	Peter Robinson	4	Ivan Kessell	1
B Roger	9	Hancox	0	Pete Lansdale	4	Wally Matthews	1

20 July NATIONAL LEAGUE DIVISION 3

TAMWORTH 46				EXETER 38			
Bill Harris	11	Steve Langton	2	B Roger	10	Hardy	3
Basil Harris	11	Peter Orpwood	2	Hodson	9	Clay	2
Cyril Page	11	Jack Baxter	2	C Roger	7	Geddes	2
Bill Dalton	5	Charlie Oates	2	Pilgrim	5	Slade	0

22 July NATIONAL LEAGUE DIVISION 3

HANLEY 51				EXETER 33			
Ray Harris	10	Lindsay Mitchell	5	C Roger	10	Pilgrim	4
Les Jenkins	10	Dick Howard	4	B Roger	8	Hardy	2
Gil Blake	10	Vic Pitcher	2	Clay	4	Slade	1
Dave Anderson	8	Ken Adams	2	Hodson	4	Geddes	0

23 July NATIONAL LEAGUE DIVISION 3

WOMBWELL 37				EXETER 47			
Harry Welch	12	Len Tupling	2	Bert Roger	11	Geddes	6
Harry Saunders	10	Son Mitchell	2	Clay	8	Hardy	3
Harwood Pike	5	Jeff Bishop	1	Hodson	8	Pilgrim	3
Stan Beardsall	4	Red Hamley	1	Cyril Roger	6	Slade	2

26 July NATIONAL LEAGUE DIVISION 3

EXETER 53				HANLEY (STOKE) 30			
B Roger	11	Pilgrim	6	Gil Blake	8	Ken Adams	4
Clay	10	Slade	5	Ray Harris	6	Lindsay Mitchell	2
Hardy	10	Taylor	1	Les Jenkins	5	Vic Pitcher	1
C Roger	9	Geddes	1	Dick Howard	4	Dave Anderson	0

31 July CHALLENGE

EXETER 57				BRISTOL 27			
Clay	11	C Roger	6	Roger Wise	7	Cyril Quick	2
Hardy	11	Geddes	5	Fred Tuck	6	Johnny Myson	1
Pilgrim	10	Hodson	4	Nobby Stock	6	Eric Salmon	1
B Roger	9	Taylor	1	Billy Hole	3	Jack Mountford	1

2 August FROUD INDIVIDUAL TROPHY

Norman Clay	15	Alf Bottoms	10	Don Hardy	7	Reg Robins	3
Cyril Roger	11	Hugh Geddes	10	Harry Welch	7	Dingo Davey	3
Bert Roger	11	Arthur Pilgrim	9	Stan Hodson	5	Johnny Myson	1
Roger Wise	11	Bob Oakley	9	Herbie Plain	5		

9 August NATIONAL LEAGUE DIVISION 3

EXETER 61				WOMBWELL 23			
Clay	12	B Roger	9	Harry Welch	5	Sonny Mitchell	3
Geddes	11	Pilgrim	6	Lionel Tupling	4	Harry Saunders	3
Hardy	10	Plain	2	Jeff Bishop	4	Pedlar Palmer	1
Hodson	11			Red Hamley	3	Stan Beardsall	0

11 August NATIONAL LEAGUE DIVISION 3

HASTINGS 41				EXETER 43			
Wally Green	9	Ken Middleditch	6	B Roger	11	Hardy	5
Ken Tidbury	7	Dan English	4	Hodson	7	Geddes	5
Jock Grierson	6	Pete Mold	2	Pilgrim	7	Mike Wood	1
Ron Clark	6	Ken Smith	1	Clay	6	Plain	1

14 August CHALLENGE

RAYLEIGH 41				EXETER 40			
Bruce Abernethy	9	Ron Howes	4	B Roger	11	Geddes	5
Percy Brine	9	Jimmy Dunn	2	Clay	8	Plain	3
Arthur Pilgrim	9	Jim Gregory	2	Hodson	7	Bill Williams	0
Roy Uden	5	Stan Crouch	1	Hardy	6	Wood	0

16 August NATIONAL LEAGUE DIVISION 3

EXETER 53				POOLE 30			
Clay	12	Pilgrim	8	Allan Chambers	9	Charlie Hayden	2
B Roger	10	Geddes	3	Joe Bowkis	6	Frank Holcombe	2
Hardy	10	Plain	1	Sid Clark	5	George Butler	1
Hodson	8	Waddell	1	Fred Pawson	4	Sid Hazzard	1

17 August NATIONAL LEAGUE DIVISION 3

SOUTHAMPTON 38				EXETER 43			
Jim Squibb	9	Alf Kaines	4	B Roger	11	Pilgrim	5
Cecil Bailey	8	George Bason	3	Hardy	9	Geddes	4
Alf Bottoms	6	Ernie Rawlins	2	Clay	9	Doug Smith	0
Tom Oakley	5	Bill Griffiths	1	Hodson	5	Waddell	dnr

20 August NATIONAL LEAGUE DIVISION 3

WOMBWELL 41				EXETER 43			
Harry Welch	10	Jeff Bishop	4	B Roger	11	Pilgrim	6
Stan Beardsall	8	Charlie Oates	4	Hardy	10	Myson	1
Jack Baxter	6	Harwood Pike	3	Clay	8	Mike Wood	0
Len Tupling	4	Red Hamley	2	Hodson	7	Plain	0

23 August BEST PAIRS CHAMPIONSHIP

NORWICH 24		COVENTRY 21		HASTINGS 19		HANLEY 16	
Paddy Mills	14	Lionel Levy	11	Jock Grierson	12	Ray Harris	13
Ted Bravery	10	Vic Emms	10	Wally Green	7	Gil Blake	3
BRISTOL 16		**PLYMOUTH 15**		**TAMWORTH 8**			
Roger Wise	8	Vic Gent	8	Steve Langton	4		
Jack Mountford	8	Len Read	7	Bill Dalton	4		

23 August NATIONAL LEAGUE DIVISION 3

POOLE 46				EXETER 38			
Joe Bowkis	10	Sid Clarke	5	B Roger	11	Pilgrim	5
Allan Chambers	10	George Butler	2	Clay	9	Myson	0
Sid Pawson	9	Sid Hazzard	2	Hardy	8	Plain	0
Charlie Hayden	6	Frank Holcombe	2	Hodson	5	Wood	0

30 August NATIONAL LEAGUE DIVISION 3

EXETER 41				PLYMOUTH 43			
Hodson	9	Stan Lanfear	4	Len Read	11	Bonny Waddwll	4
Clay	9	Hancox	2	Pete Lansdale	9	Wally Matthews	4
B Roger	9	Lew Coffin	2	Vic Gent	6	Ivan Kessell	2
Geddes	5	Myson	1	Ted Gibson	5	Bill Sobey	2

6 September NATIONAL LEAGUE DIVISION 3

EXETER 57				YARMOUTH 27			
Clay	12	Hodson	8	Paddy Hammond	6	Billy Bales	3
Hardy	10	Geddes	3	Roy Duke	5	Reg Morgan	2
Pilgrim	9	Lanfear	3	Bert Rawlinson	4	Bob Womack	2
B Roger	9	Myson	3	Sid Hipperson	4	Bill Carruthers	1

7 September NATIONAL LEAGUE DIVISION 3

TAMWORTH 50				EXETER 33			
Harry Saunders	10	Steve Langton	5	Hardy	10	Geddes	3
Bill Harris	9	Peter Orpwood	4	Clay	8	Myson	1
Cyril Page	8	Howard Chipman	3	Pilgrim	6	Hodson	0
Bill Dalton	8	Cecil Hookham	3	B Roger	5	Lanfear	0

13 September NATIONAL LEAGUE DIVISION 3

EXETER 65				TAMWORTH 19			
Hardy	12	Hodson	8	Bill Harris	6	Steve Langton	1
Clay	12	Geddes	6	Peter Orpwood	5	Howard Chipman	1
B Roger	10	Myson	5	Harry Saunders	3	Cecil Hookham	1
Pilgrim	9	Lanfear	3	Bill Dalton	2	Herbie Plain	0

16 September NATIONAL LEAGUE DIVISION 3

STOKE 39				EXETER 45			
Ken Adams	9	Stan Bradbury	4	Pilgrim	11	Geddes	4
Gil Blake	8	Dave Anderson	3	B Roger	11	Lanfear	2
Ray Harris	7	Dick Howard	2	Hardy	10	Myson	0
Vic Pitcher	4	Jack Dawson	2	Clay	7	Coffin	0

17 September NATIONAL LEAGUE DIVISION 3

CRADLEY HEATH 55				EXETER 29			
Gil Craven	12	Bill Kemp	5	Pilgrim	6	Hardy	3
Eric Irons	12	Roy Moreton	4	B Roger	6	Clay	3
Alan Hunt	9	Bill Clifton	3	Geddes	6	Myson	1
Les Beaumont	9	Phil Malpass	1	Lanfear	4	Coffin	0

20 September NATIONAL LEAGUE DIVISION 3

EXETER 48				COVENTRY 36			
B Roger	12	Hodson	4	Lionel Levy	11	Bert Lacey	3
Clay	9	Geddes	4	Vic Emms	11	Crusty Pye	2
Hardy	7	Lanfear	4	George Smith	5	Fred Yates	1
Pilgrim	5	Myson	3	Bob Fletcher	3	John Yates	0

27 September NATIONAL LEAGUE DIVISION 3

POOLE 31				EXETER 52			
Allan Chambers	10	Fred Pawson	2	B Roger	10	Geddes	6
George Butler	7	Fred Holcombe	2	Pilgrim	10	Hardy	6
Dick Howard	5	Charlie Hayden	0	Clay	9	Myson	3
Sid Clark	5			Hodson	7	Lanfear	1

27 September OPEN PAIRS CHAMPIONSHIP

BRISTOL 25		SOUTHAMPTON 19		SHEFFIELD 18		CRADLEY HEATH 17	
Roger Wise	12	Bob Oakley	12	Bruce Semmens	15	Alan Hunt	8
Jack Mountford	13	Alf Bottoms	7	John Hancox	3	Gil Craven	9
PLYMOUTH 13		**HANLEY 12**		**HASTINGS 9**		**TAMWORTH 7**	
Peter Robinson	8	Ken Adams	4	Jock Grierson	7	Jimmy Squibb	4
Len Read	5	Ray Harris	8	Ron Clark	2	Vic Gent	3

28 September NATIONAL LEAGUE DIVISION 3

PLYMOUTH 38				EXETER 46			
Len Read	10	Wally Matthews	3	Clay	12	Hodson	6
Alex Gray	7	Vic Gent	2	B Roger	9	Geddes	3
Peter Robinson	7	Ted Gibson	2	Pilgrim	7	Myson	2
Pete Lansdale	6	Bonny Waddell	1	Hardy	6	Lanfear	1

1 October (SECOND HALF. 5 HEATS)

BRISTOL JUNIORS 13				EXETER 17			
Johnny Hole	7	Graham Hole	2	Clay	7	Geddes	4
Dick Bradley	2	Ginger Nicholls	2	Pilgrim	6	Hodson	0

4 October NATIONAL LEAGUE DIVISION 3

EXETER 60				YARMOUTH 24			
B Roger	12	Hodson	8	Reg Morgan	8	Bill Carruthers	1
Hardy	12	Pilgrim	4	Billy Bales	7	Bert Rawlinson	1
Clay	11	Myson	4	Roy Duke	3	Arthur Bush	1
Geddes	8	Lanfear	1	Sid Hipperson	3	Bill Coding	0

11 October NATIONAL LEAGUE DIVISION 3

EXETER 57				TAMWORTH 27			
Clay	12	Hodson	7	Pete Orpwood	7	Lionel Watling	2
B Roger	10	Pilgrim	7	Cyril Page	6	Harry Saunders	2
Hardy	10	Myson	2	Bill Dalton	6	Basil Harris	0
Geddes	8	Lanfear	1	Will Harris	4	Howard Chipman	0

16 October NATIONAL LEAGUE DIVISION 3

HULL 50				EXETER 34			
Mick Mitchell	11	George Craig	5	Clay	10	Myson	3
Johnny White	10	Norman Johnson	4	Pilgrim	8	Hodson	2
Dick Shepherd	9	Derek Glover	4	B Roger	6	Hardy	1
Bob Baker	6	Alf Webster	1	Geddes	4	Lanfear	0

18 October NATIONAL LEAGUE DIVISION 3

EXETER 46				SOUTHAMPTON 38			
B Roger	11	Geddes	7	Alf Bottoms	10	Bob Oakley	3
Pilgrim	9	Lanfear	2	Jim Squibb	8	George Bason	3
Clay	8	Myson	1	Cecil Bailey	7	Bill Griffiths	1
Hodson	7	Hancox	1	Tom Oakley	6	Johnny Bradford	0

25 October NATIONAL LEAGUE DIVISION 3

EXETER 62				HULL 22			
Geddes	12	Pilgrim	8	George Craig	7	Derek Glover	2
B Roger	12	Hancox	5	Alf Webster	4	Johnny White	2
Clay	11	Lanfear	4	Bob Baker	3	Mick Mitchell	1
Myson	9	Hodson	1	Norman Johnson	3	Peter Dodds	0

Bert Roger.

STATISTICS 1949

28 March NATIONAL LEAGUE	EXETER 54				POOLE 30			
	Norman Clay	11	Hugh Geddes	7	Cyril Quick	8	Frank Holcombe	3
	Johnny Myson	9	Arthur Pilgrim	5	Fred Pawson	6	Ticker James	1
	Broncho Slade	8	Stan Hodson	4	Dick Howard	6	Bernard Tennant	1
	Vic Gent	8	John Hancox	2	Charlie Hayden	5	Ken James	0

4 April NATIONAL TROPHY	EXETER 62				PLYMOUTH 45			
	Clay	15	Geddes	8	Pete Lansdale	14	George Wall	4
	Pilgrim	12	Hancox	4	Peter Robinson	11	Bonnie Waddell	3
	Myson	12	Hodson	2	Len Read	6	Ivan Kessell	1
	Slade	9	Gent	0	Alan Smith	5	Ted Gibson	1

7 April NATIONAL TROPHY	PLYMOUTH 54				EXETER 54			
	Pete Lansdale	15	Bonnie Waddell	4	Clay	16	Myson	5
	Peter Robinson	12	Ted Gibson	4	Pilgrim	8	Stan Lanfear	4
	Ivan Kessell	8	George Wall	3	Hodson	8	Gent	3
	Len Read	7	Alan Smith	1	Geddes	8	Slade	2

11 April NATIONAL LEAGUE	EXETER 40				YARMOUTH 42			
	Geddes	11	Pilgrim	4	Bert Rawlinson	11	Sid Hipperson	4
	Gent	8	Slade	4	Billy Bales	10	John White	1
	Hodson	7	Myson	1	Bill Carruthers	9	Stan Page	1
	Lanfear	5	Clay	0	Reg Morgan	6	Joe Rodwell	0

13 April — NATIONAL LEAGUE

HALIFAX 34				EXETER 49			
Vic Emms	11	Jack Dawson	1	Geddes	10	Gent	5
Al Allison	9	Bill Crossland	1	Pilgrim	9	Lanfear	5
Arthur Forrest	9	Eric Mason	1	Slade	7	Hodson	4
Jerk Smith	2			Myson	5	Hancox	4

15 April — NATIONAL LEAGUE

LIVERPOOL 55				EXETER 29			
Alex Gray	12	Douglas Serrurier	6	Gent	8	Slade	3
Fred Wills	10	George Bason	5	Lanfear	6	Myson	2
Harry Welch	8	Tom Turnham	4	Hodson	4	Hancox	2
Charlie Oates	7	Stan Bedford	3	Geddes	4	Goog Hoskin	0

18 April — NATIONAL LEAGUE

EXETER 60				OXFORD 24			
Slade	12	Hodson	7	Bert Croucher	9	Alf Elliott	1
Pilgrim	10	Myson	7	Dennis Gray	7	Alf Viccary	1
Geddes	9	Hancox	4	Bill Downton	3	Maurice Hutchings	0
Lanfear	9	Gent	2	Bob Aldridge	3	Johnny Fry	0

21 April — NATIONAL LEAGUE

PLYMOUTH 44				EXETER 40			
Len Read	12	Ivan Kessell	5	Hardy	9	Pilgrim	5
Pete Lansdale	10	Bonnie Waddell	3	Hodson	8	Myson	3
George Wall	6	Wally Matthews	2	Gent	8	Slade	2
Johnny Bradford	5	Mott Jones	1	Hancox	5	Geddes	dnr

25 April — NATIONAL LEAGUE

EXETER 57				STOKE 51			
Don Hardy	10	Pilgrim	7	Gil Blake	14	Bill Pitcher	7
Slade	10	Geddes	6	Ray Harris	10	Frank Evans	4
Gent	9	Hodson	5	Ken Adams	7	Les Jenkins	2
Myson	7	Hancox	3	Lindsay Mitchell	7	Stan Bradbury	0

30 April — NATIONAL LEAGUE

RAYLEIGH 46				EXETER 37			
Jack Unstead	12	Jim Gregory	4	Hardy	9	Myson	3
Ron Howes	8	Roy Uden	3	Pilgrim	8	Slade	3
Percy Brine	7	Vic Gooden	3	Gent	8	Hancox	0
Charlie Mugford	7	Alan Briggs	2	Hodson	6	Plain	0

2 May — NATIONAL LEAGUE

EXETER 38				LEICESTER 44			
Pilgrim	11	Myson	5	Cyril Page	9	Harwood Pike	6
Gent	7	Hardy	3	Vic Pilcher	8	Ted Rawlinson	4
Hancox	6	Ernie Noakes	1	Jack Baxter	7	George Gower	2
Hodson	5	Slade	0	Ron Wilson	7	Pedlar Palmer	1

6 May — NATIONAL LEAGUE

LEICESTER 59				EXETER 25			
Ron Wilson	11	Ted Rawlinson	8	Hardy	10	Hodson	1
Vic Pilcher	11	Harwood Pike	6	Pilgrim	6	Lanfear	0
Jack Baxter	10	George Gower	5	Gent	6	Hancox	0
Cyril Page	8	Pedlar Palmer	0	Myson	2	Bill Rundle	0

7 May — NATIONAL TROPHY

STOKE 75				EXETER 33			
Les Jenkins	18	Frank Evans	8	Gent	10	Hodson	1
Gil Blake	15	Lindsay Mitchell	7	Hardy	7	Myson	1
Ray Harris	11	Dave Anderson	5	Pilgrim	7	Rundle	1
Ken Adams	8	Stan Bradbury	3	Geddes	6	Lanfear	0

9 May — NATIONAL LEAGUE

EXETER 48				RAYLEIGH 35			
Slade	10	Geddes	5	Jack Unstead	9	Toby Boschoff	4
Pilgrim	9	Hardy	5	Percy Brine	6	Ron Howes	4
Gent	8	Myson	3	Pat Clarke	5	Charlie Mugford	2
Hodson	6	Herbie Plain	2	Jim Gregory	5	Vic Gooden	0

11 May — NATIONAL LEAGUE

TAMWORTH 55				EXETER 28			
Bill Dalton	12	Steve Langton	5	Gent	8	Myson	3
Basil Harris	10	Lionel Walling	5	Hodson	6	Geddes	2
Harry Saunders	9	Cecil Hookham	4	Hardy	6	Bill Horne	0
Peter Orpwood	8	Ray Beaumont	2	Pilgrim	3	Hoskin	0

12 May NATIONAL LEAGUE

OXFORD 51				EXETER 33			
Bert Croucher	12	Bill Downton	6	Pilgrim	8	Geddes	3
Dennis Gray	11	Jimmy Wright	3	Hardy	8	Noakes	3
Alf Viccary	9	Roy Court	2	Gent	7	Hodson	0
Ernie Rawlins	7	Alf Elliott	1	Myson	4	Hoskin	0

16 May WCQR

Jack Mountford	15	Roy Craighead	11	Vic Gent	7	Billy Baird	4
Len Read	13	Herbie King	9	Bertil Karlsson	7	Jack Arthur	3
Gil Blake	11	Ken LeBreton	9	Graham Hole	4	Jack Arnfield	2
George Craig	11	Bob Fletcher	7	Roy Moreton	4	Harry Long	2

23 May NATIONAL LEAGUE

EXETER 61				HASTINGS 23			
Clay	10	Hodson	7	Jock Grierson	6	Buddy Fuller	2
Gent	10	Slade	6½	Ken Middleditch	6	Ken Smith	1
Hardy	9	Geddes	6	Pete Mold	3	Ken Tidbury	1
Pilgrim	9	Myson	3½	Norman Street	3	Stan English	1

28 May NATIONAL LEAGUE

HANLEY/STOKE 52				EXETER 32			
Ray Harris	11	Frank Evans	6	Hardy	10	Slade	3
Les Jenkins	10	Ken Adams	3	Gent	6	Geddes	2
Gil Blake	10	Stan Bradbury	3	Pilgrim	5	Myson	2
Lindsay Mitchell	8	Johnny Fitzpatrick	1	Hodson	4	Clay	0

30 May CHALLENGE

EXETER 45				NORWICH 39			
Pilgrim	12	Myson	4	Bob Leverenz	12	Syd Littlewood	4
Hardy	10	Geddes	2	Phil Clarke	7	Ted Bravery	3
Slade	8	Hodson	2	Paddy Mills	7	Fred Rogers	0
Gent	5	Nicholls	2	Jack Freeman	6	Bert Spencer	0

6 June NATIONAL LEAGUE

EXETER 48				HANLEY 36			
Clay	8	Geddes	5	Les Jenkins	8	Ken Adams	4
Slade	8	Gent	5	Frank Evans	7	Ray Harris	3
Hodson	7	Pilgrim	5	Les Blake	6	Stan Bradbury	1
Hardy	6	Myson	4	Lindsay Mitchell	6	Johnny Fitzpatrick	1

7 June NATIONAL LEAGUE

LIVERPOOL 49				EXETER 35			
Harry Welch	11	Douglas Serrurier	7	Hodson	10	Geddes	3
Alex Gray	8	Fred Wills	5	Clay	8	Slade	3
Charlie Oates	7	Stan Bedford	3	Gent	5	Pilgrim	2
George Bason	7	Ron Burnett	1	Hardy	4	Myson	0

8 June NATIONAL LEAGUE

HALIFAX 49				EXETER 35			
Vic Emms	12	Jack Hughes	3	Hodson	9	Myson	4
Arthur Forrest	12	Jack Dawson	3	Hardy	8	Slade	2
Dick Seers	10	Eric Mason	3	Clay	7	Pilgrim	0
Bill Crossland	5	Jock Shead	1	Geddes	5	Gent	0

15 June NATIONAL LEAGUE

HASTINGS 48				EXETER 36			
Buddy Fuller	11	Ken Middleditch	4	Pilgrim	9	Lanfear	2
Ken Smith	11	George Butler	3	Hardy	8	Myson	2
Ron Clark	8	Harold Tapscott	3	Geddes	7	Ed Williams	2
Norman Street	6	Dan English	2	Clay	5	Slade	1

20 June NATIONAL LEAGUE

EXETER 48				HULL 36			
Clay	11	Geddes	5	Bob Baker	8	Derek Glover	5
Hardy	10	Williams	3	Alf Webster	7	George Craig	4
Pilgrim	9	Hoskin	2	Mick Mitchell	6	Jack Watts	1
Slade	6	Myson	2	Norman Johnson	5	Ken Allick	0

23 June NATIONAL LEAGUE

PLYMOUTH 51				EXETER 33			
Pete Lansdale	12	Ivan Kessell	6	Clay	9	Hoskin	2
Alan Smith	10	George Wall	5	Hardy	8	Myson	1
Peter Robinson	8	Bob Wigg	3	Geddes	6	Slade	1
Len Read	7	Johnny Bradford	0	Pilgrim	6	Williams	0

27 June
NATIONAL LEAGUE

EXETER 49				TAMWORTH 35			
Pilgrim	11	Slade	6	Harry Saunders	11	Steve Langton	4
Clay	11	Myson	3	Peter Orpwood	5	Bill Dalton	3
Geddes	8	Hoskin	1	Ray Beaumont	4	Cecil Hookham	2
Hardy	8	Williams	1	Basil Harris	4	Lional Watling	2

28 June
NATIONAL LEAGUE

YARMOUTH 59				EXETER 23			
Reg Morgan	12	Bert Rawlinson	5	Clay	8	Hoskin	2
Tip Mills	11	Stan Page	5	Pilgrim	5	Williams	1
Billy Bales	9	Johnny White	5	Hardy	4	Myson	0
Bill Carruthers	9	Cliff Ladbrooke	3	Geddes	3	Slade	0

5 July
NATIONAL LEAGUE

EXETER 45				POOLE 38			
Hardy	12	Pilgrim	6	Ernie Pawson	10	Peter Lloyd	3
Clay	8	Myson	5	Cyril Quick	8	Frank Holcombe	2
Geddes	6	Hoskins	2	Charlie Hayden	7	Ticker James	1
Lanfear	6			Alan Chambers	7	Ken James	0

11 July
NATIONAL LEAGUE

EXETER 36				HALIFAX 48			
Clay	8	Lanfear	3	Arthur Forrest	10	Al Allison	6
Pilgrim	8	Myson	3	Vic Emms	9	Bill Crossland	3
Hardy	6	Hoskin	2	Jock Shead	8	Jack Dawson	3
Geddes	4	Slade	2	Dick Seers	7	Jack Hughes	2

12 July
CHALLENGE

ST AUSTELL (The Badgers) 38				EXETER 46			
Mick Mitchell	12	Cecil Macey	3	Hardy	11	Pilgrim	7
George Craig	8	Adrian Kessell	2	Clay	9	Gent	1
Ken James	8	Des Tamblyn	2	Geddes	9	Bob Turner	1
Alan Chambers	3	Ken Blair	0	Lanfear	8	Myson	0

19 July
NATIONAL LEAGUE

EXETER 60				LIVERPOOL 24			
Hardy	12	Gent	7	Angus Maguire	7	Ern Steers	2
Pilgrim	10	Lanfear	7	Doug Serrurier	6	George Bason	1
Clay	9	Slade	6	Harry Welch	5	Fred Wills	0
Myson	8	Williams	1	Charlie Oates	3		

22 July
NATIONAL LEAGUE

LEICESTER 40				EXETER 43			
Cyril Page	8	Harwood Pike	4	Clay	11	Lanfear	4
Johnny Carpenter	7	Vic Pitcher	4	Hardy	9	Myson	4
Jack Baxter	6	George Gower	4	Geddes	5	Gent	4
Ron Wilson	5	Pedlar Palmer	2	Pilgrim	5	Slade	1

23 July
NATIONAL LEAGUE

HULL 40				EXETER 44			
Mick Mitchell	8	Alf Webster	4	Clay	11	Lanfear	5
Johnny Green	8	Jack Watts	3	Geddes	8	Gent	5
Bob Baker	7	Ken Allick	3	Hardy	7	Myson	1
Norman Johnson	6	George Craig	1	Pilgrim	6	Slade	1

25 July
NATIONAL LEAGUE

EXETER 53				TAMWORTH 31			
Hardy	12	Gent	4	Basil Harris	8	Ray Beaumont	1
Clay	10	Geddes	3	Steve Langton	8	Cecil Hookham	1
Pilgrim	10	Myson	3	Harry Saunders	7	Peter Orpwood	1
Lanfear	8	Slade	3	Bill Dalton	4	Lionel Watling	1

30 July
DEVON DERBY

EXETER 54				PLYMOUTH 29			
Clay	11	Gent	6	Pete Lansdale	10	Toby Boschoff	1
Hardy	10	Myson	6	Len Read	9	Ivan Kessell	1
Pilgrim	9	Lanfear	3	Peter Robinson	4	Geoff Woodger	1
Geddes	6	Slade	3	Alan Smith	2	Johnny Bradford	1

1 August
NATIONAL LEAGUE

EXETER 53				YARMOUTH 31			
Clay	12	Myson	6	Billy Bales	10	Fred Brand	2
Hardy	9	Slade	6	Bert Rawlinson	7	Stan Page	2
Pilgrim	7	Gent	5	Bill Carruthers	4	Joe Rodwell	1
Geddes	6	Lanfear	2	Tip Mills	4	Reg Morgan	1

6 August
CHALLENGE

SWINDON 42				EXETER 41			
Harry Hughes	10	Tom Wilson	5	Hardy	12	Noakes	4
Reg Lambourne	9	Bonny Good	3	Pilgrim	11	Hancox	2
Bill Downton	7	Ginger Nicholls	2	Salde	6	Ed Williams	1
Norman Meek	5	Mike Collett	1	Hoskins	5	Bob Turner	0

8 August
NATIONAL LEAGUE

EXETER 52				HASTINGS 31			
Clay	12	Lanfear	5	Ken Middleditch	10	George Butler	2
Geddes	10	Gent	4	Jock Grierson	8	Dave English	2
Hardy	8	Pilgrim	3	Harold Tapscott	3	KenTidbury	2
Myson	8	Slade	2	Norman Street	3	Ken Smith	1

10 August
NATIONAL LEAGUE

TAMWORTH 55				EXETER 28			
Peter Orpwood	10	Cecil Hookham	7	Clay	8	Gent	2
Harry Saunders	10	Lionel Watling	6	Hardy	8	Myson	2
Basil Harris	9	Bill Dalton	3	Pilgrim	4	Slade	1
Steve Langton	7	Ray Beaumont	3	Geddes	3	Lanfear	0

13 August
NATIONAL LEAGUE

RAYLEIGH 42				EXETER 40			
Jim Gregory	11	Les McGillivray	5	Clay	11	Myson	4
Jack Unstead	8	Wally Mawdsley	3	Hardy	9	Lanfear	3
Vic Gooden	7	Peter Clarke	2	Pilgrim	6	Noakes	2
Ron Howes	5	Percy Brine	1	Geddes	5	Gent	0

15 August
NATIONAL LEAGUE

EXETER 47				PLYMOUTH 36			
Hardy	12	Geddes	5	Len Read	10	Alan Smith	2
Clay	12	Gent	5	Pete Lansdale	9	Toby Boschoff	2
Pilgrim	6	Hoskins	2	Peter Robinson	7	Geoff Woodger	1
Myson	5	Slade	0	George Wall	5	Johnny Bradford	0

18 August
NATIONAL LEAGUE

OXFORD 41				EXETER 42			
Dennis Gray	11	Bill Reynolds	4	Clay	12	Myson	4
Bob MacFarlane	10	Ernie Rawlins	3	Hardy	9	Pilgrim	1
Alf Viccary	5	Jimmy wright	2	Geddes	9	Noakes	0
Frank Boyle	4	Peter Lloyd	2	Gent	7	Hoskins	0

22 August
NATIONAL LEAGUE

EXETER 57				LEICESTER 27			
Clay	12	Myson	5	Harwood Pike	7	Vic Pitcher	3
Geddes	12	Gent	3	Cyril Page	6	Jack Baxter	2
Hardy	12	Lanfear	3	Sid Hipperson	4	George Gower	1
Pilgrim	8	Hoskin	2	Ron Wilson	4	Johnny Carpenter	0

29 August
NATIONAL LEAGUE

EXETER 60				RAYLEIGH 24			
Clay	11	Lanfear	7	Pat Clarke	10	Jim Gregory	2
Geddes	10	Gent	6	Jack Unstead	4	Doug Ibles	2
Hardy	10	Myson	6	Les McGillivray	3	Ron Howes	0
Pilgrim	9	Hoskin	1	Vic Gordon	3	Wally Mawdsley	0

31 August
NATIONAL LEAGUE

HASTINGS 44				EXETER 40			
Ken Middleditch	12	George Butler	4	Clay	11	Gent	4
Jock Grierson	11	Harold McNaughton	3	Hardy	9	Myson	1
Dave English	5	Ken Smith	2	Geddes	8	Hancox	0
Norman Street	5	Harold Tapscott	2	Pilgrim	7	Hoskin	0

3 September
NATIONAL LEAGUE

HANLEY 50				EXETER 34			
Lindsay Mitchell	10	Bill Harris	7	Hardy	8	Gent	4
Ken Adams	8	Johnny Fitzpatrick	4	Clay	8	Pilgrim	3
Gil Blake	8	Stan Bradbury	4	Myson	5	Hoskin	1
Les Jenkins	8	Ray Harris	1	Geddes	5	Lanfear	0

5 September
NATIONAL LEAGUE

EXETER 52				OXFORD 30			
Hardy	9	Pilgrim	7	Bob McFarlane	9	Alf Viccary	3
Clay	9	Lanfear	6	Jim Boyle	8	Jack Peck	1
Geddes	7	Myson	4	Jim Coy	5	Bill Reynolds	1
Gent	7	Hoskin	3	Ernie Rawlins	3	Bill Kemp	0

12 September BEST PAIRS

FLEETWOOD 22		CRADLEY HEATH 22		YARMOUTH 20		HALIFAX 19	
Wilf Plant	12	Alan Hunt	13	Tip Mills	11	Vic Emms	14
George Newton	10	Eric Williams	9	Reg Morgan	9	Arthur Forrest	5
HASTINGS 18		**BRISTOL 16**		**TAMWORTH 8**			
Ken Middleditch	14	Jack Mountford	14	Harry Saunders	6		
Jock Grierson	4	Eric Salmon	2	Cecil Hookham	2		

12 September NATIONAL LEAGUE

POOLE 45				EXETER 39			
Ticker James	12	Frank Holcombe	3	Clay	10	Lanfear	3
Fred Pawson	10	Terry Small	3	Geddes	9	Pilgrim	3
Cyril Quick	8	Charlie Hayden	2	Hardy	9	Hoskin	1
Dick Howard	7	Dave Anderson	0	Myson	4	Gent	0

19 September NATIONAL LEAGUE

EXETER 42				HALIFAX 41			
Hardy	11	Gent	3	Dick Seers	8	Bill Crossland	5
Pilgrim	10	Lanfear	2	Al Allison	7	Jack Dawson	5
Clay	9	Hoskin	1	Arthur Forrest	7	Jack Hughes	2
Geddes	6	Myson	0	Vic Emms	6	Ken Brown	1

26 September NATIONAL LEAGUE

EXETER 58				SWINDON 26			
Clay	10	Gent	8	George Craig	9	Reg Lambourne	2
Myson	10	Pilgrim	8	Bob Jones	8	Harry Hughes	1
Hardy	9	Hoskin	3	Derek Glover	3	Mick Mitchell	1
Geddes	8	Rusty Russell	2	Bill Downton	2	Paul Best	0

27 September NATIONAL LEAGUE

YARMOUTH 51				EXETER 33			
Billy Bales	12	Fred Brand	4	Clay	9	Lanfear	3
Bill Carruthers	12	Johnny White	4	Geddes	8	Pilgrim	2
Tip Mills	11	Stan Page	2	Hardy	7	Myson	1
Reg Morgan	5	Bert Rawlinson	1	Gent	3	Hoskin	0

3 October NATIONAL LEAGUE

EXETER 32				HANLEY 52			
Clay	6	Geddes	4	Bill Harris	12	Les Jenkins	6
Lanfear	6	Myson	4	Lindsay Mitchell	10	Frank Evans	3
Hardy	5	Russell	2	Ken Adams	8	Ray Harris	3
Pilgrim	5	Gent	0	Gil Blake	7	Brian Pritchett	3

10 October NATIONAL LEAGUE

POOLE 46				EXETER 38			
Dick Howard	12	Terry Small	4	Clay	11	Pilgrim	3
Fred Pawson	11	Roy Bartlett	2	Geddes	9	Myson	2
Cyril Quick	9	Charlie Hayden	2	Hardy	9	Gent	1
Fred Holcombe	5	Frank Wheeler	1	Lanfear	3	Russell	0

11 October NATIONAL LEAGUE

EXETER 57				LIVERPOOL 27			
Clay	12	Myson	6	Charlie Oates	9	Angus Maguire	3
Hardy	11	Pilgrim	6	Alex Gray	5	Stan Bedford	2
Geddes	10	Gent	2	Doug Serrurier	4	Percy Brine	0
Lanfear	9	Russell	1	Harry Welch	4	Reg Duval	0

13 October DEVON DERBY

PLYMOUTH 57				EXETER 26			
George Wall	12	Peter Robinson	8	Geddes	8	Slade	2
Len Read	11	Ivan Kessell	3	Myson	6	Gent	1
Alan Smith	10	Bob Wigg	3	Hardy	5	Lanfear	0
Johnny Bradford	8	Pete Lansdale	2	Pilgrim	4	Russell	0

15 October NATIONAL LEAGUE

SWINDON 56				EXETER 28			
George Craig	12	Derek Glover	7	Hardy	9	Gent	1
Bob Jones	10	Reg Lambourne	6	Pilgrim	8	Russell	1
Bill Downton	8	Harry Hughes	3	Geddes	7	Slade	0
Alf Webster	8	Tom Wilson	2	Myson	2		

17 October FROUD TROPHY

Harry Saunders	15	George Craig	9	Goog Hoskin	5	Ernie Noakes	1
Arthur Pilgrim	14	Bill Harris	9	Vic Gent	3	Peter Robinson	1
Lindsay Mitchell	12	Hugh Geddes	8	Alan Kidd	3	Don Hardy	0
Ken Middleditch	10	Bob Jones	8	Rusty Russell	2		
Johnny Myson	10	Broncho Slade	7	Ken Tidbury	2		

Broncho Slade.

Rusty Russell.

STATISTICS 1950

28 March CHALLENGE	ST AUSTELL 43				EXETER 41			
	Maurie McDermott	11	Larry Young	5	Arthur Pilgrim	11	Ted Moore	4
	Ken James	9	Norman Street	3	Don Hardy	9	Vic Gent	3
	George Gower	7	Rusty Wainwright	2	Hugh Geddes	7	Bill Grimes	2
	Alf Viccary	5	Broncho Slade	1	Goog Hoskin	4	Johnny Myson	1

31 March CHALLENGE	EXETER 53				ST AUSTELL 30			
	Don Hardy	11	Hugh Geddes	6	Norman Street	11	Alf Viccary	3
	Vic Gent	9	Ted Moore	6	George Gower	4	Ken James	3
	Arthur Pilgrim	9	Goog Hoskin	2	Larry Young	4	Broncho Slade	1
	Johnny Myson	8	Bill Grimes	2	Maurie McDermott	3	Rusty Wainwright	1

3 April NATIONAL LEAGUE	POOLE 43				EXETER 41			
	Cyril Quick	11	Ernie Noakes	5	Hardy	9	Hoskin	2
	Dick Howard	8	Frank Wheeler	3	Pilgrim	9	Walsh	2
	Charlie Hayden	6	Roy Bartlett	3	Geddes	9	Moore	2
	Terry Small	5	George Wall	2	Gent	8	Myson	0

7 April NATIONAL TROPHY	LEICESTER 66				EXETER 42			
	Harwood Pike	17	Jack Watts	7	Hardy	14	Gent	5
	Cyril Page	10	Ron Wilson	7	Pilgrim	9	Hoskin	3
	Johnnie Carpenter	9	Vic Pitcher	6	Moore	6	Myson	0
	Pedlar Palmer	8	Sid Hipperson	2	Geddes	5	Walsh	0

8 April CHALLENGE

OXFORD 52				EXETER 32			
Eric Irons	9	Frank Boyle	6	Geddes	10	Gent	2
Bob McFarlane	8	Jimmy Wright	6	Hardy	8	Pilgrim	2
Bill Kemp	8	Pat Clarke	5	Hoskin	6	Grimes	1
Buster Brown	6	Ernie Rawlins	4	Myson	3	Walsh	0

10 April NATIONAL TROPHY

EXETER 65				LEICESTER 41			
Hardy	18	Pilgrim	6	Cyril Page	9	Ron Wilson	5
Geddes	11	Myson	6	Vic Pitcher	7	Jack Watts	3
Gent	11	Walsh	6	Pedlar Palmer	6	Sid Hipperson	3
Moore	7	Hoskin	0	Harwood Pike	6	Johnny Carpenter	2

14 April NATIONAL LEAGUE

EXETER 46				SWINDON 38			
Hardy	12	Myson	6	Ron Clark	8	Alex Gray	2
Geddes	8	Gent	4	George Craig	8	Mick Mitchell	2
Pilgrim	8	Walsh	1	Bob Jones	7	Reg Lambourne	4
Moore	6	Jack Bedkober	1	Danny Malone	7	Bill Downton	0

15 April NATIONAL LEAGUE

SWINDON 54				EXETER 30			
Mick Mitchell	11	Ron Clark	6	Hardy	11	Myson	1
George Craig	9	Reg Lambourne	6	Pilgrim	7	Bedkober	1
Bob Jones	9	Danny Malone	4	Gent	6	Moore	1
Alex Gray	8	Bill Downton	1	Walsh	3		

17 April NATIONAL TROPHY

EXETER 62				LEICESTER 45			
Hardy	18	Gent	4	Vic Pitcher	9	Cyril Page	5
Geddes	13	Myson	4	Harwood Pike	8	Jack Winstanley	5
Pilgrim	12	Hoskin	2	Ron Wilson	7	Jack Watts	3
Moore	9	Walsh	0	Johnny Carpenter	6	Pedlar Palmer	2

21 April FALCON TROPHY

George Craig	14	Mick Mitchell	11	Herbie Plain	7	Rusty Russell	3
Norman Street	12	Ray Ellis	9	Jack Bedkober	6	Bob Turner	3
Bill Downton	11	Cyril Quick	9	Goog Hoskin	6	Bob Emery	0
Ken Middleditch	11	Dick Howard	8	Ken James	4	George Wall	0
				Paul Best	3	Reg Robins	0

21 April NATIONAL TROPHY

LEICESTER 53				EXETER 55			
Harwood Pike	15	Jack Watts	5	Hardy	15	Gent	7
Jock Grierson	14	Ron Wilson	4	Geddes	13	Moore	3
Johnny Carpenter	6	Vic Pitcher	3	Pilgrim	8	Grimes	2
Cyril Page	6	Pedlar Palmer	0	Walsh	7	Myson	0

25 April CHALLENGE

ST AUSTELL 29				EXETER 31			
Ken James	9	Ray Ellis	3	Hardy	9	Gent	3
Norman Street	5	Maurie McDermott	2	Moore	8	Walsh	2
Rusty Wainwright	5	George Gower	1	Geddes	6	Bedkober	0
Larry Young	3	Peter Moore	1	Pilgrim	3	Grimes	0

(Abandoned after 10 heats due to rain)

27 April NATIONAL TROPHY

OXFORD 83				EXETER 24			
Eric Irons	18	Frank Boyle	10	Hoskin	5	Pilgrim	3
Pat Clarke	15	Jimmy Wright	9	Geddes	4	Gent	3
Bob MacFarlane	12	Ernie Rawlins	5	Hardy	4	Grimes	2
Buster Brown	11	Bill Kemp	3	Moore	3	Walsh	0

28 April NATIONAL LEAGUE

EXETER 35				OXFORD 49			
Hardy	12	Myson	2	Frank Boyle	9	Eric Irons	6
Geddes	7	Walsh	2	Pat Clarke	9	Jimmy Wright	5
Pilgrim	6	Gent	1	Bob MacFarlane	8	Buster Brown	3
Moore	4	Bedkober	1	Bill Kemp	6	Ernie Rawlins	3

5 May NATIONAL TROPHY

EXETER 54				OXFORD 53			
Hardy	15	Moore	6	Ernie Rawlins	15	Bob MacFarlane	4
Pilgrim	13	Myson	3	Pat Clarke	11	Eric Irons	3
Walsh	9	Bedkober	2	Jimmy Wright	10	Buster Brown	1
Geddes	6	Gent	0	Frank Boyle	8	Bill Kemp	1

10 May
NATIONAL LEAGUE

ALDERSHOT 55				EXETER 29			
Basil Harris	12	Joe Rodwell	6	Gent	10	Grimes	3
Trevor Redmond	11	Bob Bunney	5	Hardy	5	Bedkober	2
Doug Ibele	8	Bob Harrison	3	Moore	5	Geddes	0
Pat Flanagan	7	Doug Papworth	3	Pilgrim	4	Walsh	0

11 May
NATIONAL LEAGUE

OXFORD 49				EXETER 35			
Frank Boyle	10	Bill Kemp	7	Hardy	12	Walsh	5
Pat Clarke	8	Ernie Rawlins	4	Geddes	6	Myson	1
Eric Irons	8	Jimmy Wright	2	Gent	6	Hoskin	0
Buster Brown	8	Ron Carvill	2	Moore	5	Grimes	0

12 May
CHALLENGE

EXETER 33				SOUTHAMPTON 50			
Walsh	9	Moore	3	Roy Craighead	11	Bill Griffiths	5
Geddes	7	Myson	3	Steve Langton	10	Bob Oakley	5
Hardy	6	Plain	2	Tom Oakley	8	Phil Bishop	3
Gent	3	Grimes	0	Jimmy Squibb	6	Buck Whitby	2

19 May
NATIONAL LEAGUE

EXETER 41				LEICESTER 42			
Gent	11	Walsh	5	Jock Grierson	11	Vic Pitcher	4
Hardy	8	Moore	2	Harwood Pike	9	Cyril Page	3
Pilgrim	7	Myson	2	Joe Bowkis	7	Ron Wilson	2
Geddes	5	Bedkober	1	Johnny Carpenter	5	Lionel Benson	1

26 May
NATIONAL LEAGUE

EXETER 58				LIVERPOOL 25			
Hardy	12	Geddes	9	Reg Duval	5	Alf Webster	3
Gent	11	Bedkober	3	Buddy Fuller	5	Harry Welch	3
Pilgrim	10	Moore	3	Angus McGuire	5	Stan Bedford	1
Walsh	10	Alf Kaines	0	Percy Brine	3	Derek Glover	0

29 May
CHALLENGE

EXETER 41				PLYMOUTH 43			
Geddes	10	Walsh	3	Pete Lansdale	11	Alan Smith	4
Hardy	9	Gent	3	Len Read	10	George Wall	2
Pilgrim	9	Kaines	2	Peter Robinson	9	Bill Thatcher	1
Moore	4	Myson	1	Cecil Bailey	5	Johnny Bradford	1

2 June
NATIONAL LEAGUE

EXETER 60				ST AUSTELL 24			
Hardy	12	Walsh	7	Norman Street	7	Ken James	1
Gent	12	Myson	6	Ray Ellis	6	Bill Sobey	1
Pilgrim	8	Moore	4	John Yates	5	Harold Bull	0
Geddes	8	Bedkober	3	Ed Williams	4	Maurie McDermott	0

4 June
CHALLENGE
IN DUBLIN

SHELBOURNE TIGERS 57				EXETER 49			
Jack Wright	17	Jim Gregory	3	Hardy	11	Myson	4
Ronnie Moore	12	Les Moore	3	Moore	9	Walsh	4
Dick Harris	11	Reg Trott	1	Geddes	8	Bedkober	3
Barry Pickering	9	Rod Landrum	1	Pilgrim	8	Gent	2

5 June
NATIONAL LEAGUE

LIVERPOOL 47				EXETER 35			
Harry Welch	9	Alf Webster	6	Geddes	10	Walsh	3
Reg Duval	8	Derek Glover	5	Hardy	9	Bedkober	2
Doug Serrier	7	Stan Bedford	3	Gent	4	Pilgrim	2
Percy Brine	6	Buddy Fuller	3	Moore	4	Myson	1

7 June
NATIONAL LEAGUE

TAMWORTH 51				EXETER 32			
Lionel Watling	12	Eric Boothroyd	6	Hardy	7	Gent	3
Brian Wilson	12	John Hutchings	4	Geddes	8	Myson	2
Cecil Hookham	7	Ivor Davies	3	Pilgrim	5	Alf Kaines	2
Brian Shepherd	7	Laurie Schofield	0	Bedkober	4	Moore	1

9 June
NATIONAL LEAGUE

EXETER 55				TAMWORTH 29			
Hardy	12	Bedkober	5	Eric Boothroyd	8	Cecil Hookham	2
Pilgrim	11	Gent	5	Brian Wilson	7	Brian Shepherd	2
Geddes	9	Moore	5	Lionel Watling	6	Ivor Davies	0
Walsh	6	Myson	2	Laurie Schofield	4	John Hitchings	0

16 June
WCQR

Bob MacFarlane	14	Willie Wilson	10	Ron Howes	5	John Dore	2
Tommy Miller	13	Eskil Carlsson	8	Brian Pritchett	5	Goog Hoskin	2
Pat Clarke	12	Bill Carruthers	8	Maurie McDermott	4	Bob Geary	0
Harwood Pike	10	Cyril Quick	7	Les Tolley	4	Johnny Sargeant	0
Jack Unstead	10	Pat Flanagan	5				

23 June
NATIONAL LEAGUE

EXETER 45				POOLE 39			
Hardy	11	Bedkober	5	Ken Middleditch	11	Frank Wheeler	4
Pilgrim	10	Walsh	3	Ticker James	9	Charlie Hayden	3
Geddes	6	Moore	3	Cyril Quick	5	Dick Howard	2
Gent	6	Bill Downton	1	Alan Kidd	4	Tony Lewis	1

24 June
NATIONAL LEAGUE

RAYLEIGH 50				EXETER 34			
Jack Unstead	11	Charlie Mugford	4	Geddes	9	Walsh	3
Les McGillivray	10	Gerald Jackson	3	Hardy	7	Bedkober	2
Vic Gooden	10	Ted O'Connor	2	Pilgrim	7	Gent	0
Ron Howes	9	Ted Argall	1	Moore	6	Bill Downton	0

30 June
GRAND TRIANGULAR CONTEST

OXFORD 40		SWINDON 25		ALDERSHOT 29	
Bob MacFarlane	12	Mick Mitchell	10	Trevor Redmond	9
Frank Boyle	11	Ron Clarke	6	Basil Harris	9
Eric Irons	11	George Craig	5	Pat Flanagan	6
Pat Clarke	6	Bob Jones	4	Doug Ibele	5

30 June
NATIONAL LEAGUE

LEICESTER 48				EXETER 35			
Cyril Page	12	Jack Watts	6	Hardy	10	Downton	2
Jock Grierson	7	Les Beaumont	6	Geddes	10	Gent	2
Sid Hipperson	7	Ron Wilson	4	Pilgrim	5	Bedkober	1
Joe Bowkis	6	Lionel Benson	0	Moore	5	Walsh	0

7 July
CHALLENGE

EXETER 48				KEN LE BRETON'S TEAM 35			
Hardy	9	Pilgrim	6	Sune Karlsson	12	Jonhnny Sargeant	3
Gent	8	Walsh	5	Ken Le Breton	9	Bob Legge	2
Arthur Forrest	8	Downton	4	Lindsay Mitchell	4	Len Williams	1
Bedkober	8	Moore	0	Goog Hoskin	3	Jack Summers	1

11 July
NATIONAL LEAGUE

ST AUSTELL 52				EXETER 31			
Norman Street	12	Ray Ellis	6	Moore	9	Downton	1
Harold Bull	9	Ed Williams	5	Geddes	9	Bedkober	1
Bill Sobey	8	John Yates	3	Hardy	6	Gent	0
Ken James	7	Maurie McDermott	2	Walsh	5	Sargeant	0

14 July
NATIONAL LEAGUE

EXETER 52				LEICESTER 31			
Moore	12	Geddes	7	Les Beaumont	9	Cyril Page	4
Pilgrim	9	Sargeant	7	Jock Grierson	7	Joe Bowkis	2
Gent	9	Bedkober	0	Ron Wilson	4	Johnnie Carpenter	1
Walsh	8	Downton	0	Lionel Benson	4	Sid Hipperson	0

17 July
NATIONAL LEAGUE

POOLE 56				EXETER 28			
Ticker James	11	Frank Wheeler	7	Geddes	10	Pilgrim	3
Ken Middleditch	9	Terry Small	6	Sargeant	3	Moore	3
Tony Lewis	9	Dick Howard	4	Walsh	3	Gent	2
Cyril Quick	9	Charlie Hayden	1	Bedkober	3	Hoskin	1

19 July
NATIONAL LEAGUE

ALDERSHOT 53				EXETER 31			
Basil Harris	12	Doug Papworth	7	Geddes	7	Walsh	4
Doug Ibele	11	Ivor Powell	4	Moore	7	Pilgrim	2
Trevor Redmond	9	Ken Smith	2	Hoskin	5	Bedkober	1
Joe Rodwell	7	Pat Flanagan	1	Gent	5	Sargeant	0

20 July
NATIONAL LEAGUE

OXFORD 61				EXETER 23			
Harry Saunders	12	Bill Kemp	8	Pilgrim	7	Hoskin	2
Eric Irons	10	Bob McFarlane	8	Geddes	6	Gent	0
Pat Clarke	9	Buster Brown	3	Moore	6	Sargeant	0
Frank Boyle	9	Ernie Rawlins	2	Bedkober	2	Walsh	0

21 July — NATIONAL LEAGUE

EXETER 51				ALDERSHOT 33			
Geddes	12	Pilgrim	6	Trevor Redmond	11	Ken Smith	3
Bedkober	8	Gent	4	Ivor Powell	7	Joe Rodwell	1
Moore	7	Hoskin	4	Basil Harris	6	Doug Papworth	1
Walsh	7	Sargeant	3	Doug Ibele	4	Pat Flanagan	0

27 July — CHALLENGE

LONG EATON 39				EXETER 45			
Frank Malouf	12	Eric Mason	4	Wigg	9	Walsh	5
Pedlar Palmer	9	Fred Siggins	3	Gent	8	Hoskin	4
Eric Minall	5	Bob Ibbotson	2	Moore	8	Pilgrim	3
Basil Humphries	4	Russell Davey	0	Bedkober	7	Sargeant	1

28 July — NATIONAL LEAGUE

EXETER 48				OXFORD 36			
Walsh	12	Moore	4	Bob MacFarlane	9	Harry Saunders	4
Bedkober	9	Wigg	3	Eric Irons	6	Bill Kemp	2
Pilgrim	7	Gent	3	Ernie Rawlins	6	Buster Brown	2
Hoskin	7	Sargeant	3	Pat Clarke	5	Frank Boyle	2

1 August — NATIONAL LEAGUE

ST AUSTELL 50				EXETER 34			
Harold Bull	12	Bill Sobey	5	Bedkober	11	Sargeant	2
Norman Street	11	John Yates	4	Hoskin	7	Larry Young	2
Ken James	7	Maurie McDermott	2	Pilgrim	6	Moore	0
Ray Ellis	7	Ed Williams	2	Walsh	6	Gent	0

4 August — NATIONAL LEAGUE

EXETER 42				POOLE 42			
Walsh	11	Sargeant	5	Charlie Hayden	11	Tony Lewis	3
Pilgrim	9	Hoskin	2	Ken Middleditch	10	Dick Howard	2
Bedkober	9	Gent	1	Cyril Quick	9	Terry Small	2
Moore	5	Larry Young	0	Alan Kidd	4	George Wall	1

5 August — NATIONAL LEAGUE

SWINDON 53				EXETER 30			
Bob Jones	12	George Craig	7	Walsh	9	Sargeant	4
Hugh Geddes	10	Reg Lambourne	2	Pilgrim	5	Gent	2
Alex Gray	10	Danny Malone	2	Bedkober	4	Moore	2
Frank Evans	9	Ron Clark	1	Hoskin	4	Young	0

7 August — NATIONAL LEAGUE

EXETER 36				SWINDON 48			
Walsh	9	Hoskin	5	Hugh Geddes	12	Reg Lambourne	5
Gent	7	Sargeant	2	Frank Evans	10	Bob Jones	4
Moore	6	Young	2	Danny Malone	9	Alex Gray	1
Pilgrim	5	Russell	0	George Craig	7	Tom Wilson	0

11 August — NATIONAL LEAGUE

EXETER 52				ST AUSTELL 32			
Walsh	9	Hardy	6	Norman Street	11	Maurice McDermott	1
Pilgrim	8	Bedkober	5	Harold Bull	7	Max Rech	1
Moore	8	Slade	5	John Yates	6	Ken James	1
Gent	7	Sargeant	4	Ray Ellis	5	Bill Sobey	0

18 August — NATIONAL LEAGUE

EXETER 63				RAYLEIGH 21			
Gent	12	Pilgrim	7	Oz Osborne	5	Ron Howes	3
Walsh	11	Hoskin	6	Frank Bettis	4	Gerald Jackson	1
Hardy	10	Bedkober	5	Vic Godden	4	Mike Wood	0
Moore	8	Broncho Slade	4	Jack Unstead	4	Charlie Mugford	0

24 August — DEVON DERBY

PLYMOUTH 44				EXETER 40			
George Wall	10	Bill Thatcher	4	Hardy	10	Moore	4
Pete Lansdale	10	Alan Smith	2	Walsh	7	Pilgrim	3
Len Read	10	Johnny Bradford	1	Gent	6	Hoskin	3
Peter Robinson	7	Wally Mawdsley	0	Bedkober	5	Sargeant	2

25 August — NATIONAL LEAGUE

LEICESTER 59				EXETER 25			
Harwood Pike	12	Jock Grierson	6	Gent	9	Pilgrim	2
Lionel Benson	11	Joe Bowkis	5	Hardy	7	Walsh	2
Les Beaumont	11	Ron Wilson	4	Moore	2	Sargeant	1
Cyril Page	8	Johnnie Carpenter	2	Bedkober	2	Hoskin	0

26 August NATIONAL LEAGUE

RAYLEIGH 41				EXETER 43			
Frank Bettis	10	Vic Gooden	3	Walsh	9	Hoskin	4
Ron Howes	10	Jack Unstead	3	Hardy	9	Pilgrim	3
Les McGillivray	9	Charlie Mugford	2	Gent	7	Sargeant	3
Gerald Jackson	4	Oz Osborne	0	Bedkober	6	Moore	2

1 September NATIONAL LEAGUE

EXETER 66				LIVERPOOL 18			
Walsh	11	Sargeant	8	Harry Welch	6	Doug Serrurier	1
Gent	10	Bedkober	8	Bill Griffiths	4	Derek Glover	1
Pilgrim	9	Moore	6	Percy Brine	4	Alf Webster	0
Hardy	9	Slade	5	Reg Duval	2	Arthur Bush	0

4 September NATIONAL LEAGUE

EXETER 65				TAMWORTH 19			
Gent	12	Hardy	8	Lionel Watling	7	Cecil Hookham	1
Pilgrim	11	Hoskin	7	Ivor Davies	5	Ray Beaumont	1
Bedkober	10	Moore	4	Harry Bastable	3	John Hitchings	0
Walsh	9	Slade	4	Dick Tolley	2	Geoff Newman	0

7 September (AT PLYMOUTH)

DEVON & CORNWALL 39				HANTS & WILTS 45			
Don Hardy	9	Jack Bedkober	5	Alex Gray	9	Trevor Redmond	6
Ken Walsh	9	Vic Gent	3	Frank Evans	9	Doug Ibele	3
Norman Street	6	Harold Bull	1	Hugh Geddes	9	Danny Malone	3
John Yates	6	Wally Mawdsley	0	Basil Harris	6	Doug Papworth	0

11 September NATIONAL LEAGUE

LIVERPOOL 43				EXETER 40			
Bill Griffiths	9	Derek Glover	5	Hardy	12	Gent	3
Harry Welch	9	Percy Brine	3	Pilgrim	8	Moore	3
Reg Duval	7	Arthur Bush	3	Walsh	8	Sargeant	1
Doug Serrurier	5	Alf Webster	2	Bedkober	4	Hoskin	1

13 September NATIONAL LEAGUE

TAMWORTH 38				EXETER 46			
Dick Tolley	10	Cecil Hookham	3	Hoskin	11	Walsh	6
Lionel Watling	9	Ray Beaumont	1	Hardy	8	Gent	4
Ivor Davies	9	John Hitchings	1	Pilgrim	7	Sargeant	3
Harry Bastable	5	Geoff Newman	0	Bedkober	6	Moore	1

15 September NATIONAL LEAGUE

EXETER 61				ALDERSHOT 23			
Gent	11	Moore	6	Trevor Redmond	10	Doug Papworth	2
Bedkober	11	Hoskin	5	Doug Ible	4	Bill Grimes	1
Hardy	10	Pilgrim	5	Basil Harris	3	Ron Burnett	0
Walsh	9	Sargeant	4	Ivor Powell	3	Joe Rodwell	0

18 September DEVON DERBY

EXETER 54				PLYMOUTH 30			
Walsh	12	Hoskin	6	Pete Lansdale	11	George Wall	2
Hardy	8	Bedkober	6	Len Read	8	Bill Holden	0
Pilgrim	7	Sargeant	5	Peter Robinson	6	Dennis Hayles	0
Gent	6	Moore	4	Alan Smith	3	Wally Mawdsley	0

25 September NATIONAL LEAGUE

EXETER 27				RAYLEIGH 14			
Hoskin	7	Pilgrim	1	Jack Unstead	4	Frank Bettis	2
Gent	6	Bedkober	1	Ron Howes	3	Vic Gooden	0
Hardy	6	Moore	1	Gerald Jackson	3	Oz Osborne	0
Walsh	5	Sargeant	dnr	Tom O'Connor	2	Mike Wood	dnr

Abandoned after heat 7

2 October CHALLENGE

EXETER 48				OXFORD 36			
Gent	9	Sargeant	6	Pat Clarke	10	Harry Saunders	4
Walsh	9	Moore	4	Eric Irons	9	Bob MacFarlane	2
Hardy	8	Pilgrim	3	Ernie Rawlins	7	Brian Wilson	0
Bedkober	7	Hoskin	2	Bill Osborne	4	Buster Brown	0

9 October NATIONAL LEAGUE

EXETER 55				RAYLEIGH 29			
Bedkober	11	Moore	7	Gerald Jackson	9	Mike Wood	3
Gent	11	Walsh	5	Jack Unstead	7	Oz Osborne	2
Pilgrim	8	Sargeant	5	Frank Bettis	3	Charlie Mugford	1
Hardy	7	Hoskin	1	Tom O'Connor	3	Ron Howes	1

STATISTICS 1951

26 March CHALLENGE	EXETER 42				SWINDON 37			
	Vic Gent	10	Ted Moore	4	Buster Brown	7	Danny Malone	5
	Don Hardy	8	Jack Bedkober	4	Frank Evans	7	Reg Lambourne	4
	Goog Hoskin	6	Bob Roger	3	Ron Clark	5	Dennis Newton	3
	Johnny Sargeant	5	Paul Best	2	Hugh Geddes	5	Ken Wiggins	1

2 April NATIONAL TROPHY	EXETER 77				PLYMOUTH 30			
	B Roger	16	Sargeant	11	Alan Smith	12	Johnny Bradford	2
	Hardy	14	Rusty Russell	7	George Wall	6	Denis Hayles	1
	Gent	12	Best	6	Brian Hitchcock	5	Bill Thatcher	1
	Moore	11			Broncho Slade	3	Ray Thackwell	0

5 April NATIONAL TROPHY	PLYMOUTH 54				EXETER 54			
	Alan Smith	16	Denis Hayles	5	Sargeant	14	Best	5
	George Wall	14	Broncho Slade	3	Hardy	10	Bedkober	3
	Johnny Bradford	8	Brian Hitchcock	1	Moore	10	Roger	3
	Bill Thatcher	7	Ray Thackwell	0	Gent	6	Russell	3

7 April FESTIVAL OF BRITAIN TROPHY	ALDERSHOT 89				EXETER 30			
	Basil Harris	15	Bob Harrison	9	Roger	6	Best	3
	Trevor Redmond	14	Pat Flanagan	5	Sargeant	5	Legge	3
	Ivor Powell	13	Johnnie Dore	5	Moore	4	Russell	2
	Geoff Mardon	12	Bill Grimes	3	Hardy	3	Bedkober	1
	Doug Papworth	11	Joe Rodwell	2	Gent	3	Sparkes	0

9 April FESTIVAL OF BRITAIN TROPHY	EXETER 71				ALDERSHOT 47			
	Sargeant	13	Russell	7	Trevor Redmond	9	Bill Grimes	4
	Hardy	11	Gent	6	Geoff Mardon	9	Basil Harris	2
	Moore	11	Ivan Sparkes	2	Ivor Powell	7	John Dore	2
	Best	11	Bob Legge	0	Bob Harrison	7	Doug Papworth	0
	B Roger	10			Pat Flanagan	7		

14 April NATIONAL TROPHY	RAYLEIGH 56				EXETER 52			
	Ron Howes	17	Tom O'Connor	5	Sargeant	12	Hoskin	6
	Maurie Dunn	12	Gerald Jackson	3	Hardy	10	Bedkober	5
	Les McGillivray	9	Oz Osborne	2	Moore	9	Roger	3
	Frank Bettis	7	Geoff Woodger	1	Gent	7	Russell	0

16 April NATIONAL TROPHY	EXETER 73				RAYLEIGH 35			
	Gent	17	Moore	9	Gerald Jackson	11	Geoff Woodger	4
	Hardy	13	Sargeant	6	Maurie Dunn	7	Oz Osborne	2
	Roger	12	Bedkober	4	Tom O'Connor	6	Vic Gooden	0
	Hoskin	11	Russell	1	Frank Bettis	5	Ron Howes	0

21 April NATIONAL TROPHY	SWINDON 47				EXETER 61			
	Hugh Geddes	15	Buster Brown	4	Roger	13	Moore	8
	Bob Jones	10	Ray Ellis	2	Hardy	10	Gent	6
	Danny Malone	9	Frank Evans	1	Hoskin	9	Bedkober	5
	Ken Wiggins	6	Dennis Newton	0	Sargeant	8	Best	2

23 April NATIONAL TROPHY	EXETER 63				SWINDON 45			
	Gent	16	Moore	8	Hugh Geddes	15	Ray Ellis	4
	Hoskin	10	Hardy	8	Frank Evans	7	Ken Wiggins	4
	Sargeant	10	Bedkober	2	George Craig	6	Bob Jones	3
	Roger	9	Bert Fryer	0	Danny Malone	5	Buster Brown	1

24 April FESTIVAL OF BRITAIN TROPHY

POOLE 70				EXETER 50			
Ken Middleditch	18	Charlie Hayden	8	Hardy	9	Moore	4
Tony Lewis	10	Alan Kidd	6	Roger	8	Best	4
Brian Crutcher	9	Johnny Thomson	2	Hoskin	8	Bedkober	4
Terry Small	9	Viv Thyer	0	Gent	7	Fryer	2
Dick Howard	8	Jack Cunningham	0	Sargeant	4	Maurice Hard	0

1 May FESTIVAL OF BRITAIN TROPHY

EXETER 67				POOLE 53			
Sargeant	16	Best	6	Ken Middleditch	17	Viv Thyer	4
Hardy	12	Hoskin	5	Terry Small	10	Tony Lewis	3
Roger	12	Gent	1	Charlie Hayden	4	Jack Cunningham	3
Bedkober	9	Fryer	0	Johnny Thomson	4	Allan Kidd	2
Moore	6	Hard	0	Dick Howard	4	Jimmy Coughlan	2

3 May FESTIVAL OF BRITAIN TROPHY

PLYMOUTH 69				EXETER 51			
Alan Smith	18	Rusty Wainwright	5	Roger	12	Hoskin	4
George Wall	12	Denis Hayles	4	Hardy	11	Gent	2
Johnny Bradford	11	Tony Lockyer	3	Sargeant	8	Best	1
Bill Thatcher	6	Denis Baker	3	Bedkober	7	Fryer	1
George Watts	6	Frank Holcombe	1	Moore	5	Hard	0

7 May FESTIVAL OF BRITAIN TROPHY

EXETER 81				PLYMOUTH 39			
Hardy	14	Bedkober	9	George Wall	10	George Watts	2
Gent	11	Hoskin	8	Alan Smith	10	Denis Baker	2
Roger	11	Best	6	Johnny Bradford	6	Rusty Wainwright	1
Sargeant	10	Hard	3	Denis Hayles	5	Tony Lockyer	0
Moore	9	Sparkes	0	Ray Thackwell	3	Bill Thatcher	0

8 May NATIONAL LEAGUE

ST AUSTELL 36				EXETER 48			
Allan Quinn	10	Bill Rundle	4	Hoskin	12	Sargeant	6
Stan Bedford	7	Maurice Hutchens	4	Hardy	11	Moore	2
Norman Street	5	Ken Monk	2	Roger	10	Bedkober	1
Ken James	4	Harold Bull	0	Gent	6	Best	0

10 May NATIONAL TROPHY

OXFORD 80				EXETER 28			
Ernie Rawlins	16	Bob McFarlane	10	Hardy	8	Sargeant	2
Pat Clark	14	Bill Kemp	7	Hoskin	6	Gent	2
Harry Saunders	12	Frank Boyle	5	Roger	6	Moore	0
Bill Osborne	12	Eric Irons	4	Bedkober	4	Best	0

14 May NATIONAL TROPHY

EXETER 60				OXFORD 47			
Roger	15	Gent	7	Eric Irons	12	Pat Clarke	3
Hardy	13	Walsh	5	Harry Saunders	11	Bill Kemp	3
Hoskin	8	Bedkober	4	Bill Osborne	8	Frank Boyle	2
Sargeant	7	Moore	1	Ernie Rawlins	8	Bob McFarlane	0

17 May NATIONAL LEAGUE

LONG EATON 39				EXETER 44			
Jack Winstanley	8	Percy Brine	5	Roger	10	Hoskin	5
Peter Moore	7	Frank Malouf	5	Gent	8	Walsh	5
Eric Minall	6	Eric Mason	3	Bedkober	6	Sargeant	3
Pedlar Palmer	5	Bill Humphries	0	Hardy	6	Moore	1

18 May NATIONAL LEAGUE

WOLVERHAMPTON 22				EXETER 62			
Roy Moreton	8	Peter Harris	2	Gent	12	Hoskin	7
John Hitchings	4	Allan Sutcliffe	2	Hardy	10	Walsh	6
Derek Timms	3	Bob Harrison	1	Roger	10	Bedkober	5
Ted Gibson	2	Syd George	0	Sargeant	8	Moore	4

21 May NATIONAL LEAGUE

EXETER 52				CARDIFF 32			
Hardy	11	Sargeant	6	Arthur Pilgrim	9	Ray Beaumont	2
Bedkober	9	Walsh	4	Mick Holland	9	Kevin Hayden	2
Roger	8	Moore	4	Frankie Johnson	5	Gerald Pugh	1
Hoskin	7	Gent	3	Jimmy Wright	4	Mick Callaghan	0

24 May NATIONAL LEAGUE

PLYMOUTH 41				EXETER 42			
Alan Smith	12	Brian Hitchcock	2	J Sargeant	8	Hoskin	4
George Wall	12	George Watts	2	Roger	8	Gent	3
Bill Thatcher	8	Fred Holcombe	2	Walsh	7	Bedkober	3
Johnny Bradford	3	Rusty Wainwright	0	Hardy	6	Moore	3

28 May
NATIONAL LEAGUE

EXETER 65				LONG EATON 18			
B Roger	11	Bedkober	9	Eric Minall	6	Jack Winstanley	1
Gent	11	Sargeant	7	Percy Brine	4	Eric Mason	1
Walsh	10	Hoskin	5	Frank Malouf	3	Johnny Jones	1
Hardy	10	Moore	2	Pedlar Palmer	2	Peter Moore	0

31 May
CHALLENGE

IPSWICH 39				EXETER 45			
Stan Clark	10	Derek Hewitt	3	Walsh	11	Roger	6
Wal Morton	9	Joe Baldwin	2	Bedkober	8	Gent	3
Rod Laudrum	6	John (Jack) Davis	2	Hardy	7	Moore	3
Alby Smith	5	George Flower	2	Sargeant	7	Paul Best	0

4 June
WCQR

Johnny Sargeant	13	Ken Walsh	10	Ray Harris	8	Ted Moore	3
Don Hardy	13	Bob Roger	9	Bob McFarlane	5	Fred Rogers	3
Vic Gent	12	Nick Nicholaides	9	Charlie Hayden	5	Ernie Rawlins	2
Harold Fairhurst	12	Don Hawley	8	Eddie Lack	4	Trevor Davies	1

11 June
NATIONAL LEAGUE

EXETER 45				SWINDON 38			
Bedkober	10	Gent	6	Buster Brown	12	Frank Evans	3
Hardy	8	Moore	3	Ray Ellis	8	Ken Wiggins	3
Sargeant	8	Walsh	2	Bob Jones	7	Hugh Geddes	0
Hoskin	6	B Roger	2	Reg Lambourne	5	Danny Malone	0

16 June
NATIONAL LEAGUE

ALDERSHOT 59				EXETER 23			
Trevor Redmond	12	Brian Wilson	9	Gent	6	Hoskin	1
Basil Harris	10	Bert Edwards	4	Sargeant	6	Moore	1
Ivor Powell	9	Doug Papworth	4	Hardy	5	Walsh	0
Geoff Mardon	9	Bill Grimes	2	Bedkober	4	B Roger	0

18 June
NATIONAL LEAGUE

EXETER 56				ALDERSHOT 28			
Hardy	11	Walsh	8	Trevor Redmond	11	Brian Wilson	2
Gent	10	Bedkober	4	Geoff Mardon	7	Doug Papworth	1
Sargeant	9	Hoskin	3	Basil Harris	4	Bill Grimes	0
B Roger	8	Moore	3	Ivor Powell	3	Ron Burnett	0

26 June
NATIONAL LEAGUE

EXETER 43				POOLE 41			
Hoskin	8	Hardy	6	Allan Kidd	9	Dick Howard	4
Walsh	8	Moore	4	Ken Middleditch	8	Frank Wheeler	3
Bedkober	7	B Roger	3	Terry Small	7	Tony Lewis	3
Sargeant	7	Best	0	Charlie Hayden	5	Brian Crutcher	2

30 June
NATIONAL LEAGUE

RAYLEIGH 61				EXETER 23			
Les McGillivray	12	Gerald Jackson	8	Gent	10	Bedkober	1
Ron Howes	9	Tom O'Connor	8	Hardy	5	Moore	1
Maurie Dunn	8	Jules Benson	5	Walsh	3	Hoskin	0
Vic Gooden	8	Mike Wood	3	B Roger	3	Best	0

2 July
NATIONAL LEAGUE

EXETER 54				PLYMOUTH 30			
Bedkober	10	Walsh	7	George Wall	10	Johnnie Bradford	2
Hoskin	9	Hardy	6	Alan Smith	8	Bill Thatcher	1
Gent	9	Sargeant	4	Brian Hitchcock	6	Denis Hayles	0
B Roger	7	Moore	2	George Craig	3	Tom Turnham	0

3 July
NATIONAL LEAGUE

POOLE 53				EXETER 31			
Ken Middleditch	11	Charlie Hayden	7	Walsh	10	Hoskin	4
Terry Small	11	Bill Holden	4	Gent	5	B Roger	3
Alan Kidd	7	Brian Crutcher	3	Bedkober	4	Moore	1
Tony Lewis	7	Frank Wheeler	3	Hardy	4	Best	0

9 July
NATIONAL LEAGUE

EXETER 67				WOLVERHAMPTON 16			
B Roger	12	Gent	9	Roy Moreton	5	John Hitchings	1
Walsh	12	Hoskin	8	Jack Cunningham	4	Cliff Biggs	1
Bedkober	10	Best	4	Gundy Harris	3	Derek Timms	0
Hardy	10	Moore	2	Harry Wardropper	2	Allan Sutcliffe	0

12 July DEVON DERBY	PLYMOUTH 35				EXETER 49			
	Bill Thatcher	12	Brian Hitchcock	3	Gent	9	B Roger	7
	George Wall	8	Johnnie Bradford	2	Bedkober	9	Hardy	6
	Alan Smith	5	Tom Turnham	1	Hoskin	8	Moore	1
	Denis Hayles	4	George Craig	0	Walsh	8	Best	

16 July NATIONAL LEAGUE	EXETER 58				LONG EATON 25			
	Hardy	10	Gent	9	Frank Malouf	9	Jack Winstanley	2
	Walsh	9	Hoskin	5	Eric Mason	4	Ray Binfield	2
	Bedkober	9	Best	4	Eric Minall	4	Pedlar Palmer	1
	B Roger	9	Moore	3	Johnny Jones	3	Peter Moore	0

23 July NATIONAL LEAGUE	EXETER 59				RAYLEIGH 25			
	Walsh	11	Hardy	8	Gerald Jackson	9	Maurie Dunn	2
	B Roger	10	Gent	5	Ted O'Connor	5	Frank Bettis	2
	Bedkober	9	Moore	5	Ron Howes	3	Vic Gooden	1
	Hoskin	8	Best	3	Jules Benson	3	Jack Unstead	0

26 July NATIONAL LEAGUE	LONG EATON 48				EXETER 35			
	Eric Mason	10	Peter Moore	6	Hoskin	8	Hardy	4
	Johnny Jones	7	Jack Winstanley	5	Gent	6	B Roger	3
	Eric Minall	7	Ray Binfield	3	Bedkober	5	Best	3
	Frank Malouf	7	Pedlar Palmer	3	Walsh	5	Moore	1

28 July NATIONAL LEAGUE	ALDERSHOT 56				EXETER 28			
	Geoff Mardon	12	Basil Harris	8	Hardy	8	B Roger	2
	Trevor Redmond	10	Brian Wilson	6	Hoskin	6	Bedkober	1
	Ivor Powell	9	John Dore	1	Moore	5	Walsh	1
	Bert Edwards	9	Bill Grimes	1	Gent	4	Best	1

30 July NATIONAL LEAGUE	EXETER 63				ST AUSTELL 21			
	Hardy	12	Bedkober	7	Maurice Hutchens	6	Ticker James	2
	Walsh	11	B Roger	7	Norman Street	4	Ken James	2
	Hoskin	10	Moore	4	Ken Monk	3	Alan Quinn	2
	Gent	9	Best	3	Max Rech	2	Harold Bull	0

2 August NATIONAL LEAGUE	CARDIFF 43				EXETER 41			
	Kevin Hayden	11	Arthur Pilgrim	3	Sargeant	11	B Roger	6
	Charlie May	10	Chum Taylor	3	Hardy	8	Gent	2
	Gerald Pugh	8	Mick Holland	1	Walsh	6	Bedkober	1
	Les Moore	7	Ray Bartlett	0	Hoskin	6	Moore	1

4 August NATIONAL LEAGUE	SWINDON 41				EXETER 43			
	Ray Ellis	7	Danny Malone	6	Roger	12	Gent	4
	Frank Evans	7	Buster Brown	5	Sargeant	10	Hoskins	3
	Hugh Geddes	6	Ken Wiggins	3	Hardy	6	Bedkober	2
	Bob Jones	6	Dudley Smith	1	Walsh	5	Best	1

6 August INTERNATIONAL	ENGLAND 'C' 61				SWEDEN 46			
	Ken Middleditch	15	George Wall	8	Olle Nygren	18	Lennart Carlstrom	4
	Vic Gent	9	Buster Brown	7	Olle Segerstrom	8	Sune Karlsson	3
	Bob Roger	8	Don Hardy	6	Bo Andersson	6	Dan Forsberg	1
	Jack Unstead	8	Terry Small	0	Rune Sormander	5	Eskil Carlsson	1

9 August CHALLENGE	IPSWICH 38				EXETER 46			
	Wal Morton	8	Dick Shepherd	4	B Roger	10	Hoskin	6
	Sid Clarke	8	Jimmy Grant	2	Sargeant	9	Gent	6
	Alby Smith	7	Allan Briggs	2	Bedkober	7	Moore	1
	Harold McNaughton	6	Rod Laudrum	1	Walsh	6	Best	1

13 August NATIONAL LEAGUE	EXETER 53				PLYMOUTH 31			
	Gent	12	B Roger	7	Alan Smith	11	Doug Fursey	2
	Hoskin	10	Walsh	6	George Wall	8	Brian Hitchcock	1
	Sargeant	8	Moore	2	George Craig	5	Ron Barrett	0
	Bedkober	7	Best	1	Frank Wheeler	4	Viv Thyer	0

16 August
NATIONAL LEAGUE

PLYMOUTH 35				EXETER 49			
Alan Smith	10	Ron Barrett	4	B Roger	11	Walsh	7
Johnnie Bradford	6	Frank Wheeler	4	Sargeant	9	Gent	4
George Wall	5	George Craig	1	Hoskin	8	Best	2
Brian Hitchcock	5	Doug Fursey	0	Bedkober	8	Moore	0

20 August
NATIONAL LEAGUE

EXETER 53				SWINDON 31			
Roger	11	Bedkober	6	Bob Jones	10	Frank Evans	3
Sargeant	9	Best	6	Hugh Geddes	6	Buster Brown	2
Walsh	8	Moore	4	Danny Malone	5	Reg Lambourne	2
Hoskin	8	Gent	1	Ray Ellis	3	Dudley Smith	0

23 August
NATIONAL LEAGUE

CARDIFF 41				EXETER 42			
Charlie May	11	Les Moore	4	Sargeant	11	Gent	4
Kevin Hayden	8	Gerald Pugh	3	B Roger	11	Hoskin	3
Mick Holland	7	Arthur Pilgrim	1	Walsh	7	Morris Barnett	1
Chum Taylor	6	Vic Brinkworth	1	Hardy	5	Bedkober	0

27 August
NATIONAL LEAGUE

EXETER 54				ALDERSHOT 29			
Sargeant	12	Hardy	6	Geoff Mardon	9	Ivor Powell	4
B Roger	9	Walsh	5	Trevor Redmond	7	Basil Harris	1
Hoskin	7	Gent	5	Bert Edwards	4	Craig Jones	0
Bedkober	6	Moore	4	Brian Wilson	4	Doug Papworth	0

3 September
DEVON DERBY

EXETER 53				PLYMOUTH 30			
Sargeant	10	Hardy	7	George Wall	6	Johnnie Bradford	4
Gent	9	Walsh	5	Ron Barrett	6	Frank Wheeler	3
Hoskin	9	Bedkober	3	Alan Smith	5	Tom Turnham	1
B Roger	7	Moore	3	George Craig	5	Doug Fursey	0

10 September
NATIONAL LEAGUE

EXETER 55				POOLE 29			
Walsh	10	Sargeant	8	Ken Middleditch	11	Brian Crutcher	2
Gent	9	Hardy	6	Terry Small	6	Tony Lewis	1
Hoskin	9	Moore	3	Roy Craighead	5	Bill Holden	1
B Roger	8	Best	2	Charlie Hayden	3	Alan Kidd	0

11 September
CHALLENGE

ST AUSTELL 43				EXETER 41			
Allan Quinn	10	Norman Street	4	Hardy	10	Walsh	3
Maurice Hutchens	9	Ticker James	4	Hoskin	9	Best	3
Harold Bull	7	Ken Monk	2	Sargeant	8	Gent	0
Ken James	6	Max Rech	1	B Roger	8	Moore	0

17 September
NATIONAL LEAGUE

EXETER 64				WOLVERHAMPTON 19			
B Roger	12	Walsh	8	Derek Timms	5	Cyril Maidment	2
Hoskin	11	Moore	7	Jack Cunningham	4	Ronnie Genz	1
Sargeant	10	Morris Barnett	3	Roy Moreton	4	Dick Harris	0
Hardy	10	Best	3	Gundy Harris	3	Ted Stevens	0

24 September
NATIONAL LEAGUE

POOLE 54				EXETER 30			
Tony Lewis	10	Brian Crutcher	7	Hoskin	9	Gent	2
Terry Small	10	Allan Kidd	4	B Roger	8	Sargeant	1
Ken Middleditch	9	Roy Craighead	4	Hardy	7	Moore	0
Bill Holden	8	Charlie Hayden	2	Walsh	3	Best	0

29 September
NATIONAL LEAGUE

RAYLEIGH 37				EXETER 47			
Jack Unstead	10	Johnny Guilfoyle	3	Hoskin	12	Moore	5
Les McGillivray	8	Tom O'Connor	2	B Roger	11	Gent	2
Frank Bettis	6	Ron Howes	2	Hardy	10	Best	1
Gerald Jackson	5	Jules Benson	1	Walsh	6	Sargeant	0

1 October
NATIONAL LEAGUE

EXETER 62				ST AUSTELL 22			
Walsh	12	Moore	8	Max Rech	5	Norman Street	2
Hardy	12	Gent	4	Ticker James	5	Ken Monk	1
B Roger	12	Barnett	3	Ken James	4	Maurice Hutchens	1
Hoskin	9	Best	2	Allan Quinn	3	Stan Bedford	1

2 October
CHALLENGE

ST AUSTELL 44				EXETER 40			
Maurice Hutchens	8	Ken Monk	6	Walsh	12	Gent	2
Allan Quinn	8	Ken James	3	B Roger	11	Best	1
Harold Bull	7	Ticker James	3	Hardy	7	Barnett	1
Max Rech	7	Norman Street	2	Hoskin	6	Moore	0

5 October
NATIONAL LEAGUE

WOLVERHAMPTON 40				EXETER 44			
Ronnie Genz	9	Jack Cunningham	5	Walsh	10	Best	5
Roy Moreton	8	Ron Wilson	5	Hoskin	10	Gent	4
Derek Timms	6	Dick Harris	1	B Roger	7	Barnett	2
Harry Wardropper	6	John Hitchings	0	Walsh	5	Moore	1

6 October
NATIONAL LEAGUE

SWINDON 38				EXETER 46			
Hugh Geddes	10	Bob Jones	4	Walsh	10	Gent	3
Buster Brown	6	Mike Beddoe	3	Hoskin	10	Moore	3
Danny Malone	6	Ken Wiggins	3	B Roger	10	Barnett	0
Reg Lambourne	5	Frank Evans	1	Hardy	10	Best	0

8 October
NATIONAL LEAGUE

EXETER 54				RAYLEIGH 29			
Walsh	11	Hardy	7	Jack Unstead	10	Johnny Guilfoyle	2
Gent	10	Hoskin	6	Gerald Jackson	9	Ron Howes	2
B Roger	9	Best	4	Frank Bettis	4	Jim McGillivray	0
Moore	7	Colin Selley	0	Les McGillivray	2		

15 October
CHALLENGE

EXETER 42				WEMBLEY 42			
B Roger	10	Gent	4	Freddie Williams	12	Eric Williams	6
Hardy	7	Jack Unstead	4	Bob Oakley	8	George Wilks	3
Hoskin	7	George Wall	3	Bruce Abernethy	7	Jimmy Gooch	0
Hugh Geddes	6	Moore	1	Trevor Redmond	6	Tommy Price	0

22 October
CARNIVAL TROPHY

Don Hardy	11	Charlie Plain	8	Bob Emery	3	Reg Robins	2
Vic Gent	10	Hugh Geddes	7	Broncho Slade	3	Colin Selley	1
Goog Hoskin	10	Ted Moore	5				

Morris Barnett

STATISTICS 1952

7 April
INTERNATIONAL CHALLENGE

EXETER 42				SMERDERNA 42			
Don Hardy	12	Vic Gent	4	Joel Jansson	7	Rune Sormander	5
Goog Hoskin	9	Jack Hart	4	Bosse Andersson	7	Olle Nygren	5
Johnnie Sargeant	5	Jack Geran	3	Sven Skoglund	7	Olle Segerstrom	4
Ron Barrett	5	Neil Street	0	Bert Lindarw	5	Lars Erik Andersson	2

11 April
SOUTHERN LEAGUE

PLYMOUTH 57				EXETER 27			
George Wall	12	Frank Wheeler	5	Goog Hoskin	7	Johnny Sargeant	3
Alan Smith	12	Doug Fursey	4	Ron Barrett	6	Colin Selley	1
Pete Lansdale	11	Denis Hayles	3	Don Hardy	5	Neil Street	1
Bill Thatcher	8	Brian Hitchcock	2	Jack Geran	4	Vic Gent	0

21 April
NATIONAL TROPHY

EXETER 73				WOLVERHAMPTON 34			
Hardy	16	Geran	9	Jimmy Grant	10	Benny King	3
Sargeant	13	Street	6	Ken Brown	9	Derek Timms	3
Hoskin	12	Barrett	5	Charlie Hayden	4	Roy Moreton	1
Gent	10	Selley	2	Cyril Quick	3	Syd George	1

25 April
SOUTHERN LEAGUE

WOLVERHAMPTON 49				EXETER 59			
Cyril Quick	13	Benny King	6	Hoskin	18	Selly	4
Jimmy Grant	8	Charlie Hayden	5	Hardy	15	Barrett	4
Ken Brown	8	Roy Moreton	1	Geran	8	Gent	3
Derek Timms	8	Eric Irons	0	Sargeant	5	Street	2

28 April
NATIONAL TROPHY

EXETER 57				PLYMOUTH 51			
Hardy	16	Sargeant	5	Pete Lansdale	16	George Wall	4
Gent	10	Geran	4	Alan Smith	11	Frank Wheeler	4
Hoskin	8	Street	4	Bill Thatcher	6	Doug Fursey	3
Barrett	7	Selley	3	Brian Hitchcock	5	Denis Hayles	2

29 April
SOUTHERN LEAGUE

ST AUSTELL 29				EXETER 55			
Norman Street	6	Ken James	3	Hoskin	12	Geran	7
Max Rech	5	Alan Quinn	3	Hardy	10	Sargeant	5
Ticker James	4	Maurice Hutchens	3	Barrett	9	Selley	2
Mitch Mitchell	4	Harold Bull	1	Gent	9	Street	1

1 May
NATIONAL TROPHY

PLYMOUTH 67				EXETER 41			
Bill Thatcher	14	Frank Wheeler	7	Hoskin	18	Geran	3
Alan Smith	11	Johnny Bradford	6	Hardy	8	Barrett	1
Pete Lansdale	11	Brian Hitchcock	5	Gent	8	Selley	0
George Wall	10	Denis Hayles	3	Street	3	Barnett	0

3 May
SOUTHERN TROPHY

SWINDON 48				EXETER 36			
Frank Evans	11	Ian Williams	7	Hoskin	9	Street	2
Reg Lambourne	10	Bob Wells	5	Hardy	9	Gent	2
Buster Brown	7	Bob Jones	1	Barrett	8	Geran	2
Danny Malone	7	Ken Wiggins	0	Barnett	3	Selley	1

5 May
SOUTHERN LEAGUE

EXETER 49				SWINDON 35			
Hoskin	12	Geran	5	Danny Malone	9	Ian Williams	4
Hardy	11	Barnett	4	Buster Brown	6	Bob Wells	3
Barrett	9	Street	0	Bob Jones	5	Ken Wiggins	2
Gent	8	Selley	0	Frank Evans	4	Reg Lambourne	2

12 May SOUTHERN LEAGUE

EXETER 63				LONG EATON 20			
Gent	12	Barnett	8	Peter Moore	5	Johnnie Jones	2
Hardy	11	Barrett	8	Wilf Plant	5	Jack Winstanley	2
Hoskin	9	Ronnie Swaine	4	Frank Malouf	3	Roy Browning	0
Geran	8	Selley	3	Cyril Page	3	Lionel Pugh	0

19 May SOUTHERN LEAGUE

EXETER 53				ST AUSTELL 30			
Swaine	10	Gent	7	Norman Street	8	Ticker James	2
Hoskin	9	Geran	5	Ken James	8	Maurice Hutchins	2
Barrett	9	Selley	3	Alan Quinn	5	Harold Bull	1
Hardy	8	Barnett	2	Max Rech	4	Mitch Mitchell	0

22 May SOUTHERN LEAGUE

IPSWICH 42				EXETER 41			
Sid Clarke	11	Vic Sage	4	Hoskin	12	Geran	2
Harold McNaughton	10	Tich Read	3	Hardy	11	Barrett	2
Dennis Day	6	Arthur Pilgrim	1	Gent	8	Swaine	2
Dick Shepherd	6	Rod Laudrum	1	Sargeant	3	Street	1

24 May SOUTHERN LEAGUE

RAYLEIGH 49				EXETER 35			
Jack Unstead	12	Ron Howes	5	Gent	10	Barnett	2
Gerald Jackson	8	Pat Clark	5	Hoskin	9	Swaine	1
Les McGillivray	6	Ted O'Connor	4	Barrett	7	Geran	0
Jules Benson	6	Maurie McDermott	3	Hardy	6	Sargeant	0

26 May WCQR

Goog Hoskin	15	Johnny Sargeant	9	Jack Geran	6	Ronnie Swaine	3
Harold Fairhurst	14	Bill Thatcher	9	Frank Malouf	5	Jimmy Cox	2
Les Hewitt	13	Chum Taylor	6	Tip Mills	4	Vic Ridgeon	2
Ron Barrett	11	Derek Tailby	6	Max Rech	5	Herbie King	0
Vic Gent	9						

2 June SOUTHERN LEAGUE

EXETER 46				CARDIFF 38			
G Hoskin	12	R Swaine	3	Gerald Pugh	9	Kevin Hayden	3
R Barrett	12	J Sargeant	3	Charlie May	8	Chum Taylor	2
J Geran	10	V Gent	2	Mick Holland	7	Jimmy Wright	2
M Barnett	4	D Hardy	0	Hugh Geddes	7	Bambi Royle	0

3 June CHALLENGE

ST AUSTELL 43				EXETER 41			
Norman Street	12	Allan Quinn	4	Hoskin	11	Geran	4
Ken Monk	7	Ken James	3	Hardy	8	Gent	3
Ticker James	7	Harold Bull	3	Sargeant	8	Selley	2
Maurice Hutchens	5	Max Rech	2	Barrett	5	Swaine	0

5 June SOUTHERN LEAGUE

CARDIFF 58				EXETER 26			
Gerald Pugh	12	Kevin Hayden	6	Hoskin	9	Gent	3
Charlie May	10	Mick Holland	6	Geran	4	Sargeant	2
Hugh Geddes	9	Jimmy Wright	4	Hardy	4	Selley	0
Chum Taylor	8	Derek Clark	3	Barrett	4	Street	0

6 June CHALLENGE

WIGAN 44				EXETER 40			
Dick Harris	10	Harry Welch	4	Hoskin	8	Barrett	7
Alf Webster	9	Eric Liddell	4	Hardy	8	Sargeant	3
Peter Robinson	8	Ralph Horne	3	Geran	7	Swaine	0
Archie Windmill	4	Ron Hart	2	Gent	7	Barnett	0

9June SOUTHERN LEAGUE

EXETER 52				ALDERSHOT 29			
G Hoskin	11	R Barrett	6	Ivor Powell	11	Doug Papworth	2
D Hardy	8	J Geran	5	Bert Edwards	9	Charles Frenzel	1
V Gent	7	N Street	5	John Dore	4	Basil Harris	0
J Sargeant	6	C Selley	4	Bill Grimes	2	Vic Gooden	0

16 June SOUTHERN LEAGUE

EXETER 54				IPSWICH 30			
R Barrett	10	J Geran	7	Arthur Pilgrim	9	Rod Laudrum	1
D Hardy	9	R Swaine	7	Sid Clarke	9	Vic Sage	1
N Street	8	J Sargeant	5	Dick Shepherd	5	Alby Smith	0
V Gent	8			Harold McNaughton	5	Tich Read	0

18 June SOUTHERN LEAGUE	ALDERSHOT 58				EXETER 25			
	Ivor Powell	11	Vic Gooden	7	Geran	5	Street	3
	Basil Harris	11	Bill Grimes	5	Barrett	5	Swaine	2
	Bert Edwards	8	Ron Burnett	5	Hardy	4	Sargeant	2
	Doug Papworth	8	Charles Frenzel	3	Gent	3	Barnett	1

23 June SOUTHERN LEAGUE	EXETER 58				SOUTHAMPTON 26			
	Gent	12	Hoskin	8	Mike Tams	7	Jack Vallis	3
	Hardy	9	Barrett	6	Brian McKeown	6	Aston Quinn	1
	Sargeant	8	Barnett	5	Den Hayles	5	Dudley Smith	1
	Geran	8	Swaine	2	Ted Moore	3	Dennis Cross	0

30 June SOUTHERN LEAGUE	EXETER 40				RAYLEIGH 44			
	Geran	11	Street	3	Jack Unstead	10	Maurie McDermott	4
	Sargeant	9	Barnett	2	Gerald Jackson	10	Jules Benson	3
	Gent	7	Swaine	2	Tom O'Connor	9	Johnny Applegate	3
	Hardy	5	Barrett	1	Peter Clark	5	Ron Howes	0

1 July SOUTHERN LEAGUE	SOUTHAMPTON 39				EXETER 45			
	Bert Croucher	8	Den Cross	5	Gent	12	Hardy	5
	Jack Vallis	6	Maurie Mattingley	5	Sargeant	9	Barrett	4
	Brian Mckeown	6	Mike Tamms	4	Geran	7	Barnett	1
	Dudley Smith	5	Dennis Hayles	0	Street	6	Swaine	1

3 July SOUTHERN LEAGUE	LONG EATON 53				EXETER 29			
	Wilf Plant	11	Bill Harris	7	Gent	10	Swaine	2
	Cyril Page	8	Jack Winstanley	7	Geran	6	Street	1
	Peter Moore	8	Fred Siggins	3	Hardy	6	Barrett	1
	Lionel Watling	8	Roy Browning	1	Sargeant	2	Barnett	1

4 July SOUTHERN LEAGUE	WOLVERHAMPTON 59				EXETER 25			
	Cyril Quick	12	Ken Brown	7	Hardy	6	Sargeant	3
	Benny King	12	Derek Timms	6	Geran	5	Barrett	1
	Jimmy Grant	11	Jack Cunningham	3	Gent	5	Swaine	1
	Eric Irons	7	Charlie Hayden	1	Hoskin	4	Street	0

10 July SOUTHERN LEAGUE	PLYMOUTH 40				EXETER 44			
	Bill Thatcher	10	Doug Fursey	3	Hoskin	11	Barrett	6
	George Wall	9	Ted Stevens	2	Gent	10	Geran	2
	Brian Hitchcock	8	Bill Rundle	2	Hardy	8	Street	1
	Alan Smith	6			Sargeant	5	Swaine	1

14 July SOUTHERN LEAGUE	EXETER 44				PLYMOUTH 40			
	Hardy	11	Sargeant	4	George Wall	12	Brian Hitchcock	4
	Gent	11	Barrett	4	Alan Smith	9	Doug Fursey	2
	Hoskin	6	Swaine	1	Pete Lansdale	6	Ted Stevens	1
	Geran	6	Street	1	Bill Thatcher	6	Bill Rundle	0

21 July SOUTHERN LEAGUE	EXETER 52				ST AUSTELL 31			
	Hardy	12	Barrett	6	Norman Street	9	Harold Bull	2
	Hoskin	8	Sargeant	5	Allan Quinn	8	Johnny Bradford	1
	Gent	7	Barnett	5	George Newton	7	Lloyd Goffe	0
	Geran	6	Swaine	3	Ken Monk	4	Aston Quinn	0

26 July SOUTHERN LEAGUE	SWINDON 49				EXETER 35			
	Bob Jones	12	Ian Williams	5	Hoskin	7	Geran	5
	Danny Malone	8	Reg Lambourne	5	Gent	7	Barrett	5
	Frank Evans	8	Buster Brown	3	Sargeant	5	Swaine	1
	Ray Ellis	7	Bob Wells	1	Hardy	5	Barnett	0

28 July INTERNATIONAL	ENGLAND 'C' 70				SWEDEN 38			
	Pete Lansdale	12	Ivor Powell	9	Sune Karlsson	17	Gote Olsson	3
	Jack Unstead	12	Vic Gent	8	Gunnar Karlsson	9	Rune Sormander	1
	Goog Hoskin	11	George Wall	7	Olle Nygren	4	Bengt Gustavsson	0
	Gerald Pugh	9	Norman Street	2	Stig Pramberg	4		

29 July SOUTHERN LEAGUE

ST AUSTELL 41				EXETER 43			
Ken Monk	10	Allan Quinn	4	Hoskin	12	Sargeant	3
George Newton	9	Norman Street	3	Hardy	9	Swaine	3
Harold Bull	8	Dick Harris	1	Gent	7	Barrett	3
Lloyd Goffe	5	Johnny Bradford	1	Geran	5	Street	1

4 August SOUTHERN LEAGUE

EXETER 33				RAYLEIGH 51			
Hoskin	8	Hardy	2	Maurice McDermott	10	Jack Unstead	7
Gent	8	Swaine	2	Gerald Jackson	9	Las McGillivray	5
Barrett	6	Barnett	2	Tom O'Connor	8	Johnny Applegate	3
Geran	4	Sargeant	1	Peter Clark	8	Jules Benson	1

6 August SOUTHERN LEAGUE

EXETER 39				SWINDON 45			
Hoskin	8	Street	4	Danny Malone	12	Buster Brown	4
Geran	8	Barrett	3	Frank Evans	10	Reg Lambourne	2
Gent	7	Swaine	2	Bob Jones	9	Ray Ellis	1
Barnett	6	Sargeant	1	Bob Wells	7	Ian Williams	0

9 August SOUTHERN LEAGUE

IPSWICH 38				EXETER 46			
Sid Clarke	8	Charles Mugford	4	Hoskin	11	Gent	7
Dick Shepherd	8	Alby Smith	4	Barrett	9	Swaine	2
Harold McNaughton	6	Tich Read	3	Geran	8	Barnett	2
Dennis Day	5	Arthur Pilgrim	0	Sargeant	7	Street	0

11 August SOUTHERN LEAGUE

EXETER 43				WOLVERHAMPTON 41			
Barrett	10	Barnett	5	Eric Irons	12	Jimmy Grant	4
Geran	7	Swaine	3	Dick Howard	9	Bill Jemison	3
Hoskin	7	Sargeant	2	Benny King	6	Jack Cunningham	2
Gent	7	Street	2	Ken Brown	5	Cyril Quick	0

22 August SOUTHERN LEAGUE

WOLVERHAMPTON 42				EXETER 42			
Cyril Quick	10	Jack Cunningham	4	Hoskin	11	Gent	4
Eric Irons	9	Stan Bradbury	4	Barrett	11	Barnett	2
Benny King	6	Ken Brown	2	Geran	10	Eric Minall	0
Jimmy Grant	5	Dick Howard	2	Sargeant	4	Swaine	0

25 August SOUTHERN LEAGUE

EXETER 55				IPSWICH 29			
Gent	12	Barrett	6	Sid Clarke	9	Doug Papworth	2
Sargeant	10	Barnett	4	Harold McNaughton	7	Charlie Mugford	2
Hoskin	9	Swaine	3	Dick Shepherd	4	Geoff Woodger	1
Geran	8	Minall	3	Dennis Day	3	Tich Read	1

30 August SOUTHERN LEAGUE

RAYLEIGH 52				EXETER 32			
Jack Unstead	11	Jules Benson	3	Barrett	8	Gent	4
Gerald Jackson	11	Les McGillivray	3	Geran	7	Sargeant	3
Peter Clarke	11	Alby Smith	2	Barnett	5	Minall	0
Maurice McDermott	10	Tom O'Connor	1	Hoskin	5	Street	0

1 September SOUTHERN LEAGUE

EXETER 47				SOUTHAMPTON 36			
Hoskin	12	Barrett	4	Brian McKeown	11	Dudley Smith	4
Gent	11	Barnett	3	Bert Croucher	9	Frank Malouf	2
Geran	7	Minall	2	Mike Tams	5	Maurie Mattingley	1
Sargeant	6	Street	2	Ernie Brecknell	4	Jack Vallis	0

3 September SOUTHERN LEAGUE

ALDERSHOT 62				EXETER 22			
Ivor Powell	12	Tom Turnham	8	Hoskin	8	Sargeant	1
Vic Gooden	12	Bill Grimes	7	Geran	7	Barrett	1
Basil Harris	8	Archie Windmill	4	Gent	3	Barnett	0
Charles Frenzel	8	Ron Burnett	3	Minall	2	Street	0

8 September SOUTHERN LEAGUE

EXETER 51				WOLVERHAMPTON 33			
Barrett	11	Gent	7	Ken Brown	8	Jack Cunningham	4
Sargeant	10	Street	4	Dick Howard	6	Benny King	2
Hoskin	9	Minall	1	Eric Irons	6	Jimmy Grant	2
Geran	9	Barnett	0	Bill Jemison	5	Cyril Quick	0

12 September SOUTHERN LEAGUE

CARDIFF 65				EXETER 19			
Charlie May	12	Hugh Geddes	6	Hoskin	6	Sargeant	1
Chum Taylor	12	Frank Johnson	6	Barrett	5	Minall	1
Mick Holland	11	Kevin Hayden	5	Geran	4	Barnett	0
Gerald Pugh	8	Bert Edwards	5	Gent	2	Street	0

15 September SOUTHERN LEAGUE

EXETER 63				ALDERSHOT 21			
Sargeant	12	Gent	8	Ivor Powell	6	Jack Taylor	2
Hoskin	12	Barnett	5	Bill Grimes	5	Johnnie Dore	1
Barrett	11	Street	4	Vic Gooden	4	Basil Harris	1
Geran	8	Minall	3	Charles Frenzel	2	Archie Windmill	0

22 September SOUTHERN LEAGUE

EXETER 48				PLYMOUTH 35			
Hoskin	10	Sargeant	4	Alan Smith	10	Brian Hitchcock	3
Gent	9	Barnett	3	Bill Thatcher	9	Roy Moreton	1
Barrett	9	Minall	3	George Wall	5	Bill Rundle	1
Geran	9	Swaine	1	Ted Stevens	5	Alan Dobinett	1

29 September SOUTHERN LEAGUE

EXETER 45				CARDIFF 39			
Barrett	10	Barnett	5	Gerald Pugh	11	Chum Taylor	5
Hoskin	7	Street	5	Hugh Geddes	9	Charlie May	2
Gent	6	Sargeant	5	Bert Edwards	6	Kevin Hayden	1
Swaine	6	Minall	1	Mick Holland	5	Frank Johnson	0

7 October SOUTHERN LEAGUE

SOUTHAMPTON 62				EXETER 21			
Dudley Smith	12	Brian McKeown	7	Gent	6	Sargeant	1
Ernie Brecknell	10	Bert Croucher	6	Hoskin	5	Swaine	0
Maurie Mattingley	10	Jack Vallis	5	Barrett	5	Street	0
Mike Tams	9	Brian Hanham	3	Barnett	4	Wally Monckton	0

20 October CARNIVAL TROPHY

Ron Barrett	12	Brian Hitchcock	8	Gordon Leigh	4	Wally Monckton	2
Vic Gent	10	Johnny Sargeant	7	Hugh Geddes	3	Neil Street	1
Morris Barnett	8	George Wall	6				

STATISTICS 1953

4 April CHALLENGE

ST AUSTELL 46				EXETER 38			
Harold Bull	11	Ken Monk	5	Hoskin	12	Gent	2
Norman Street	10	Maury McHugh	3	Hardy	8	Street	2
Jackie Gates	9	Graham Williams	2	Barrett	7	Sargeant	2
Alf Webster	6	Roy Thomas	0	Barnett	5	Minall	0

6 April INTERNATIONAL CHALLENGE

EXETER 47				FILBYTERNA 37			
Goog Hoskin	8	Ron Barrett	6	Ove Fundin	8	Sven Skoglund	5
Don Hardy	8	Eric Minall	4	Joel Jansson	7	Gunnar Johansson	4
Johnnie Sargeant	8	Vic Gent	4	Jan Jonsson	7	Per Tage Svensson	1
Morris Barnett	7	Neil Street	2	Torsten Karlsson	5	Gosta Zanderholm	0

13 April NATIONAL LEAGUE

EXETER 56				ST AUSTELL 28			
Hoskin	12	Barnett	5	Norman Street	7	Ken Monk	3
Hardy	12	Gent	5	Alf Webster	7	Jackie Gates	2
Barrett	12	Street	3	Graham Williams	4	Roy Thomas	1
Sargeant	6	Wally Monckton	1	Harold Bull	3	Maury McHugh	1

18 April SOUTHERN LEAGUE

RAYLEIGH 39				EXETER 45			
Maurie McDermott	9	Frank Bettis	4	Hoskin	10	Barnett	4
Gerald Jackson	8	Tom O'Connor	3	Hardy	10	Street	2
Peter Clark	8	Ron Howes	2	Barrett	10	Sargeant	0
Las McGilivray	5	Alby Smith	0	Jack Geran	9	Gent	0

20 April NATIONAL TROPHY

EXETER 60				SWINDON 48			
Hoskin	15	Barnett	5	Danny Malone	10	Ronnie Swaine	6
Barrett	15	Sargeant	3	Bob Wells	10	Ian Williams	5
Hardy	11	Gent	3	Bob Jones	7	Frank Evans	3
Geran	8	Street	0	Ken Wiggins	7	Maurice Hard	0

25 April NATIONAL TROPHY

SWINDON 68				EXETER 40			
Bob Wells	16	Len Williams	8	Hoskin	13	Barnett	4
Frank Evans	14	Maurice Hard	7	Barrett	7	Hart	4
Bob Jones	10	Ken Wiggins	2	Geran	6	Sargeant	2
Danny Malone	9	Ronnie Swaine	2	Hardy	4	Street	0

27 April SOUTHERN LEAGUE

EXETER 69				IPSWICH 15			
Hoskin	12	Street	8	Dick Shepherd	5	Len Silver	1
Barnett	12	Barrett	8	Stan Clark	4	Doug Papworth	0
Geran	12	Hart	5	Nobby Stock	3	Tich Read	0
Hardy	9	Sargeant	3	Jim Blythe	2	Charlie Mugford	0

1 May NATIONAL LEAGUE

PLYMOUTH 41				EXETER 43			
Bill Thatcher	12	Brian Hitchcock	2	Hoskin	10	Street	4
Alan Smith	11	Frank Wheeler	2	Barrett	10	Geran	3
Pete Lansdale	6	Dick Howard	2	Barnett	7	Gent	2
Doug Fursey	6	Dick Harris	0	Hardy	5	Hart	2

4 May SOUTHERN LEAGUE

EXETER 55				CARDIFF 29			
Hoskin	9	Street	6	Charlie May	6	Jimmy Wright	4
Hardy	9	Hart	6	Gerald Pugh	6	Mick Holland	3
Barnett	8	Geran	5	Bert Edwards	6	Mick Callaghan	0
Barrett	8	Gent	4	Hugh Geddes	4	Kevin Hayden	0

11 May CHALLENGE

EXETER 40				HARRINGAY STARS 44			
Hoskin	9	Barnett	5	Maury Dunn	12	Bill Longley	5
Geran	7	Hardy	5	Split Waterman	10	Jeff Lloyd	3
Hart	6	Sargeant	3	Ken Walsh	8	Bob Meyer	0
Street	5	Gent	0	Hugh Geddes	6	Wally Monckton	0

21 May SOUTHERN LEAGUE

CARDIFF 45				EXETER 39			
Hugh Geddes	11	Mick Holland	4	Barnett	8	Street	6
Charlie May	10	Kevin Hayden	3	Hoskin	7	Hart	4
Bert Edwards	9	Mick Callaghan	2	Hardy	7	Gent	0
Frankie Johnson	5	Jimmy Wright	1	Geran	7	Sargeant	0

25 May DEVON DERBY

EXETER 53				PLYMOUTH 31			
Hoskin	12	Hart	6	Alan Smith	9	George Wall	3
Hardy	9	Gent	5	Pete Lansdale	7	Len Read	3
Barnett	7	Geran	4	Bill Thatcher	6	Derek Timms	0
Street	7	Sargeant	3	Brian Hitchcock	3	Dick Harris	0

25 May DEVON DERBY

PLYMOUTH 67				EXETER 40			
Alan Smith	18	George Wall	7	Hardy	11	Sargeant	3
Pete Lansdale	10	Dick Harris	5	Street	9	Gent	2
Doug Fursey	9	Len Read	5	Geran	7	Hart	2
Bill Thatcher	9	Derek Timms	3	Barnett	5	Meyer	1

28 May SOUTHERN LEAGUE

IPSWICH 41				EXETER 43			
Jim Blythe	8	Jim Grant	5	Hoskin	12	Hart	5
Dick Shepherd	8	Harold McNaughton	3	Street	8	Geran	3
Nobby Stock	7	Stan Clark	2	Barnett	6	Gent	3
Charlie Mugford	6	Len Silver	2	Hardy	6	Sargeant	0

1 June CORONATION BEST PAIRS

Goog Hoskin	12	20	Dick Shepherd	7	16	Harold Bull	4	10
Don Hardy	8		Nobby Stock	9		Jackie Gates	6	
Jack Geran	9	16	Bert Edwards	3	13	Ian Williams	4	9
Morris Barnett	7		Charlie May	10		Danny Malone	5	

6 June SOUTHERN LEAGUE

SWINDON 41				EXETER 43			
Bob Wells	9	Ronnie Swaine	4	Hoskin	12	Barnett	4
Ian Williams	9	Bob Jones	2	Hardy	11	Gent	4
Frank Evans	9	Maurice Hard	2	Street	5	Charlie May	2
Danny Malone	6	Reg Lambourne	0	Geran	5	Hart	0

8 June SOUTHERN LEAGUE

EXETER 54				OXFORD 30			
Hoskin	10	Street	8	Jim Gregory	12	Bill Kemp	3
Geran	9	Barnett	4	Jim Boyd	5	Benny King	2
May	8	Hart	4	Bob MacFarlane	4	Bill Codling	1
Hardy	8	Sargeant	3	Bill Osborne	3	Frank Boyle	0

15 June SOUTHERN LEAGUE

EXETER 58				SWINDON 26			
Geran	11	Street	7	Danny Malone	9	Ronnie Swaine	2
Hoskin	10	Gent	6	Ian Williams	6	Ken Wiggins	1
Hart	10	May	4	Bob Wells	6	Bill Grimes	0
Hardy	8	Meyer	2	Bob Jones	2	Frank Evans	0

18 June SOUTHERN LEAGUE

OXFORD 51				EXETER 33			
Jim Boyd	11	Bob MacFarlane	5	Geran	8	Hart	4
Bill Kemp	11	Herbie King	5	Street	6	May	4
Jim Gregory	10	Bill Osborne	2	Hoskin	5	Gent	1
Benny King	6	Frank Boyle	1	Hardy	5	Meyer	0

20 June SOUTHERN LEAGUE

RAYLEIGH 53				EXETER 31			
Maurie McDermott	10	Frank Bettis	6	Hart	8	Hardy	3
Gerald Jackson	9	Tom O'Connor	5	Hoskin	7	May	1
Peter Clark	9	Ron Howes	3	Geran	6	Street	1
Les McGillivray	8	Alby Smith	3	Gent	5	Meyer	0

22 June SOUTHERN LEAGUE

EXETER 49				RAYLEIGH 35			
Geran	12	Street	6	Gerald Jackson	10	Peter Clark	2
Hoskin	10	Gent	5	Maurie McDermott	9	Alby Smith	2
Hardy	7	May	3	Les McGillivray	7	Ron Howes	1
Hart	6	Meyer	0	Tom O'Connor	4	Frank Bettis	0

29 June QUEEN'S CUP

EXETER 72				STOKE 36			
Hoskin	18	Street	10	Ray Harris	10	Johnnie Fitzpatrick	4
Geran	13	Gent	5	Don Potter	6	Jackie Hughes	3
Hart	12	Minall	3	Ken Adams	4	Bill Dalton	3
Hardy	11	Monckton	0	Les Jenkins	4	Ron Peace	2

30 June SOUTHERN LEAGUE

ST AUSTELL 40				EXETER 44			
Harold Bull	9	Norman Street	3	Geran	10	Gent	4
Jackie Gates	8	Alf Webster	2	Hoskin	9	Street	4
Ken Monk	8	John Yates	2	Hart	7	Dick Howard	3
Bob Duckworth	7	Graham Williams	1	Hardy	7	Minall	0

6 July SOUTHERN LEAGUE

EXETER 59				PLYMOUTH 25			
Geran	11	Gent	7	Pete Lansdale	11	Brian Hitchcock	1
Hart	9	Street	7	Alan Smith	6	Johnnie Sargeant	1
Hardy	8	Howard	5	Bill Thatcher	5	Len Read	0
Hoskin	7	May	5	George Wall	1	Derek Timms	0

13 July SOUTHERN LEAGUE

EXETER 49				SWINDON 35			
Hoskin	12	Hardy	7	Danny Malone	10	Gordon Leigh	3
Gent	9	Howard	4	Bob Wells	7	Ronnie Swaine	2
Hart	7	May	3	Ian Williams	6	Bill Grimes	2
Street	7	Minall	0	Bob Jones	4	Frank Evans	1

20 July SOUTHERN LEAGUE

EXETER 50				SOUTHAMPTON 34			
Hoskin	12	Gent	5	Brian McKeown	9	Brian Hanham	4
Hardy	9	May	4	Maurie Mattingley	7	Dudley Smith	2
Geran	7	Hart	4	Ernie Brecknell	6	Mike Tams	1
Howard	6	Street	3	Lionel Levy	4	Ernie Rawlins	1

23 July
SOUTHERN LEAGUE

OXFORD 46				EXETER 38			
Bob MacFarlane	9	Frankie Johnson	5	Hoskin	11	Gent	4
Jim Boyd	8	Bill Osborne	4	Geran	10	Hart	2
Jim Gregory	8	Benny King	3	Street	6	May	1
Bill Kemp	7	Herbie King	2	Hardy	4	Howard	(dnr)

27 July
QUEEN'S CUP

EXETER 69				RAYLEIGH 39			
Hoskin	16	Street	7	Gerald Jackson	13	Peter Clark	4
Hardy	13	Gent	7	Tom O'Connor	5	Alby Smith	4
Geran	11	May	5	Frank Bettis	4	Ron Howes	3
Hart	10	Meyer	0	Maurie McDermott	4	Les McGillivray	2

28 July
SOUTHERN LEAGUE

SOUTHAMPTON 39				EXETER 45			
Ernie Rawlins	8	Maurie Mattingley	5	Geran	10	May	6
Ernie Brecknell	8	Hugh Geddes	3	Street	9	Hardy	3
Dudley Smith	6	Brian Hanham	2	Hart	7	Gent	3
Brian Mckeown	6	Mike Tams	1	Hoskin	7	Johnny Applegate	0

3 August
SOUTHERN LEAGUE

EXETER 51				PLYMOUTH 33			
Hoskin	11	Hart	6	Alan Smith	9	Bill Thatcher	3
Geran	11	Applegate	3	Pete Lansdale	7	Len Read	2
Hardy	7	Gent	3	George Wall	7	Derek Timms	1
May	7	Street	3	Stan Clark	3	Kevin Hayden	1

8 August
SOUTHERN LEAGUE

SWINDON 41				EXETER 43			
Mick Holland	9	Danny Malone	4	Hoskin	11	May	4
Ronnie Swaine	9	Bob Wells	3	Geran	10	Gent	4
Ian Williams	8	Bluey McCoy	1	Hardy	6	Street	2
Bob Jones	7			Hart	5	Meyer	1

10 August
SOUTHERN LEAGUE

EXETER 53				IPSWICH 31			
Geran	12	Gent	6	Tich Read	8	Dick Shepherd	4
Street	11	Hardy	4	Harold McNaughton	6	Charlie Mugford	3
Hoskin	9	May	3	Sid Clark	6	Nobby Stock	0
Hart	6	Meyer	2	Dennis Day	4		

15 August
SOUTHERN LEAGUE
4 TEAM TOURNAMENT
AT RAYLEIGH

EXETER 33		OXFORD 31		RAYLEIGH II 29		RAYLEIGH I 27	
Geran	14	Jim Gregory	12	Maurie McDermott	14	Gerald Jackson	12
Hart	8	Jim Boyd	8	Peter Clark	7	Las McGillivray	9
Hardy	8	Bob MacFarlane	8	Alby Smith	6	Tom O'Connor	6
Gent	3	Benny King	3	Ron Howes	2	Frank Bettis	0
Fred Badcock	(dnr)	Peter Mould	dnr	Bert Little	0	Eric Ebbs	0

17 August
SOUTHERN LEAGUE

EXETER 61				ST AUSTELL 23			
Hoskin	12	Hart	5	Johnnie Sargeant	8	Alf Webster	3
May	12	Street	5	Jackie Gates	4	Cyril Maidment	1
Geran	11	Gent	5	Bob Duckworth	3	Dennis Newton	1
Hardy	7	Meyer	4	Kevin Bock	3	Ken Monk	0

24 August
SOUTHERN LEAGUE

EXETER 57				OXFORD 27			
Hoskin	9	May	8	Jim Boyd	9	Peter Robinson	2
Geran	9	Hart	8	Jim Gregory	6	Frank Boyle	2
Hardy	9	Gent	3	Frankie Johnson	4	Bill Osborne	1
Street	9	Meyer	2	Bob MacFarlane	3	Benny King	0

31 August
QUEEN'S CUP

EXETER 69				WHITE CITY (GLASGOW) 39			
Hoskin	14	May	8	Tommy Miller	11	Larry Lazarus	3
Hardy	12	Street	6	Ken McKinley	11	Doug Templeton	2
Geran	11	Gent	6	Peter Dykes	8	Harry Welch	0
Hart	8	Meyer	4	Junior Bainbridge	4	Don Wilkinson	0

3 September
SOUTHERN LEAGUE

PLYMOUTH 36				EXETER 48			
Alan Smith	11	Dick Harris	3	Hoskin	12	Hardy	4
Pete Lansdale	10	Kevin Hayden	1	Geran	10	May	4
Len Read	8	Jack Hillard	0	Street	7	Gent	4
Bill Thatcher	3	Derek Timms	0	Hart	7	Meyer	0

7 September
CHALLENGE

EXETER 48				SOUTHERN LEAGUE STARS 36			
Hoskin	12	Geran	6	Jim Gregory	9	Brian McKeown	3
Street	10	May	4	Danny Malone	9	Jackie Gates	2
Hardy	7	Gent	3	Hugh Geddes	6	Johnnie Sargeant	2
Hart	6	Meyer	0	Pete Lansdale	4	Jim Boyd	1

8 September
SOUTHERN LEAGUE

ST AUSTELL 43				EXETER 40			
Cyril Maidment	10	Bob Duckworth	5	Hoskin	12	Street	2
Jackie Gates	9	Johnnie Sargeant	5	Hardy	9	Gent	2
Ken Monk	8	Johnny Greenwood	1	Geran	9	May	2
Alf Webster	5	Harold Bull	0	Hart	4	Meyer	0

14 September
SOUTHERN LEAGUE

EXETER 60				SOUTHAMPTON 24			
Geran	12	Street	8	Ernie Brecknell	6	Dudley Smith	3
Hoskin	11	Howard	4	Hugh Geddes	6	Brian Hanham	2
Hart	10	Gent	3	Ernie Rawlins	3	Maurie Mattingley	1
Hardy	9	May	3	Brian McKeown	3	Jack Gleed	0

18 September
SOUTHERN LEAGUE

IPSWICH 59				EXETER 25			
Tich Read	11	Nobby Stock	9	Hoskin	11	May	2
Jimmy Grant	10	Dennis Day	5	Geran	4	Gent	2
Harold McNaughton	9	Len Silver	4	Hart	3	Howard	0
Bert Edwards	9	Doug Papworth	2	Hardy	3	Street	0

23 September
QUEEN'S CUP

WHITE CITY (GLASGOW) 72				EXETER 36			
Tommy Miller	18	Don Wilkinson	5	Geran	10	Street	2
Ken McKinley	16	Bob Sharp	5	Hoskin	8	May	2
Larry Lazarus	13	Peter Dykes	5	Gent	7	Hardy	1
Junior Bainbridge	7	Harry Welch	3	Hart	6	Howard	0

28 September
SOUTHERN LEAGUE

EXETER 60				RAYLEIGH 24			
Geran	11	Street	8	Gerald Jackson	5	Frank Bettis	3
Hoskin	10	Howard	7	Peter Clark	5	Ron Howes	2
Hardy	9	May	4	Maurie McDermott	4	Tom O'Connor	1
Hart	8	Gent	3	Alby Smith	4	Eric Ebbs	0

29 September
SOUTHERN LEAGUE

SOUTHAMPTON 42				EXETER 42			
Ernie Rawlins	11	Jim Gleed	4	Hardy	11	Hart	3
Hugh Geddes	9	Ernie Brecknell	3	May	10	Howard	1
Maurie Mattingley	7	Brian Hanham	3	Geran	9	Street	0
Dudley Smith	5	Jack Vallis	0	Hoskin	8	Gent	0

Goog Hoskin and Plymouth's Bill Thatcher battle it out in a local derby.